Development Studies

Development Studies

Volume 1

Edited by

Prasenjit Maiti

ATLANTIC

PUBLISHERS & DISTRIBUTORS (P) LTD

Published by
ATLANTIC
PUBLISHERS & DISTRIBUTORS (P) LTD
B-2, Vishal Enclave, Opp. Rajouri Garden,
New Delhi-110027
Phones : 25413460, 25429987, 25466842

Sales Office
7/22, Ansari Road, Darya Ganj,
New Delhi-110002
Phones : 23273880, 23275880, 23280451
Fax : 91-11-23285873
web : www.atlanticbooks.com
e-mail : info@atlanticbooks.com

ISBN 81-269-0765-7 (Vol.1)
ISBN 81-269-0764-9 (Set)

Printed and bound in India
at Syndicate Binders, Noida

Foreword

The current rhetoric of sustainable development indicates an increasing propensity to inform the discourses of globalization in our postmodern era. The academic as well as activist viewpoints, whether consonant or dissonant, impact upon the limited choices and suppressed voices of the stakeholders who are at the receiving end of the critical logistics of integrated markets and segregated polities. The inevitable questions that often confront us in this context happen to focus on the basic tenets of the concept of development.

What is and who are the target(s) of development? What normative principles determine these targets and, equally appropriately, the agencies? What are the costs and benefits of development? To whose account(s) are these credited, or from whose, debited? What, if any, is the interplay between politics and development?

These are questions that do not have any ready answers; more so if we ignore the importance of the polemics that underpin them. The issues and concerns of development affect the entire gamut of nations—*developed, developing* and *least developed*—either directly or indirectly. In addition, the impacts of development are also perceived at the levels of society, culture, market and politics worldwide.

The multi-volume book series, *Development Studies*, edited by Dr Prasenjit Maiti, makes a commendable effort to answer such questions in experiential, empirical and/or theoretical terms. Contributors to this book series have analytically deliberated upon the various aspects of development to explore the viable alternatives that seek to recalibrate and reconcile the theories and praxes of development. Their efforts would be duly rewarded if they receive critical acclaim from their readers.

S.S. Chakraborty
Managing Director,
Consulting Engineering Services (India)
Private Limited, New Delhi

Preface

The Volumes on Development Studies covers an extensive range of critical areas that have one common theme of questioning the accepted parameters of development from different angles informed by multiple academic backgrounds. An attempt has been made to accommodate conflicting points of view that would facilitate the reader to arrive at his/her own understanding of the problems under purview.

Contributors to these Volumes have tried to argue the different issues and concerns of development paradigms. Their atricles indicate the different choices of development that are necessarily context-bound and issue-driven in approach.

Choices entail alternatives from among a range of viable options that tend to determine development projects. Both primary and secondary stakeholders are required under the imperatives determined by the project to choose among this or that in order to optimize their given baskets of utilities. Development projects more often than not involve the politics of choice that is underpinned by the who gets what, how, when, where and why scenario.

The very first choice that is exercised on the part of primary stakeholders relates to the feasibility study of the inception stage of development projects. Such studies examine the overall practicability of projects and determine whether proposed physical interventions would disproportionately affect man and environment in an adverse manner.

Projects that have been allowed to continue till the feasibility study stage are in effect projects that would be subsequently implemented. So the next logical stage is to justify the suggested mitigation measures by implying that sustainable development can be ensured by due compliance to the project prescriptions.

It is argued in this context that primary stakeholders do not exercise any effective choices in real terms so far as planned project interventions are concerned. It is true that bilateral donor agencies almost always insist that the choices of the affected persons should be reflected during the project planning stage in order to ensure participatory development. But it is an everyday reality that such grass-roots representation is not incorporated in a uniform manner.

This is due to the fact that less or even least developed countries do not have easy access to civil societal resources such as primary education, civic awareness, ability to question and capacity for independent decision-making based on both knowledge as well as experience. Such limited access indicates a straitjacketed democratic system that does not offer equal opportunities or political resources to the end-users of political development.

So, affected persons in most cases are individuals who are generally without any affluence or influence in their everyday lives. They are without any representation, without any collective bargaining power, without any adequate level of social capital formation and without any organized platform to sustain informed debates and dialogues.

The only collectivity available to the archetypal individual at the grass roots is the resource called politics that is often defined by attributes of religion, caste, feudal identities, patriarchy, culture, language and several other regional specifics. So, politics becomes almost an enabling factor while exercising independent choices based on a cost-benefit analysis of losses and gains related to the project.

Choices are related to arguments, as options do not assume any meaning without polemics. That is why informed debates almost always facilitate discussions focused on the range of available choices as viable alternatives. So the entire logic of choices is underpinned by the exercise of debates.

Dialogues should continue irrespective of resistance to change. There may be aversion to change in a civil society but this should not deter the free flow of polyphony within the public sphere. Change management as a negotiating art must be able to handle repulsion, rebellion and resurgence in a creative manner in order to make development projects meaningful in the larger context of societal empathy.

Choices are resources of power that may be deployed by pressure groups to promote certain ideologies as preferences. Hence, the central assumption in this context is—negotiate change to negate the possibility of subversion that may ultimately come across as an idiom of static manipulations exercised by vested interests.

But the critical inquiry remains—should change be only for the sake of change or should change assume a larger ascription of potentiality and strategy that requires a deft understanding of the politics of everyday life? This is in itself ponderable—whether to exercise choice and facilitate change or to conform to the conventional and continue as such?

These are difficult questions with no ready answers. We can at best cite certain hypothetical case studies and try to analyze the best solutions under the given set of circumstances. Such analytical models would help us better appreciate the pros and cons of choices and the difficulties associated with the exercise of choices as an assumption of free will.

For instance, the various incidents of actual and potential evictions of encroachers who illegally occupy different canal banks, pavements and government land along railway tracks in several large metropolitan cities such as Kolkata. It is a fact that these unauthorized persons do not have any legal right whatsoever to occupy these strategic points that are critical to sustain urban development. The issue here is—to what extent the space of human rights can be stretched to empower encroachers.

But should one also be concerned with an assertion of their moral right to stay wherever they are? Or should they be relegated to the footnotes of history? Such underprivileged persons cater to the everyday requirements of the city as domestic helps, drivers, shop assistants, etc.

Their contribution to the everyday life of cities cannot be undermined. So the moral, legal and administrative stance of the State vis-à-vis the development versus displacement debate in the context of liberal democracies can be re-examined by bureaucrats, policy-makers and political masters to ensure a certain modicum of human dignity for such marginal men and women.

The postcolonial bureaucratic Indian State cannot perhaps conceptualize that development implies dignity on the part of the stakeholders/beneficiaries concerned in the larger perspective of human progress. The managerial Indian State apparatus still continues with its repressive colonial legacy and so cannot appreciate the ontological consequences of development induced/defined by displacement.

This phenomenon may be observed elsewhere with minor changes conditioned by local-level specifics. But the central inquiry remains the same—can development studies be examined without its human (if not humane) context? Can development be always managed/explained in terms of numbers? Can development be justified in ethical terms even if a few persons are unevenly affected due to project interventions?

These questions do not have any ready answers. It is not always practicable to allow encroachers to pollute common urban resources such as lakes and parks and road networks. It is also not always feasible to rehabilitate evicted persons due to economic constraints. It is not always viable on the part of the State to accept the financial responsibility of these persons.

Two other prominent actors have to be actively considered before the conclusion of our development versus displacement debate, i.e. the Civil Society and the Market. The Market more often than not dictates its priorities and preferences to the State while the Civil Society can (and does) occasionally intervene as the Third Actor in order to mediate between the worldviews of the State and the Market.

The rhetoric of development is underpinned at times by variables such as opportunities and competencies. The project proponent and funding agencies have to decide on the final terms of reference that design the scope and purpose of development projects. Such examination of alternative proposals is an exercise in the deployment and utilization of limited resources of power that decide on the ultimate outcome of the futuristic (and perhaps ambitious) roadmaps of development.

PRASENJIT MAITI

Contents

1

Social Capital and Poverty: An Analysis of the Efficacy of the Social Capital Approach to Understand a Culture of Poverty Situation*

DHAMMIKA HERATH

Poverty is a complex and multi-dimensional social problem affecting both developed and developing countries. In Sri Lanka too poverty is widespread despite many gains in social development in recent decades. More than 6% of Sri Lanka's population lives in absolute poverty of less than $ 1 a day and 46% live on less than $ 2 a day (World Development Report, 2000-01). As a result, there is always an expectation that the Government of Sri Lanka will spend a substantial proportion of its resources on welfare for the poor, even though this might not be in line with the capacity or the intentions of the government or other stakeholders in development. However, the gravity of the problem of poverty in Sri Lanka is reflected by the fact that eradication of poverty forms the talking point of many academic and political discussions and conventions. Every government elected since the independence so far has had a programme of action intended to deal with this serious issue. It is also understood that all the time, poverty has been politically manipulated to get the all-important edge in elections. Nevertheless, the fact remains that poverty continues to be part and parcel of the lives of many individuals and families.

Before any effort to understand the explanations of poverty, it is necessary to have a poignant conception of what poverty

---

* This paper was presented at the "18th European Conference of Modern South Asian Studies", 6-9 July 2004, Lund, Sweden.

is. For this purpose let's examine some of the definitions that try to describe poverty.

"Poverty is that condition in which a person, either because of inadequate income or unwise expenditures, does not maintain a scale of living high enough to provide for his physical and mental efficiency and to enable him and his natural dependents to function usefully according to the standards of society of which he is a member" (Gilling and Gilling quoted in Shankar, 1998).

"Individuals, families and groups in the population can be said to be in poverty when they lack resources to obtain the type of diet, participate in the activities and have living conditions and amenities, which are customary...in the societies to which they belong" (Townsend, 1977—quoted in Alcock, 1993).

"The absence or the under-utilization of material or non-material resources for the basic satisfaction and well-being of all human beings" (Ratnapala, 1981).

From a human development perspective, poverty means the denial of choices and opportunities for a tolerable life. Poverty can mean more than a lack of what is necessary for material well-being. It can also mean the denial of opportunities and choices most basic to human development; to lead a long, healthy, creative life and to enjoy a decent standard of living with freedom, dignity, self-esteem and the respect of others (Human Development Report, 1997, p. 6).

Poverty consists in experiencing a whole bundle of undesirable circumstances. These circumstances can vary between different poverty groups. These different poverty groups may experience under-nourishment, exposure to cold, hunger, indebtedness, poor living conditions, poor health and so on according to their circumstances (Richards; Gooneratne, 1980, p. 53).

Poverty differs from one social context to the other. Issues of poverty in developing countries involve hunger, illiteracy, epidemics, lack of health services and safe drinking water and so on. In developed countries, hunger is rare, literacy is close to universal, and conditions of life are far more satisfactory (Human Development Report, 1997, p. 17). Some people lift themselves from poverty, others stay poor and, still others become newly poor. Poverty is constantly being created and recreated (H.D.R., 1997, p. 31).

Explanations of poverty fall into two groups, one blaming the victim and the other blaming the system. The first set of theories emphasizes the characteristics, attributes and behavior of the poor. They often confuse the cause and the effect. They assume that the lifestyle of those suffering from certain social conditions is the cause of those conditions. Such explanations have been used to divert critical attention away from serious structural problems in the economy and the social system (Daly, 1996, p. 29). These explanations include pathological explanations of indolence, fecklessness, etc. They also include generic explanations, which refer to social status with supposedly inherited characteristics such as intelligence and psychological approaches, which explain individual achievements by reference to acquired or developed personality traits. However, these explanations deal more with nature rather than nurture. They blame the victim for his or her own poverty. And many people question the availability of evidence to substantiate their arguments (Alcock, 1993).

In the US in 60s the pathological tradition was taken up once again in response to the rediscovery of poverty within the affluent post-war American society. One of the significant catalysts for this re-emphasis on the categorization of the poor was the detailed research carried out by Oscar Lewis into the lives of poor Puerto Rican families. Lewis described how such families and the communities in which they lived had learned to cope with their higher levels of poverty and deprivation, in part, by suppressing expectations of greater wealth and even secure employment, developing a culture, which focused upon the day-to-day strategies, adopted by poor families and individuals to survive without affluence in an affluent society. Lewis referred to it as the culture of poverty (Alcock, 1993). Lewis and his followers saw poverty not merely as a lack of adequate income, but rather as a way of life, handed down from generation to generation through well-defined social networks. This theory holds that the uprooted slum dwellers, while rejecting the dominant values of the larger society, have certain values of their own, conditioned by their upbringing, migration experience, economic circumstances, lifestyle and social segregation (Silva; Athukorala, 19).

The main intention of this paper is not to fall back on pathological explanations of poverty but to make an analysis on the efficacy of the social capital approach to understand a culture of poverty situation based mainly on an empirical study on the culture of poverty. But I also draw facts from another ongoing study on social capital and poverty in a rural village in Sri Lanka. My first study on poverty was undertaken in 2000-01 where I took "the culture of poverty" as a conceptual tool.

The Theory of Culture of Poverty

Oscar Lewis did the pioneering work on the culture of poverty and following him, scholars around the world have focused on this concept and, at times, valued its relevance to understand the persistence of poverty and while some others have made damaging criticisms against it. In this backdrop, I adopted a neutral position and carried out my research work.

Lewis attempts to understand poverty and its associated traits as a culture or as he says "more accurately as a subculture with its own structure and rationale, as a way of life, which is passed down from generation to generation along family lines". So, the culture of poverty is not simply a case of economic deprivation, of disorganization, or of the absence of something. It is also something positive and provides some rewards without which the poor can hardly carry on.

Lewis explains that there are some conditions under which culture of poverty tends to grow and flourish. In my study I have studied whether these conditions are prevalent in my study community and whether these conditions have given rise to a culture of poverty situation in that community. Following are those conditions:

- A cash economy, wage labour and production for profits.
- A persistently high rate of unemployment and under-employment for unskilled labour.
- Low wages.
- The failure to provide social, political and economic organization, either on a voluntary basis or by government imposition for the low-income population.
- The existence of a bilateral kinship system rather than a unilateral one.
- The existence of a set of vales in the dominant class which stress the accumulation of wealth and property, the possibility of upward mobility and thrift and explains the low economic status as the result of personal inadequacy or inferiority.

Moreover, as Lewis describes it, the culture of poverty is more likely to come into existence when a stratified social and economic system is breaking down or is being replaced by another. Often, this is brought in by imperial conquest in which the native social and economic structure is smashed and the natives are maintained in a servile colonial status. It can also occur in the process of detribalization.

Lewis holds that the way of life, which develops among the poor under these conditions, is the "culture of poverty". According to him, this is clearly visible in urban or rural slums and is characterized by around seventy interrelated social and psychological traits. However, the number of traits and their interrelations may vary from society to society and family to family.

The culture of poverty is both an adaptation and a reaction of the poor to their marginal position in a class-stratified highly individuated and capitalistic society. It stands for an attempt to cope with the feelings of hopelessness and despair, which develops from the realization of the improbability of achieving success in terms of the values and goals of the larger society. According to Lewis, many of the traits of the culture of poverty can be considered as local solutions for problems, not met by existing institutions and agencies because people are not eligible for them, cannot afford them or are ignorant or suspicious of them. For example, ignorant of banks, they use their own resources or organize informal credit devices without interests.

Lewis is of the opinion that the culture of poverty is not only an adaptation to a set of objective conditions in the larger society. Once, it is established, it tends to perpetuate itself from generation to generation as a consequence of its impact on children, who acquire and absorb the basic values and attitudes of their culture. So, they are, then, not psychologically geared to capitalize on the changing conditions or increased opportunities, which they may come across in their lifetime.

Those people, who come from the lower strata of a rapidly changing society in which they have been alienated, are likely to be in the culture of poverty. Thus, as Lewis puts it, the landless rural workers who migrate to cities can be expected to develop a culture of poverty much more readily than migrants from peasant villages with well-established traditional cultures. For example, he says, the rural population of Latin America made the transition from tribal to peasant society a long time ago, but Africa is still close to its tribal heritage. Due to the more corporate nature of the many of the African societies and also due to the persistence of village ties, the emergence of a full-blown culture of poverty has been inhibited or delayed in such societies. This is in contrast to many of the Latin American societies. Furthermore, the conditions of apartheid in South Africa too, due to the institutionalization of repression and discrimination, tend to develop a greater sense of identity and group consciousness.

Lewis notes that the concept of culture of poverty can be studied from various points of view such as the relationship between the subculture and the larger society, the nature of the slum community, the nature of the family and the attitudes, values and character structure of the individual. He lists some of the characteristics of culture of poverty as follows:

1. They lack effective participation and integration of the poor in the major institutions of society. This is a complex matter for which the reasons maybe lack of economic resources, segregation, discrimination, fear, suspicion or apathy, and the development of local solutions for problems. Yet, participation in some of the institutions of society, for example, the jail, army, public relief system, does not *per se* eliminate the culture of poverty. Here, Lewis believes that a relief system, which barely keeps people alive, perpetuates both basic poverty and feelings of hopelessness.

   Low wages, chronic unemployment, underemployment lead to lack of property ownership, absence of savings, absence of food reserves at home and a chronic shortage of cash. These conditions reduce the possibility of effective participation in the larger economic system. According to Lewis, as a response to these conditions, we find in the culture of poverty a high incidence of pawning of personal goods, borrowing from local moneylenders at usurious rates of interest, spontaneous informal credit devices organized by neighbors, the use of second-hand clothing, and the pattern of frequent buying of small quantities of food many times a day as the needs arise.

   People with a culture of poverty produce very little wealth and receive very little in turn. They have a low level of literacy and education, usually do not belong to trade unions, are not members of political parties, generally do not participate in the national welfare agencies and make very little use of banks, hospitals, department stores, museums or art galleries. They maintain critical attitudes toward some of the basic institutions of dominant classes, hatred of police, mistrust of the government, and those in high positions and a cynicism, which even extends to church. This gives, in Lewis's view, culture of poverty a high potential for protests and for being used in political movements aimed against the existing social order.

Further, Lewis expresses that people afflicted with a culture of poverty are quite conscious of the middle-class values, talk about them and even claim some of them as their own, but on the whole do not live by them. Thus, what they say and what they do have to be distinguished.

2. When we look at the culture of poverty on the local community level, we find poor housing, gregariousness, crowding, but above all a minimum of organization beyond the level of nuclear family and extended family. Occasionally, there are informal temporary groupings or voluntary associations within slums. The existence of neighborhood gangs, which cut across slum settlements, represents a considerable advance from this situation. Usually, it is this low level of community organization that gives the culture of poverty its marginal and anachronistic quality in a highly complex and specialized society. Their level of socio-cultural organization is lower than that achieved by most primitive people.

   However, Lewis adds that in spite of low level of organization, there may be a sense of community and *espirit de corps* in urban slums and urban neighborhoods. Yet, this is dependent on the size of the slum, its location and physical characteristics, length of residence, incidence of land and home ownership, rentals, ethnicity, kinship-ties, freedom or lack of freedom of movement.

3. On the family level, according to Lewis's description, major traits of the culture of poverty are the absence of childhood as a specially prolonged and protected stage in the lifecycle, early initiation into sex, free-unions or consensual marriages, a relatively high incidence of abandonment of wives and children, a trend toward female or mother centered families, a strong predisposition to authoritarianism, lack of privacy, and verbal emphasis on family solidarity, which is rarely

achieved because of sibling competition and rivalry for limited goods and maternal affection.

4. On the level of the individual major characteristics of the culture of poverty are strong feelings of marginality, of helplessness, of dependence, and of inferiority. Also, there may be a high incidence of maternal deprivation, of orality, of weak ego structure, confusion of sexual identity, absence of impulse control, strong present-time orientation with relatively little ability to differentiate gratification and to plan for the future, a sense of resignation and fatalism, a widespread belief in the male superiority, and a high tolerance of psychological pathology of all sorts.

   People with a culture of poverty are provincial and locally-oriented and have little sense of history. They know only their troubles, their own local conditions, and their own way of life. Usually they do not have the knowledge, the vision or the ideology to see similarities between their problems and those of their counterparts in other countries. They are not class conscious, though they are very sensitive to status distinctions.

Lewis presents the notion that when the poor become class conscious or active members of trade union organizations or when they adopt an internationalist outlook on the world, they are no longer part of the culture of poverty, although they may still be desperately poor. Any movement, which organizes the poor and gives them hope and at the same time, which effectively promotes solidarity and a sense of identification with larger groups, destroys the social and psychological core of the culture of poverty.

According to Lewis, it is much more difficult to eliminate the culture of poverty than to eliminate poverty *per se*. He says that there are some positive aspects in the culture of poverty. However, he stresses that this is a thin culture. There is a great deal of pathos, suffering and emptiness among those, who live in the culture of poverty. It does not provide for long-term satisfaction and its encouragement of mistrust tends to magnify helplessness and isolation. The elimination of physical poverty *per se* may not be sufficient to eliminate the culture of poverty, which is a whole way of life. Lewis pinpoints that underdeveloped countries, by creating basic structural changes in society, by redistributing wealth, by organizing the poor and giving them a sense of belonging, of power, of leadership, it is possible to abolish some of the basic characteristics of the culture of poverty, even when they do not succeed in abolishing poverty itself.

How do we make sense of culture of poverty? The culture of poverty theory is now considered incomplete as theoretical tool to understand poverty. So, as was mentioned earlier, the focus of this paper is to look at the culture of poverty from a different theoretical angle; that of social capital. The idea is to see whether this would open up new ways of looking at the culture of poverty and possibly news ways to cope with poverty.

Social Capital

I understand social capital as "networks of social relations, norms and values supporting collective action, reciprocity, mutual trust among individuals and groups, the sense of empowerment and the presence of community-based organizations aimed at the well-being of all members". In the light of this definition, a hypothetical society with dense social capital is characterized by people who are well connected to each other. In such a society the social fabric should encourage people to interact constantly with each other. This society has norms and values which are supportive of collective action. People have the willingness to work together and they are conscious of the value of working together. They also are trustworthy to each other and trust each other. However, the level of this trust is subject to variation. People also have a sense of empowerment, i.e. they believe in self-reliance as far as their mobility is concerned and are not characterized by apathy, resignation and dependence. The presence of a community based organization, which organizes people to work together for the common good, could be an added feature strengthening social capital base in society.

I was strongly influenced on this concept by the work of Robert Putnam, who shows how a community can reap the benefits of coordinated actions that will be difficult in a community with low networks of social capital. Putnam emphasizes that after initially building social capital on a small-scale, then it is possible to develop it further to solve even large-scale social problems having more complex institutional arrangements.

Literature on social capital dates back to many years. But, the theory of social capital as we use it today was made popular by Robert Putnam. In his "Making Democracy Work" he defines social capital as "features of social organizations such as trust, norms and networks that improve the efficiency of society by facilitating coordinated actions (Putnam, p. 167). Pamela Paxton in "Is Social Capital Declining in United States?" presents some useful views on social capital. According to her, social capital is the idea that individuals and groups can gain resources from their relations to one another (Paxton, 1999, p. 89). Hence, it encompasses networks of social relations, norms and values supporting collective action, mutual trust, reciprocity, the level and the sense of empowerment and the presence of community based organizations aimed at the well-being of all members. This new theory has gained currency among social scientists in many countries of the world and is multidisciplinary. Especially, it focuses on social capability of people rather than material resources to better their conditions of living.

Pierre Bourdieu says that "social capital is the aggregate of actual or potential resources which are linked to possession of a durable network of more or less institutional relationships of mutual acquaintance and recognition or in other words, to membership in groups" (Bourdieu, p. 92).

For Coleman "the concept of social capital illustrates how the social structure of a group can function as a resource for the individuals of that group". He claims that social capital inheres in the structure of relations between and among actors. Social capital is not lodged in individuals themselves. They can make use of it to facilitate the production of individual or collective ends. Coleman sees social capital in trust, information, norms and effective sanctions authority relations and the extent of obligations in a group. Each is a feature of social structure that also provides social capital as a resource for the individuals of that group (Coleman, p. 92).

Social networks involve activities of civic engagement such as neighborhood associations, service and charitable clubs, volunteerism and the like. In both rural and urban communities social capital refers to the institutions and mechanisms whereby residents relate to and interact with each other to solve problems for common good (Debertin, 2002).

However, according to Paxton, there is a large gap between the concept of social capital and its measurement. There isn't a common agreement on the meaning of the term social capital. So, it is used with many different interpretations. She asserts that social capital is a general concept and thus cannot be measured with one variable (90-91). This view is supported by some others who explain that "the concept of social capital has captured the imagination of academics and practitioners alike without much agreement on its definition or content" (Uphoff and Wijayaratna, 2000). This does not in any way mean that social capital cannot be measured and that it cannot be used. There are many studies where a variety of indicators have been developed to measure social capital in different settings. And, many studies try to use social capital to address problems of development and poverty.

Scholars agree that when there is a strong presence of social capital, it usually leads to a very desirable quality of life and increases the potential for economic growth. (Debertin, 2002). Putnam says that the quality of public life and the performance of public institutions are strongly influenced by norms and networks of civic engagement. Social capital engenders a sense of solidarity and a community can reap the benefits of coordinated actions that will be difficult in a community with low networks of social capital (p. 167). Social capital accrues certain benefits to people. Paxton says that in a neighborhood where there is high level of social capital reflected by the fact that people know each other, talk to each other and trust each other, people get certain social benefits. For instance, she explains that in such a community, "a mother may feel comfortable in letting her child walk alone to a nearby park". This would not be possible in a community with low social capital and in such a case either mother has to chaperon the child or would have to hire someone to do this job (Paxton, 1999, p. 89). In fact, modern day planners have recognized the significance of social capital formation and therefore many newly designed urban neighborhoods are equipped with a club house, a swimming pool, tennis courts and other recreational facilities which permit social interaction, a necessary ingredient to form social capital (Debertin, 2002).

Social capital and poverty: It was mentioned that this paper is based on two studies one of which was carried out in one of up-country tea plantations in Sri Lanka. The selection of a plantation community for this study was mainly prompted by the pioneering study by Lewis, who did his research work in Mexican slum communities. I was also under the impression that the slum-like environment, which is found in plantation communities, can provide a fertile ground for the culture of poverty to develop. This study was a field research that modeled ethnographic study. A deep, complex and complicated phenomenon like the culture of poverty needs rigorous research work, especially qualitative investigation. Participant observation was the main technical tool with which I used to carry out my field research. And under this broad methodological framework I made case studies, unstructured and semi-structured interviews, key informant interviews and close observation.

Findings of the first study: In the next section of this paper I try to describe the conditions of poverty in the estate community and in the last part the applicability of social capital approach to explain the poverty situation is explored with the light of the findings of this study.

Chronic unemployment and underemployment are the biggest hurdles for upward mobility in this community. Sometimes, it is argued that estate dwellers report low unemployment due to the availability of wage labour and also due to the fact that with low incomes they cannot afford to be unemployed. But in this particular estate community, people report severe unemployment and underemployment. The estate tea plantation is no longer capable of providing employment for all estate dwellers, especially for the youth. So, there is a heavy dependence of youth on older generations. On the part of the people, majority of the estate dwellers do not have a strong liking for self-employment. They usually complain about not having permanent employment and consider it the responsibility of the government to provide employment. This is a kind of a dependent mentality which is almost characteristic of them. Most of all, their subculture does not have ample examples of upward mobility acquired through self-employment. Yet, their condition is not to be understood as a purely subjective condition. There are concrete objective barriers, which render self-employment a very difficult task. Some of the people do have the determination that they should move away from poverty and they make the effort. But they face an eternal lack of capital. They live by what they earn today and in many cases tomorrow is mortgaged. There is virtually no way to get capital. Banks do not accept them as they fail to produce surety. There has hardly been a comprehensive programme on the part of government to furnish them with capital, training and motivation. There is not even a non-governmental organization operating in this community to assist them in the absence of government help.

The conditions of unemployment and underemployment in the estate have been intergenerational. Despite improvements in educational levels reached, the absence of intergenerational change in vocational skills has complicated this situation. The younger generation has not been able to develop new skills, which would have assisted their development. They have, by and large, inherited the traditional skills of carpentry, masonry, plucking tealeaves and so on. This chronic lack of skills has hampered their development and further reinforced social exclusion. This situation is a definite product of the unusually high school dropout rate, weaknesses in the formal education system and poverty itself.

The income levels of estate dwellers have stagnated over generations. It can readily be observed that there is a nominal increase of incomes, but no apparent increment in real terms. Of course, the incomes of the younger generation have become more unstable because they report more underemployment than did the older generation, who had the chance to be occupied in the estate just after quitting school. But, the younger generation quits school and idles at home for a few years and then, some of them find work in the estate, but the majority opts outside jobs, which give better wages but are highly unstable and cause underemployment. And, if the incomes do not rise, it is likely that poverty would stay unabated. This informs that some of the things that have led to conditions of poverty in this community are beyond the control of the inhabitants.

Similarly, the expenditure patterns of the older and younger generations are not visibly different from each other. Estate dwellers, young or old, have always set aside the largest proportion of the household expenditure on food. Very often, many people purchase most of their essentials on credit. In fact, buying things on credit is a situation effected largely by the shortage of cash. So, both the generations have unwittingly incurred losses because buying things on credit reduces one's bargaining power. Why they spend a large proportion of their income for food is understandable. Given their low income, they have no other option. Hence, we cannot blame the poor for this situation. But this reduces their proportion of expenditure allocated for other essential areas such as education of children, savings and so on. They spend minimum amount of money for education of children. The failure to allocate sufficient amount of money for education have had lasting effects on children's mobility. Nonetheless, alcoholism is frequently observed in the community and is vitally relevant for the perpetuation of poverty. In fact, they allocate more money for alcohol than they do for the education of children. It was found that while the percentage expenditure for the education of children is around 1%, they spend around 6% of their income on alcohol. Majority of the estate dwellers are day-wage earners. When they spend a large portion of their wage for alcohol, it affects the family in several ways. First of all, given their low wages, its economic effect is substantial. Also, the quarrelsome behavior of the alcoholics affects education and personality development of children. So, the home atmosphere is not conducive for successful education. Alcoholism crippled the development of the older generation and is now crippling that of the younger generation. I saw the educated informants of the area pointing out alcoholism to be a source of destruction. However, there are obvious justifications that people make regarding the habit of constant drinking. If one asks why do you drink, the respondent would say, "I am doing hard work. It is so tiring. So I drink." "I have lot of problems. Sometimes I drink to get some fun." "I am used to drinking. I cannot give up." I do not attempt to invalidate these justifications. The fact that they do not have means of recreation and that they do strenuous labour jobs is true. But, there is little doubt that alcoholism definitely makes them eternally poor. And, there are some, who drink for the sake of drinking too. The eventual effect of all these different factors is their underdevelopment.

Since, estate dwellers did not and do not have the ability to save or the habit of saving, it is not possible for them to assist the mobility of themselves and their children. A composite of many different factors had made saving an almost impossible task for the older generation. They had to consume all what they earned. This situation remains unchanged with the younger generation as well. In many cases, savings are totally absent. So, a day or two without work can, sometimes, put them in extreme hardships. Thus, when they are not able even to sustain themselves, it is absurd to talk about savings. The unavoidable outcome of these dire conditions is the practice of frequent borrowing and pawning of personal items. Borrowing and pawning were frequently practiced in the older generation. This correlated with the absence of savings and low income. They usually borrowed from a local moneylender to whom they lost their gold (Of course jewelry is a kind of savings for the poor. But, they do not have lot of jewelry as they have already lost them to moneylenders). They were very remote from the banks. Even the younger generation is not able to secure loans from the bank without pawning, since they fail to produce guarantees. So, the moneylenders have always ruthlessly exploited the estate masses. The unavoidable repercussion of this exploitation is eternal indebtedness. The undue reliance on the moneylenders and frequent borrowing has generated a widespread and prolonged indebtedness in the younger generation. In some cases, this drains a substantial proportion from the incomes of the estate dwellers. Hence, it can be said that external determinants that prevented the development of the older generation still remain in force and prevents the development of the younger generation. I consider this an external determinant because, why people rely on moneylenders is not due to their personal fault. If the banks do not accept them, they do not have any other alternative. In fact, pawning can be done in the bank, but they are ignorant of it. And, there is nobody to tell them that such a path is possible. So, some systemic problems promoted conditions of poverty among those of the older generation and are promoting among those of the younger generation.

Estate dwellers' association with banks is very limited. Since majority of them are low-income earners, their savings are essentially low and they also do not have the habit of saving. So, they do not have a need to associate themselves with banks. A composite of many different factors had made saving an almost impossible task for the older generation. They had to consume all what they earned. This situation remains unchanged with the younger generation as well. In many cases, savings are totally absent. The absence of savings has some vital repercussions on their economy. Apart from generating some income, the fact that savings can be used in emergencies minimizes their undue reliance on private moneylenders. Absence of savings also prevents them from initiating self-employments. More importantly, this increases their indebtedness. Hence, absence of savings delays their development and mobility in many ways.

As mentioned earlier, they fail to secure credits from the formal credit institutions. In fact, they do not really feel that there is such an avenue for credits. So, even for pawning they go to local moneylenders. Most of them do not understand that they can pawn gold in the bank for much lower interest rates than that of moneylenders whose rate is 20% per month (so, effectively the annual rate is 240%). Lots of people fail to save their pawned items. Also, unlike in the banks, they receive a very low value for their gold (they pawn valuable gold and take petty loans). So, when they lose their gold to moneylenders, they lose a lot. Moreover, since people pay them in small instalments, they repay interests until they have paid many times the original sum. At times, they keep paying only the interests. So, the moneylenders have a big say in the poverty of these people. Another reason why they go to moneylenders is that banks are very slow to issue loans, but the needs of people are immediate. Whatever the reason, disassociation from the banks and the indebtedness are major causal factors hindering their mobility and development.

The local solution for this lack of access to formal credit institutions is the phenomenon of Seettu. The Seettu is an integral part of the economy of the estate dweller. Almost everybody subscribes money to one or more Seettus. In the absence of formal credit facilities Seettus come out as the only way they can have a sudden draw of money. But, money coming from the Seettus is always used for consumption purposes such as to purchase household equipment, to pay off debts, to improve the house, etc. Very few people utilize that money for generating an income. They do not understand its investment potential. When it is pointed out that this money could be invested, they accept it. But most of them have never tried it. This is further proof a culture of poverty where people do not make a desperate effort to develop themselves. Their culture does not provide them with examples (of using Seettus for investment). Hence, this aspect of their lives has a vital effect on their development and the mobility. In a sense, as Putnam says the prevalence of Seettu tells about a positive aspect of the community. Putnam says, "The rotating credit associations illustrate how problems of collective action can be overcome by drawing on external sources of social capital...lacking physical assets to offer as surety, participants, in effect, pledge their social connections. Thus, social capital is leveraged to expand credit facilities...a rotating credit association is more than a simple economic institution: it is a mechanism strengthening the overall solidarity of the village (Putnam, 1992, p. 169). The subscription of money to Seettus has been there in the community for several decades. But, neither older nor the younger generation ever understood that this could help their development. The older generation used this money to buy household equipment, to improve the houses and for general consumption. And, the same usage prevails now with little difference. I never met a person either in the older or younger generation, who ever used or thought of using Seettu money for an investment purpose. This is a deplorable reflection of their ignorance, present-time orientation, and the feelings of inferiority and status consciousness. Spending it for consumption (buying household items or improving the houses) rather than investment speaks about the present-time orientation. The fact that they are so much worried about improving their houses at the expense of their future tells about their feelings of inferiority and status consciousness.

The poor performance in respect of education is one of the crucial reasons why they have been lacking mobility and development for several generations. The school dropout rate has always been unusually high in the case of both older and younger generations. Were the circumstances that produced this high dropout rate the same for both generations? Most people of the older generation did not have parental backing for education. Very often, economic difficulties forced them out of school or due to such reasons their parents asked them to leave school and work. Their parents were mostly indifferent to their education. But in the majority of cases, parents of the younger generation, though they also had lots of financial difficulties, have not compelled their children to leave school and work. They understand the potential of education and like their children to educate themselves. They give some form of attention to the education of their children. This is not, however, to say that they were enthusiastic about education.

Many of them do not make a firm effort in that regard. Although concerned about giving the children primary education, they were not committed to give them further education. Some parents place only a verbal emphasis on education. Parents themselves being uneducated, they cannot be an example to their children. At times, even when economic reasons do not force them out of school, many people of the younger generation have not utilized the opportunity to progress through education.

It seems that the perceived poor quality of teaching in the local school is also responsible for bringing about this situation. Many people accuse that teachers of the local school are not committed to their job. They come to the school very late but leave very early. The principal is not taking any action regarding this as he has his own defects. Teachers, according to people, demotivate children. Many respondents accused that the teachers of that school underrate the value of education in front of the children. According to some estate parents, the teachers give students the notion that education is not very essential for estate children. One of the key informants revealed to me that the school principle is a morally easygoing character and has once attempted to abuse a girl-child. When this was reported to the relevant authorities, according to that respondent, he bribed them and escaped punishment. (However, it is not possible for me to confirm all the accusations.) But, one of the teachers of the school accepted that teachers are not punctual, though she denied that teachers discourage children. She stressed that conditions of the school are still favourable and if there is a skilled student, teachers always love him and encourage him. She specifically mentioned that if teachers shun their duties, it becomes a curse for them.

Further, in their subculture it has become almost a practice to quit schooling very early. It does not have many models to be followed. One of the things that lured children of the older generation out of school was the desire to earn money. The same factor is still in operation. As the school principal pinpointed, some children are attracted to work by the prospects of pocket money. So, attitudes toward education haven't undergone significant changes. I met many boys and girls of the ages between 12 and 18 who are not attending school. When they were enquired as to why they are avoiding school, the children gave no concrete answers. Their parents complained that children have abandoned school even when they were pushing them to continue education. This tells that even the third generation has not changed their attitudes very much. This, in fact, foretells a pathetic situation in the future, i.e. even the third generation will continue to stay in the same impoverished conditions that their parents are in now. Again why this happens is of vital significance. If there is parental motivation, at least, to a limited extent, if children are not working, and if there is a school at hand, but still, children shun the school, then this must be the sub-cultural influence. It is the example that children get in the community.

The rudimentary perception of education is also responsible for the above condition. The older generation vaguely understood education to be a source of employment. The younger generation also sees education as only a source of employment, specially, government jobs. Thus, they have still not perceived that apart from giving qualifications for employment, education performs other important roles. So, there has been little or no change relating to the perception of education. Hence, the children do not have a sense that education is an entitlement in itself and that it is a norm in the larger society.

It is quite obvious that poor education leads them to less remunerative and unstable jobs. This inevitably drives them to poverty. This in turn affects the education of their offspring. Therefore, this operates like an unbreakable, vicious cycle inhibiting the mobility and development of the estate dwellers. As a result, after decades of operation of the free education system, education is yet to facilitate upward mobility in this community. There is an overall improvement in the level of basic education, particularly, literacy in the younger generation. But this improvement in education has not had the potency to increase the life chances of those of the younger generation because many of them have left school prematurely (before the

O/L exam). In the older generation there are lots of people who have never set foot in a school. In the younger generation also there were several people who never had the chance to education, but this number is very small compared to the older generation.

Next, the non-ownership of property has a noticeable impact on the household economy. Even the houses they live in belong to the estate. Save for a minority, estate folk do not have fixed or moveable property that can generate income. They are totally dependent on their wages. So, long periods of underemployment can push them into dire poverty. In this sense, non-ownership of property blocks their development and mobility.

The foregoing situation is further aggravated by the inherent defects of the public welfare system intended for the poor. The Samurdhi scheme operates in an inefficient, ineffective and corrupted fashion. The selection of beneficiaries has been done with an extreme political bias. So, many people who are capable of sustaining themselves receive benefits, while the real deserved have been left out. People, annoyed about this, grumble about not having Samurdhi. They point out that some of the rich receive Samurdhi, while the poor do not. Of course, according to my observations, the rich do not receive Samurdhi, but those who are capable of maintaining themselves without Samurdhi do receive it.

Lacking physical and financial capital, they also are not rich in social capital. Their social world is very small. The chance to interact with the individuals of upper social classes is extremely limited. In some cases, some of the estate folk know a few government officials and rich businessmen outside the community. Yet, they cannot get help from them, since the rich and the powerful are not normally interested in keeping close relationship with estate dwellers. Contacts with relatives are also not very strong. They cannot normally get help from the relatives as they are also of the same economic and social position. Some of the people do have relatives in good positions, but they do not seem to be interested in helping them out of poverty. The absence of contacts affects them in securing employment, credit, finding good schools for their children, getting some work done from government offices and many other aspects of life. All these have a significant impact on their lives. For example, getting the children to a good school is crucial if children are to benefit from the public education system. It is common sense knowledge that not all the schools give children quality education, skills motivation and prestige to compete in the job market. Hence, this could be treated as one factor, which impedes their mobility and development. The relatively low level of social capital is an intergenerational issue. The older generation had too little social contacts to improve their life chances. Further, through the years they have not been able to develop new acquaintanceships with those of favourable socioeconomic standing. The younger generation, except perhaps those few who have moved themselves from poverty, has made no significant progress in their social capital. Of course, some people work outside the estate and come into contact with people of higher socioeconomic backgrounds. But, they do not generally develop intimate relationships with them. The estate women paint no better picture compared to their old counterparts. They are still hemmed in the estate.

The low level of community participation also represents skinny social capital of estate dwellers. The older generation rarely participated in community activities. The younger generation takes after the older generation in exactly the same fashion. In the community there has never been a stable community organization. They do not even have a funeral-aid society. In the village of Ooduwela, there is a funeral-aid society in which some of the economically better-off estate dwellers have obtained membership. But, the less fortunate majority are not attached to this society. A few people do have the membership, but are not able to subscribe money. So, they do not receive benefits. This shows that the low-level of income is troubling these people in multiple ways. Further, the community lacks a charismatic leader, a catalyst, who can rouse the community spirit. Hence, the younger generation has made no progress from this stalemate. This delays their mobility in two ways. One is that they are not entitled to reciprocal help that such organizations could generate. Secondly, they cannot raise a voice against the negligence of them on the part of the government.

Level of political participation presents the same pitiful situation like that of community participation. The political participation of the old generation was confined to the expression of votes and giving a bit of support for local politicians. These people rarely or never participated in active politics (except participation in strikes by estate workers). There is nothing striking about the political participation of the youth either. There isn't a powerful force to mobilize them into political action. The economic powerlessness has generated political powerlessness, which has marginalized the estate inhabitants.

The estate folk are a marginalized society. This is substantiated by their attitudes toward government officials. Some of the older dwellers are unhappy with the government officials. They talk about inefficiency, corruption and overt superiority that state officials assert over the common man. However, they are not very critical about state officials because they generally had limited needs to be fulfilled by them. So, many of the old are neither satisfied nor dissatisfied about their performances. Yet, the younger generation ridicules state officials for the aforesaid defects and for not serving the people for whom they have been appointed. They have lots of anger and hatred about the ill-treatment by the government officials. They nourish a deep sense of discrimination. This feeling stays like "cinder" in their minds. Two factors seem to be responsible for this marginalized situation. One is their poor economic standing and the other is the poor social recognition that outsiders confer on estate dwellers. The resultant feelings of marginality lead to resignation. And, this reinforces their underdevelopment. This situation also calls attention to the fact that some of the conditions, which perpetuate poverty among them, are systemic problems that are beyond their control.

However, it should be noted here that neither generation is so vociferous about exploitation. They do not think that their surplus production or simply their income is expropriated and appropriated by outside forces. They are troubled by the escalating cost of living and grumble about it, but do not necessarily cry out that they have been victimized by the unbridled forces of capitalism.

Next, a vital aspect of their poverty is the absence of planning. Both the old and the younger generations are in the same position regarding planning their future. Neither generation reported well laid-out plans for the future. If they had a plan, it was mostly an unrealistic plan. For example, some respondents pointed out that they had planned to build a new house in the next year. But it seemed to me that, given their low level of income, unemployment and underemployment, building a new house within such a short period was almost impossible. If they did not have a plan and if asked why almost everybody said that it was useless to make plans if that cannot be realized. Hence, old or young, the estate dwellers do not make plans, which would have provided them with a foundation to work upon.

The foregoing descriptions show that in the Hantana community there is very little intergenerational change in many respects of their lives. Majority of the old generation stagnated in the condition in which their parents lived. The younger generation, leaving out the few, who have escaped from poverty, now stagnates in the condition that the present older generation lived a several decades ago. Some have in a way gone poorer. It is evident that even the geographical mobility is rare, unless it happens through marriages to outsiders. However, I have not ignored the areas where there is observable intergenerational change. Now, let us examine some of those aspects, indicating some kind of change.

The housing conditions have undergone some intergenerational change. The hosing conditions of the younger generation have moderately been improved. Many of the households of both generations have now been equipped with electricity and a few electric appliances as well as some furniture. Most of the present houses have plastered walls and cemented floors. The estate has provided them with common flush toilets. The older generation did not enjoy these facilities in their past.

Yet, the type of housing, for the most part, is still the line house.

There is a vast intergeneration change regarding the willingness to stay in the estate and line houses. Almost all of the older generation did not and do not fret themselves about having to live in line houses and the estate. Only now they perceive that there is some kind of a differential treatment meted out to them by the mainstream society. But, they like estate residence for having several facilities. The younger generation, on the contrary, is very much disturbed and bothered about this discrimination. They personally feel and complain about it. As a result, they like to move out and to live in single houses, instead of line houses.

There are some minor changes in expenditure patterns especially in the realm of saving. Unlike the older generation, the younger generation, in a few cases though, is now starting to save some money for their children at a very small scale. This would not make a substantial difference in their life chances, but the habit itself is important to notice. This tendency could probably be the result of the realization that their children are bound to suffer at the hands of private moneylenders and from indebtedness, unless they have a little saving. After years of suffering, a minority of them has now realized the utility of savings. Also, while continuing to depend on moneylenders for credit, some young estate dwellers have started to explore the possibilities of pawning in the bank. A few of them now feel that the banks provide credits for much lower interest rates than moneylenders. If this awareness becomes widespread or if some outside intervention can create it, it is likely that local moneylenders will lose their strong grip on people, at least, to a certain extent and indebtedness will decrease.

Further, it was possible to note a marked intergenerational change in attitudes toward politicians. The older generation criticized the politicians for the use of violence and not helping them, but their viewpoint was blurred and they did not clearly understand what was happening in the realm of politics. Now, politics do not make an apparent impact on their lives. But, the younger generation is outrageous about the performances of the politicians. They fervently oppose corruption and the neglect of the poor. They have an intense contempt towards the behavior of the politicians. They do not take the present political situation for granted like the older generation. This change of attitudes could be due to the increased awareness on what happens in the realm of politics. It is difficult to specify how this awareness has come about. But, the impact of media and the relatively larger number of elections (due to devolution of power to provincial council, etc.) may have contributed to this situation.

Furthermore, there is an explicit intergenerational change in terms of the attitudes toward gender roles and relations. This is not to say that everybody of the older generation was authoritarian. But, the young is more conscious and concerned about women's role in the family. Women get better treatment and respect from them. The young believe that women play an equally important role as that of men in the family. And, in the decision-making in the household women actively participate. The older generation did not understand much about gender equality. So, the predisposition to authoritarianism or the sense of male superiority that Lewis described as a feature of the culture of poverty cannot be observed among the youth.

The respondents have made it very clear that they are aspiring to lead better lives. They think that their lives and those of their children will be better in the future. They hope to improve their conditions. The drawback is that these hopes do not have enough power and planning to drive them to reach their success goals.

So, is there a culture of poverty in the Hantana community? There is definitely a deep culture of poverty which is handed down from generation to generation in this community. The above description tells you that this community clearly has all the conditions necessary for the development of a culture of poverty. The community is a cash economy and most people work as labourers. They are considered unskilled and there is severe unemployment and underemployment. Wages are low from an absolute sense because their wages are not very different from other poor sections in Sri Lankan society. It was also clear that the community is not organized on any basis. The macro society is a wealth-oriented society where there is heavy stress on upward mobility and failure do so is very often considered personal fault.

Above conditions have created deep poverty culture in this community. The people are not integrated in the major institutions of the mainstream society. They are involved in the economy but are not owners of it in sense of benefiting from it. They are a marginalized society from an economic, political, social and also a spatial sense. They suffer segregation from society. The poverty they have to live in has been there form generations and it is handed down from generation to generation. The important question here is—where does this poverty come from? As I have explained in this paper, there are two major sources. One is the systemic causes and the other is the value system in the community, which perpetuates poverty or in other words culturally loaded causes. The poverty in this community is not just due to the personal fault of the people. I have cited ample evidence to show that the systemic causes have powerful influence on the poverty conditions in this community. The fact that the estate economy cannot absorb them into the work force, and that they are paid low, lack of skills, low savings, shortage of capital, absence of physical assets, lack of access to credit and weaknesses in the welfare system are beyond their control. Hence, it is not just the culture of poverty alone, which perpetuates poverty in this community. Having said that, their consumption orientation, and the lack of investment motive, lack of organization, absence of political participation, sense of apathy and resignation, absence of planning, heavy alcoholism and the like have much to do with culture of poverty. Even then the question is whether this concept gives us a comprehensive understanding on poverty. Most of the features which I have cited above as features of culture of poverty are in turn related not only to each other but also to systemic causes. It is an extremely difficult task to pinpoint their origin. Are the systemic causes the genesis of culture of poverty or vice versa? It is certain that they are interrelated and reinforce each other. But in the effort to address the issues related to culture of poverty, is necessary to get the core of it. It is my opinion that the culture of poverty is an outcome of the hostile conditions in which the estate dweller has always lived. The systemic causes led to create a pervasive poverty situation, which is now handed down from generation to generation. Now, their life style, which I see as a consequence of the systemic causes contributes to the perpetuation of poverty along with systemic causes. So, where does this knowledge lead us?

Culture of poverty as an explanation of poverty has several pros and cons. It has great potential to lend insight into a complex problem like poverty. It shows that certain conditions in society make poverty a part of people's lives, of their perception of reality and their worldview. It calls our attention to latent but vital aspects of poverty, which most other explanations would fail to notice. It brings out that once you are in poverty, it is enormously difficult for you to get out of it because poverty is a trap. It tells the policy-makers that physical alleviation of poverty is not sufficient solution to poverty. Thus, it adds a new perspective to the understanding poverty. However, this explanation has several serious flaws as well. Often, it stops after the mere description of a situation and fails to get at the root cause of a certain condition. It does not address the question of "why" in explaining the above stated conditions. So, often, it seems to hold the poor responsible for their poverty. In other words, it blames the victim. It does not capture or explain the intricate interrelations between the systemic causes and the culturally loaded causes. Further, it cannot capture national and regional variations or variations which can occur with time. The universal character that Lewis has attributed to the traits of the culture of poverty is questionable because some of its traits cannot be observed in our case. Also, the concept of the culture of poverty is a static concept. It does not have an applied orientation. A concept like social capital, presented by Putnam can explain a practical solution to this problem.

Putnam shows how social capital engenders a sense of solidarity and how a community can reap the benefits of coordinated actions that will be difficult in a community with low networks of social capital. Putnam emphasizes that after initially building social capital on a small-scale, then it is possible who develop it further to solve even large-scale social problems having more complex institutional arrangements. Unlike the theory of culture of poverty that looks at the poor pessimistically, social capital theory says that there are ways to improve the conditions of the poor by building networks. It does not assume that poor people are deadlocked into poverty. On the contrary, poor people have the potential to develop themselves. This is the reason why I am interested in applying the theory of social capital to study poverty, making it possible to construct a novel, much more humane and effective approach. This is very significant because relatively less attention has been given to the formation of social capital and the empowerment of the poor, helping them to voluntarily get out of the trap of poverty and stand on their own feet.

How could we use the social capital approach to understand the poverty situation of estate dwellers? A host of new intriguing questions come up when we try to answer this question. Is it the low level of social capital that has caused poverty? Does the level of social capital influence the economic performance of the estate dwellers? The estate community has a low level of both bonding and bridging social capital and this does have some implication on their poverty situation. My study highlights the fact that networks of social relations among the estate dwellers are minimal and thus do not generate mutually beneficial collective action, which is the expected outcome of dense social capital. It was pointed out that in many instances such as in finding employment, securing credits, getting children to school absence of strong cross-cutting networks among the estate dwellers has a considerable bearing on their life chances and poverty. Moreover, intra-communal ties too are weak. Thus, low levels of both bridging and bonding social capital are a noticeable feature of the poverty situation in this community.

This community is not characterized by strong norms of reciprocity. Their social fabric does not support collective actions. I have shown above that the socialization process that the children of this community go through does not generate norms and values which are supportive of collective action. The absence of grass-roots organizations such as a funeral aid societies, credit societies which are crematistic of rural villages in Sri Lanka, substantiate this proposition. However, one exception to this claim is the presence of trade unions among the tea-pluckers, which organizes them into some kind of collective action. In fact, the trade union has been responsible for several wage hikes that workers were able to win.

Trust is a strong component of social capital. But I have cited many examples to illustrate how a great deal of mistrust prevails among estate dwellers, against state officials, and politicians. Yet, the low level of trust, as was pointed out, is a result of the objective conditions and also harassments at the hands of the state officials and politicians. In some instances this mistrust has grown into intense hatred. Low level of interpersonal trust prevents organized actions by estate dwellers and as was pointed out earlier, deprives them of mutual benefits especially to find grievances to their problems.

Therefore, it is quite clear that low level of social capital has reinforced poverty in the estate community. It should be stressed here too that it is the systemic causes which have created poverty in this community. It is difficult to say whether poverty itself is a cause of low level of social capital. What we can say is that low level of social capital contributes to deepening of poverty. What is even more interesting is the possibility that social capital can go a long way to get people out of poverty. Social capital approach is not merely an academic tool to understand poverty but it is an action-oriented set of ideas. Through organizing the poor into groups, it is possible to give them better chances of coming out of poverty. Social mobilization can be used for productive work at the micro level such as village infrastructure development, to improve houses at low cost, to create credit societies and to remove the problem of private moneylender, to create awareness, to give them a sense of power, to overcome resignation, to create thrift and to give them some bargaining power and so on. For example, in a farming community, if all farmers can work collectively, they can influence the price of what they produce to a certain extent.

Yet it does not mean that poverty can be addressed through social capital alone. As we saw in the case of this plantation community, there are systemic factors and external dynamics involved. Social capital can only address the micro-factors in relation to development. There is a limit beyond which social capital can play no role in the development of a community. These are the macro-factors in development, which the social capital base in a society cannot address. Social capital can draw people out of poverty to a certain extent but it will not necessarily lead to a take off stage. Social capital may help in getting people to work for their development with self-reliance, in securing certain infrastructure, in overcoming micro-level barriers, and in developing a support base for economic actions but after they have come to a certain stage in their development, the step beyond that can be addressed only by macro-factors like external economic environment and macroeconomic policies. For example, some community-based organizations try to provide the members with credit for microenterprises. But, this alone cannot produce a thriving economy for microenterprises. Although social capital approach is an extremely useful instrument in understanding poverty and tackling this issue, there is a need to combine other approaches. As John Harris argues, development cannot be "depoliticized" (Harris, 2001). Especially in the case of the poor, development needs care because not all the poor can be made to be economically productive in a short period of time. (Gunatilaka, 1997, Hulme and Mosely, 1996). So, social capital approach cannot be the panacea for all the problems confronting this community.

Finally, getting back to the core of this paper, it is important to say that from an academic sense, the culture of poverty thesis can be used to understand poverty in combination with the social capital approach. The culture of poverty approach looks at certain aspects of poverty and it helps in understanding poverty. But it does not provide a comprehensive explanation. Here, the social capital approach can be combined as I have tried to do in this paper. It gives better insight and also suggests a strategy to attack poverty.

REFERENCES

Abeysekera, Gladys. 1991. "Cottage Industries and Women in Development." Colombo: Agrarian Training and Research Institute.

Alailima, Patricia. 1997. "Poverty and Unemployment in Sri Lanka." Colombo: Department of Natural Planning, Ministry of Finance and Planning.

Alcock, Pate. 1993. *Understanding Poverty*. Hong Kong: Macmillan.

Amunugama, Sarath. 1964. "Rural credit in Ceylon: Some Sociological Observations." *The Ceylon Journal of Historical and Social Studies*, July-December 1964. Vol. 7, No. 2: 135-143.

Athukorala, Karunathissa. 2000. "Viyawaharika Samaja Viddyave Bavithaya Pilibanda Hadinvemak (Sinhala)." *Samaja Viddya Vimarshana*. 1(1).

Bourdieu, Pierre. 1985. "Forms of Capital," in J.G. Richardson (ed.). *Handbook of Theory and Research for the Sociology of Education*. 241-58. New York. Greenwood.

Bourdieu, Pierre. 1999. *The Weight of the World: Social Suffering in Contemporary Society*. Stanford: Stanford University Press (Translated by Ferguson, Priscilla Parkhurst: Emanuel, Susan: Johnson, Joe and Waryn, T Shoggy).

Central Bank of Sri Lanka. 1999. Annual Report. Colombo. The Central Bank Printing Press.

Coleman, James. 1988. "Social Capital in the Creation of Human Capital." *American Journal of Sociology*: 94: 95-120

Datt, Gaurav and Dileni, Gunawardane. 1997. "Some Aspects of Poverty in Sri Lanka," 1985-90 (Policy Research Working Paper). Policy Research Department, World Bank.

Debertin, David. 2002. "A Comparison of Social capital in Rural and Urban settings." http://www.uky.edu/~deberti/socsaea.htm. The World Bank.

Gayathri, M.A. Chandima. 1998. "Dugeebawa Saha Sri Lankawe Dugeebawa Pitudekina Rajya Wedasatahan Pilibanda Agayeemak, Samaja Sameeksha."

Goodhand, Jonathan, David Hulme and Nick Lewer. 2000. "Social Capital and the Political Economy of Violence: A Case Study of Sri Lanka. Disasters," 24(4): 390-406.

Gunatilaka, Ramani. 1997. "Credit-based Participatory Poverty Alleviation Strategies in Sri Lank: What Have We Learned?" Colombo: IPS.

Harris, John. 2001. *Depoliticizing Development: The World Bank and Social Capital*. London: Anthem Press.

Lewis, Oscar. 1967. *La Vida: A Puerto Rican Family in the Culture of Poverty*. London: London Panther Modern Society.

Paxton, Pamela. 1999. "Is Social capital declining In United States? A Multiple Indicator Assessment". *American Journal of Sociology*. 105: 88-127.

Putnam, Robert, Robert Leonardi and Raffaella Nanetti. 1993. *Making Democracy Work: Civil Traditions in Modern Italy*. Princeton, New Jersey: Princeton University Press.

Putnam, Robert. 1995. "Bowling Alone: America's Declining Social Capital." *Journal of Democracy* 6:1, 65-78.

Rao, C.N. Shankar. 1998. *Sociology*. New Delhi: Chand and Chand Company Limited.

Ratnapala, Nandasena. 1986. *Drug and Narcotic Dependence in Sri Lanka*. Moratuwa. By the Author.

Ratnapala, Nandasena. 1989. *Rural Poverty in Sri Lanka*. Nugegoda. By the Author.

Ratnayake, R.M.K. 1994. "Alleviation and Reduction of Poverty, Sri Lanka." Sri Lanka Journal of Social Sciences." June\December, Vol. 17, No. 1 and 2: 25-40.

Silva, K.T. and Athukorala, Karunathissa. 1991. *The Watta Dwellers*. Lanham: University Press of America Inc.

Silva, K.T. 2000. "Poverty and Social Exclusion." A Paper presented at the Second Annual-Symposium on Poverty Research in Sri Lanka, Colombo.

UNDP. 1997. *Human Development Report*. New York/Oxford: Oxford University Press.

Uphoff, Norman and C.M. Wijayaratna. 2000. "Demonstrated Benefit from Social Capital: The Productivity of Farmer Organizations in Gal Oya, Sri Lanka." *World Development*, 28 (ii): 1875-1890.

World Bank. 1995. *Sri Lanka Poverty Assessment: Country Management Unit, South Asia Region*.

World Bank. 2000-01. *World Development Report: Attacking Poverty*. New York. Oxford University Press.

2

Improving HR's Performance in the Knowledge Age: Key to Corporate Success

TAPOMOY DEB

Performance Management is the key strategy of Human Resource Management. With globalization of economy, the focus of organizational success has shifted to human resources. With proactive and systematic management of human resources, organizational performance can be improved to attain competitive advantage in a market-place characterized by Olympian competition. It is in this context that, HRM as a function attains utmost importance for improving organizational performance. But unfortunately, HR still practices a reactive role without reference to the organizational strategy and focus. In this article, we shall explore what makes HR a truly business-aligned function for improving corporate performance.

In the words of David Ulrich (1997), "HR should not be defined by what it does, but by what it delivers—results that enrich the organization's value to customers, investors and employee."

Human resource management, in the sense of getting things done through people, is an essential part of every manager's responsibilities. "People are our most valuable asset" is a cliché which no member of any senior management team would disagree with. Yet, the reality for many organizations is that their people remain undervalued, undertrained and underutilized. The rate of change facing organizations has never been greater and organizations must absorb and manage change at a much faster rate than in the past. In order to implement a successful business strategy to face this challenge, organizations, large or small, must ensure that they have the right people capable of delivering the strategy. The marketplace for talented, skilled people is competitive and expensive. Taking on new staff can be disruptive to existing employees. Also, it takes time to develop 'cultural awareness', product/ process/ organization knowledge and experience for new staff members as every organization has its unique value system, product and process differentials on account of newer technologies and process optimization parameters, protocols and a unique set of desirable and undesirable behaviours which needs to be understood and internalized by the new employees for effective job performance. Also, at the same time, every new employee also possesses his/her own value system, expectations, different exposure to technology, process and people behaviours and unique set of desirable and undesirable behaviours as gained through personal and organizational socialization processes. All these require time and conscious effort on the part of the new employees to make congruence between the two.

As organizations vary in size, aims, functions, complexity, construction, the physical nature of their product, and appeal as employers, so do the contributions of human resource management. Some HR functions are manned by reactive people whereas others are manned by proactive people; some are manned by avid risk takers and experimenters whereas others believe in safe play; some are manned by independent people whereas others are dependent on leadership for day-to-day decision-making (typically known as poonch—poonch management), etc. It is essentially the quality of such HR functionaries, organizational environment and commitment of leadership which brings about a decisive impact on the contributions of HR function. Therefore, human resource management plays a pivotal role in proactive management of employees for effective orientation of people philosophies with organizational objectives. Therefore, human resource management is the effective use of human resources in order to enhance organizational performance as confirmed through numerous research work such as that of Huang (2000), Michie and Sheehan-Quinn (2001), Kelliher and Riley (2002), Michie and Sheehan (1999), Cooke, F.L. (2001), Rondeau and Wager (2001)[1], etc.

It is worth noting here that the problem comes back to the idea of people being labeled as 'assets' and 'resources' which John Morris (1974) tellingly exposed in his pointed distinction between 'human resources' and 'resourceful humans'. Human resources are the readily manipulated foot soldiers of organizations; resourceful humans are the managers and others, but particularly managers who initiate. The best test of resourcefulness then is to go out and start one's own business.

Performance of HR function is critically linked to the performance of human resources and ultimately the organization. Successful HR function knows that to win in today's competitive marketplace they must attract, develop, and retain talented and productive employees. Winning organizations get their competitive edge from a performance management system that helps them hire talented people; place them in the right position; align their individual performance with the organization's vision and strategic objectives; develop their abilities; and reward performance commensurate with contributions to the organization's success.

To be successful in an increasingly competitive and demanding global environment, organizations must continuously improve their performance. To do so, they require sustained performance improvement from their employees as people are central to competitive advantage of any organization. Capital can be arranged, technology can be copied/adopted but nobody can emulate a highly committed and competent workforce capable of delivering unparallel results. Therefore, organizational performance can only be substantially improved by improving performance of its human resources—the heart and life line of any contemporary business organization. Hence, organizations are increasingly realizing that performance management system is associated with significant economic returns.

Employees are the most valuable asset. Optimizing that asset through comprehensive performance management is key to organizational success. Unfortunately, in many organizations today the performance management process is flawed:

- There is little or no alignment of performance goals with the business strategy.
- Standards are likely to be missing, or inappropriately applied.
- The process is so time and labour-intensive that it interferes with productivity, rather than enhancing it.

HR function has to move to the pinnacle of organizations' objectives, along with generating revenue and managing costs and seek to link senior leadership, HR, and line management—together to drive that improved performance. Failure to connect the various parts of the performance management to business strategy of the organization at times can lead an organization to inconsistent and haphazard performance. A good performance management system designs competencies, taps into the talent pool, engages senior leadership to "own" the talent, uses technology, and ties the critical aspects of performance management system together to show consistent business performance improvement. It is the job of the HR function to mould individuals to maximize their potential, to help employees find their true talents and leverage them on the job, and to arm the workforce with the competencies necessary to perform in an exceptional manner. If HR function is able to accomplish this feat, it has increased its value to an organization.

Therefore, it is in this context that performance management assumes utmost importance. Performance Management has been defined by Stephen P. Robbins, David A. DeCenzo, Robin Stuart-Kotze and Eileen B. Stewart (2005) as:

- Integration of management practices that includes a formal review of employee performance.
- Includes establishing performance standards and reviewing the performance.
- To ensure that organizational goals are being met.

Thus, Performance Management refers to a set of techniques and procedures which the common features of:

- providing information on the contribution of human resources to the strategic objectives of the organization;
- forming a framework of techniques to secure maximum achievement of objectives for given inputs; and
- providing a means of inspecting the functioning of the process links which deliver performance against objectives.

In today's complex, turbulent and dynamic business environment—where goals, circumstances, organizational structure, staffing, and activities are constantly changing—it is the task of the HR function to organize, motivate, equip, and direct rather ordinary people to perform at their highest possible levels, helping them meet performance expectations successfully and facilitate in getting feedback, and meaningful recognition and rewards.

To be successful, a performance measurement system must generate data on required organizational results, actions and behaviour vis-à-vis the actual result, action and behaviour exemplified through financial, customer and employee datasheets, right from planning of HR strategies, individual tasks and goals to its ultimate, effective delivery. The gaps provide grounds for improving and enhancing organizational practices and achieve goals; provide accountability for all of the stated goals, improve performance, allocate resources; and make informed policy decisions. Measurement of performance begins with defining an explicit model or conceptual framework that describes what organization's purpose and goals are and trace the pathways to outputs and potential outcomes and impacts.

HR as a function has been for long on the periphery of an organization. It has enjoyed providing residual services to an organization at a cost to the organization without generating adequate revenues. A re-look at recent times has brought forth the flaws of the HR function to the forefront. It is important for HR professionals to understand that it is more than a facilitator—the real driving force behind an organization in improving performance of the organization. However, the pertinent question which arises here is, how? Based on experience, the following strategies are suggested:

1. Ownership of Performance Management System

HRM as a function has to play a vital and profound role in devising, implementing, monitoring and integrating organization through performance improvement programme. Performance management system by itself shall be grossly inadequate if the owners themselves are satisfied with the role of mere facilitators as pointed out earlier. It has to ensure that the organizational environment, processes and people are all aligned along with the business strategy of the organization as active constituent of the system and performance is the sole criteria of being member of the organization. It has to create an enabling environment so as to harness the natural talents and abilities of the people and leverage it for easy integration with performance improvement programmes.

HR function has also to see that every employee of the organization understands and speaks the language of business of the organization and visualizes success as a team, much beyond individualistic connotations.

2. Linking Work Goals to Performance Expectations

HR function has to ensure that the line management spells out clearly the role, responsibilities and behaviours necessary for effective performance of a given job especially in case of new staff members. Often, it has been found that there exists an only vague and broad job expectation which only leads to role ambiguity and conflict thereby undermining performance of the employees. HR function must act as a strategic partner in counseling line management and employees alike to develop appropriate models of actions and behaviours for appropriate results in conjunction with business strategies.

3. Change Agent

In the context of performance improvement programmes, it is worth noting that work goals are a moving target than a stationary one because of immense uncertainty, complexity and lack of dependability in the contemporary business scenario. HR function has therefore, to act as a key organizational change agent for bringing greater fit between the environment and the organization by improving adaptability, capability and capacity of the employees. This will be possible only when employees know very well the change necessary for attaining the mission and objectives of the organization.

4. Organizational Rejuvenation Initiator

It is a misnomer to believe that only mature organizations need rejuvenation. Even growing organizations need rejuvenation as a part of adaptive response to continuously changing environment. HR function has to keep on analyzing internal HR processes and procedures for congruence with mission and objectives of the organization. It has to change, adopt, modify and initiate new processes and procedures which meet the needs of the organization and changing business scenario and appraise and enable employees for greater fit between business strategy and HR strategy.

5. Ethics Custodian

There lies a number of ethical issues in performance management programmes as basic as individual biases and prejudices, liking and disliking, personal allegiances, personal references, balancing acts, etc. which demeanor the credibility of performance management system right from planning stage to appraisal stage. Therefore, HR function has to balance out all these aspects by introducing multi rater systems, multi rater feedback system, and scrutinizing all performance improving programmes from the point of an internal Systems Critic. The problem is that HR function does not work like an organizational critic as HR professionals are more concerned about their individual growth and prospects. No performance management system can be good enough if it is not critically examined and validated.

Now, the question is how to appraise performance of HR function in an organization. 'Performance Scorecard' methodology, based on balanced scorecard method, can be evolved to appraise performance of HR function. Performance scorecard enables the leadership to determine how effectively HR is leveraging on human capital as well as mobilize and galvanize the people within the organization in terms of four perspectives—Quality, Cost, Delivery, and Responsiveness. A suggested methodology is given below:

1. Operations Perspective

This perspective refers to internal business processes and their alignment with HR planning, acquisition, development, and retention of trained and developed employees who can perform their jobs effectively keeping in view the business priorities of the organization. Metrics based on this perspective allow senior leadership to know the effectiveness, efficiency and quality of these HR processes in meeting organizational and environmental requirements.

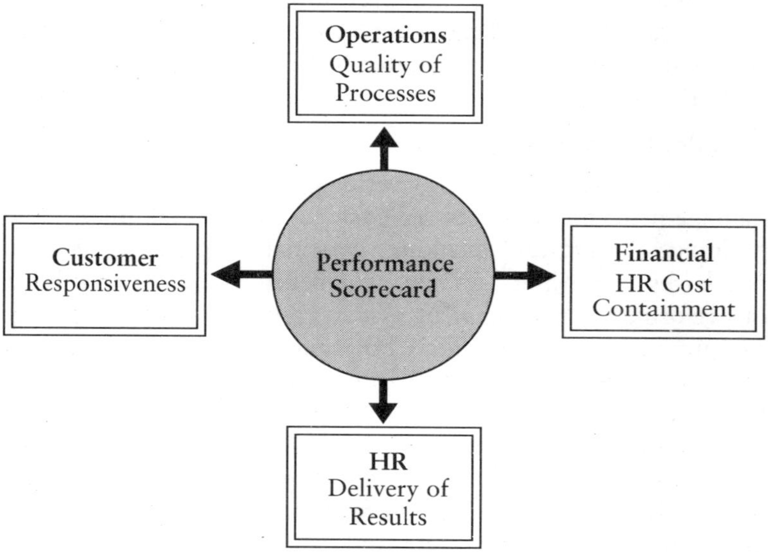

2. Financial Perspective

HR function needs to keep cost of compensation and benefits at optimal level based on organization's ability to pay, industry norms, business strategy, and growth prospects. Here, it is pertinent to emphasize that people are not costs, but an attempt should be made to equate actual/expected contributions in terms of financial data with respect to investment made on employees. After all capital is a prime necessity of an organization.

3. HR Perspective

This perspective includes employee training and corporate cultural attitudes related to both individual and corporate self-improvement. Where success was once dependent upon an organization's ability to discover and manage natural resources, success today goes to the organizations that most effectively discover and manage their human resources. The key differentiator between the corporate winners and losers in the 21st century will be the effectiveness of knowledge-worker; talented people—the only repository of knowledge—to deliver cost-effective, efficient and innovative solutions and services to create greater customer value. Today's HR function needs to develop an intrapreneur workforce capable of delivering results at all times, consistently and continuously.

4. Customer Perspective

Recent management philosophy has shown an increasing realization of the importance of customer focus and customer satisfaction in any business. These are leading indicators: if customers are not 0sfied, they will eventually find other organizations that will meet their needs. Poor performance from this perspective is thus a leading indicator of future decline, even though the current financial picture may look good.

Customer delight and loyalty can be built only through employees because happy, committed and motivated employees pass on their 'goodwill' to the customers like a true partner. Therefore, besides HR function training, motivating, developing and continually inciting them to harness their customer relationship skills and competencies in order to build and sustain customer base, HR function also needs to be responsive at all time towards its internal as well as external customers. Responsiveness includes innovation, faster decision-making, leading an industry in price or value, and effectively linking with suppliers and vendors to build a value chain for the customer. To support the value chain argument, research indicates that employee attitude correlated highly with customer attitude.

Conclusion

Human Resource Management is a philosophy of people management based on the belief that human resources are uniquely important to sustain business success. An organization gains competitive advantage by using its people effectively, drawing on their expertise and ingenuity to meet clearly defined objectives because employee actions directly influence the "intangible" assets, e.g. customer loyalty, capacity to innovate and change, brand image, intellectual capital, and leadership effectiveness depend heavily on employee capabilities and commitment—the very real assets that often account for more than half of an organization's value.[2] Intangible assets drive enhanced fiscal accountability, programme effectiveness and customer-centered service. Take the example of Microsoft Corporation, its almost entire assets lie in its people. Its people's talents, innovation and excellence skills have made it world's number one software conglomerate. Therefore, HR function has to enable employees to harness their hidden talents and potentials, see the big picture of the organization, stay flexible, innovative, young, and adaptive, capable of meeting today's and tomorrow's business opportunities and challenges on pre-emptive basis. Through such strategies HR function shall be able to ensure that the employees of the organization are utilized in such a way that the employer draws the greatest possible benefit from their abilities and the employees obtain both material and psychological rewards from their work. This will build the credibility of HR function as the key differentiator of corporate success.

REFERENCES

1. Price, Alan. 2004. *Human Resource Management in a Business Context*, 2nd edn. Thomson Learning.
2. Deb, Tapomoy. 2005. *A Conceptual Approach to Strategic Talent Management*. 1st edn. Indus Publishing Company, New Delhi.

3

Incorporating Gender into Development Studies

GINA BUIJS

EXECUTIVE SUMMARY

This paper is a brief overview of the role of gender in development thinking in the past fifty years. While women were ignored as a category in early development theorizing, they were later brought in as a separate category to men. By the end of the 20th century, gender issues were recognized as being crucial to the successful implementation of development in LDCs but gender aspects were still not being integrated into development planning at a practical level.

Introduction

It is virtually axiomatic in the 21st century that women should be key participants in and beneficiaries of policies, programmes and projects concerned with poverty eradication and improvement in livelihoods. There have been four world UN conferences on women in recent decades, in Mexico City (1975), Copenhagen (1980), Nairobi (1985) and Beijing (1995). Blueprints have been produced designed to eliminate discrimination against women (CEDAW) and to ensure women's interests and needs are reflected across the spectrum of development issues and not only in traditionally 'female' areas of health, contraception and education. Major UN and European Union development agencies (such as DFID) include frameworks to check that gender is considered even in projects that might appear gender neutral such as those involving civil engineering or famine relief.

Critics of what appears to be a more balanced approach to gender argue that development organizations have co-opted gender issues and submerged them in mainstream development activity rather than allowing gender issues to challenge ideas and institutions. Some say gender as a reference point has become another example of the way in which the priorities and discourses of the West have dominated development, imposing neo-colonial ideas on communities and countries with different priorities and understanding of gender differences and gender roles.

Gender and Ideology

Because ideas of gender roles have a strong ideological content, policy in both poor and better-off countries often reflects normative or prescriptive versions of female and male roles, rather than what men and women actually do. For example, ideology in African cattle keeping societies states that women have nothing to do with the animals. Women are not allowed to herd cattle or enter the cattle enclosure. Yet we find that an essential part of the bridewealth gifts is the cow given by the bridegroom to his mother-in-law, which remains her property to do with as she wishes and which may not be sold by her husband. Ownership of cattle and other livestock enables many rural African women to build up capital, which they may use to finance their own income generating projects.

Maxine Molyneaux (1998) suggests that planning for low income women must be based on the distinction between 'women's interests', strategic gender interests and practical gender interests. While the concept of women's interests assumes that women will share interests based on the fact of being women, in reality the position of women in any society will depend on a number of different criteria such as class and ethnicity as well as gender. Thus women may share common interests based more on class or ethnicity than the biological fact of being women. Molyneaux suggests that more important than women's interests are the gender interests that women develop because of their social positioning through gender attributes. She makes a distinction between strategic and practical gender interests.

Strategic Gender Needs

Strategic gender needs are the needs women identify because of their subordinate position to men in society. Strategic gender needs will vary according to the particular context they arise in. They relate to gender divisions of labour, power and control and may include issues such as legal rights, domestic violence and women's control over their bodies. Meeting strategic gender needs helps women to achieve greater equality. It changes existing roles and therefore challenges women's subordinate position. Strategic gender needs may include abolishing the sexual division of labour, ameliorating the burden of domestic work and child care, removing institutionalized forms of discrimination such as lack of the right to own land and property, or to get access to credit; establishing political equality and measures to prevent male violence and control over women.

Practical Gender Needs

Practical gender needs are needs women identify in their socially accepted roles in society. They do not challenge the gender division of labour or women's subordinate position in society, although they arise out of them. Practical gender needs are often concerned with inadequate living conditions, such as water provision, health care and employment. Because the gender division of labour within the household gives women the main responsibility, not only for domestic work and child care, family health and food provision but also for the community management of housing and basic services, and income production, so policies aimed at meeting practical gender needs must focus on the domestic arena, income earning activities and community level requirements of housing and basic services. While basic needs such as food, shelter and water are required by all, they are identified specifically as the practical gender needs of women, arising out of women's gendered responsibilities for their families and communities.

The early efforts to integrate women into the development process (Boserup, 1970) were based on an analysis that saw women as excluded from the development process. This approach concentrated on women's lack of access to resources as the key to their subordination without raising questions about the role of gender relations in restricting that access in the first place. In the last two decades the WID approach has been criticised and broadened into GAD (Gender and Development) and applied to a range of development policies and practices.

In the 1990s there was considerable debate about the need to distinguish between the needs of poor women, in terms of their gendered responsibilities for household survival and reproduction and the issues surrounding the importance of supporting women in challenging gender relations (meaning that women often have less access than men to the scarce resources available to the poor in developing countries). This distinction between needs and issues has often been lost sight of in anti-poverty strategies which have tended to focus on women as among the poorest of the poor instead of applying a gender analysis to the causes of poverty and the effectiveness of poverty elimination strategies (Moser, 1993).

While development is still seen in terms of structural and political inequalities, gender remains an important predictor of whether a person is 'poor'. But the 'feminization of poverty', meaning the fact that women are most often the 'poorest of the poor' may obscure the fact that structures of gender subordination cannot be reduced to poverty and that poverty analysis and policy should not be focused only on women.

Applying a GAD approach to the 'feminization of poverty' reveals problems. For instance, a commonly used measure of poverty in many countries is individual food consumption. But such measures are often based on amounts of food consumed by households which do not reveal intra-household gender inequalities of food access and distribution. Another example is the increasing masculinity ratios in South-East Asia which are a product of the widespread cultural preference in that region for male children. This preference results in systematic discrimination in many communities in the allocation of food, health care and other scarce resources. The poorer the household the more such discrimination endangers girls and the more crucial the discrimination in boy/girl food allocation. Poverty focused food security programmes therefore need to understand and work with a detailed knowledge of the dynamics of intra-household food allocation.

Dangers also exist if the gendered needs of poor women are conceptualized only in terms of the material provision of food, as other causes of female morbidity and mortality such as deliberate injury, differential access to health care, and the providing of food to male infants and children before female ones may be overlooked, (Smith 1997). While such practices are culturally based, we need to recognise that they are enforced by both men and women. The problem is to understand the ways in which gender norms and roles are reinforced and perpetuated and what opportunities exist to change these practices.

Gender Mainstreaming

Gender mainstreaming, the practice of situating gender analysis in all aspects of development, rather than leaving it to women's issues, has been a response to the lack of progress achieved by policies and projects designed to target women since the 1970s. These policies have created what Pearson (2000, p. 400) has referred to as "gender ghettos". Nevertheless, this attempt to move gender analysis from the margin to the centre has been resisted by the institutional culture of many development organizations and universities.

In order to counteract this tendency to avoid dealing with gender it is helpful to get away from an exclusive association of gender with women, whether from a WID or a GAD perspective, and instead analyse the role of men in development issues. Recently in the West there has emerged a growing concern with the problems of men and masculinity. These problems are connected to rising levels of unemployment, especially among lower skilled workers and younger males; lower educational and skill levels appearing among young men as compared to young women, as well as a culture of increasing drug-taking, criminal activity and sexual irresponsibility. These are also issues that are of major concern in South Africa.

Development analysts must begin to look at the complex and multiple roles of men and the ways in which changes in the ability and desire of men to fulfil these roles pose challenges for men as well as women. The need to provide answers to problems of domestic violence and community safety as well as the spread of HIV/AIDS, demands that men be part of the solution and not only the problem. Development analysis today still remains centred on economic (and thus 'productive' rather than 'reproductive') issues. The point to emphasize is that it is not men themselves who constitute a problem but cultural attributes and attitudes that are associated with dominance and power.

Conclusion

The teaching of Development Studies must incorporate a realistic view of gender relations which takes into account cultural norms and values and the ways in which men and women negotiate their positions in the family and community, if it is to be successful in pointing the way to meaningful change in poor societies.

REFERENCES

Boserup, E. 1970. *Women's Role in Economic Development*, London: Allen and Unwin.

Molyneaux, M. 1998. "Analysing women's movements" in C. Jackson and R. Pearson, (eds.) *Feminist Visions of Development: Gender Analysis and Policy*. London: Routledge.

Moser, C. 1993. *Gender Planning and Development: Theory, Practice and Training*. London: Routledge.

Pearson, R. 2000. "Rethinking gender matters" in A. Allen, and A. Thomas, (eds.) *Poverty and Development into the 21st Century*, Oxford: Oxford University Press for the Open University.

Smith, S.C. 1997. *Case Studies in Economic Development*, 2nd edition. New York: Addison-Wesley.

4

US-China: Free Market or Statism

JAMES PETRAS

The most striking aspect of the US (and European) trade conflict with China is Washington's systematic rejection of the free market and its resort to heavy-handed dependence on state intervention. Equally astonishing, supposedly orthodox free market economists have joined the chorus of protectionist politicos (like Robert Zoellick, Deputy Secretary of State) in questioning China's free trade policy and demanding that China abide by US directives instead of the free play of market forces (*Financial Times* Oct. 7, 2005, p. 5). Worse still, some experts like Fred Bergsten, US director of the Institute for International Economics, are demanding more concessions from China under threat of a major economic confrontation (*Financial Times* August 25, 2005, p. 11).

Political Myths and Economic Realities

The US yearly trade deficit with China (US$ 186 Billion by July 2005) is largely a result of US inefficiencies, not Chinese trade restraints. China has the lowest import barriers of any large developing country. In areas where the US has invested, innovated and is efficient, in agriculture, aeronautics and high tech, the US has a trade surplus. The US trade deficit is largely in the appliances, electronics, clothing, toys, textile and shoe industries where many US corporations have invested in Chinese subsidiaries to export back to the US. Over 50% of Chinese exports to the US are through US multinational corporations. The US trade deficit is in large part between the US state and its own MNCs located in China.

China's exports are largely based on imports of parts from overseas, which are assembled and then sold abroad. According to the *Financial Times*, "...China is merely the last stop for a lot of the goods Asia exports to the US, importing...components from elsewhere in the region—including Japan. The local value added in its exports is as low as 15% (*Financial Times* Oct. 11, 2005, p. 5)." In other words China is a huge importer from other countries with which it has a trade deficit, largely with Asian manufacturers, oil exporting countries and Third World exporters of raw materials. China's overall trade surplus is largely based on its commerce with the US. US tariff and quotas against Chinese goods will prejudice world trade.

Contrary to US political and academic ideologues, China is one of the most liberal economies in Asia. By 2003 the ratio of China's stock of inward investment (inflows of foreign investment) to GDP was 35%—against 8% in South Korea, 5% in India and just 2% in Japan (*Financial Times* Sept. 15, 2005, p. 11). Moreover, China is the world's third largest trading nation. In 2004, China's ratio of trade to GDP reached 70%, far greater than the US and Japan which have ratios to trade to GDP below 25%.

Orthodox economists and US Congressional members argue that China's currency (renminbi) is undervalued and that a larger re-valuation would reduce the US trade deficit. Over the past several years the US dollar has been devalued in relation to several currencies—including the Euro, the Pound and the Swiss franc—and yet the US trade deficit has increased. The focus on Chinese currency reform is totally beside the point. The key problem is that US capitalists are not investing in domestic productive sectors, they are not upgrading their productive sites, nor are they introducing technological innovations to lower costs. Instead they are investing overseas, in non-productive sectors at home, speculating in real estate, today (and IT, yesterday), increasing profits via cuts in labour costs—hardly a sound method to compete with low-cost labour producers.

The failure of the US MNCs to support a universal national health plan and their reliance on private medicine increases the cost of production by 10% contributing to the loss of competitiveness of US enterprises and an increase in the trade deficit.

Chinese economic policy with regard to foreign investment is far more liberal than US policy. In 2004, foreign invested enterprises in China accounted for 57% of China's exports. In contrast, in the US, the Committee on Foreign Investments in the United States (CFIUS), constantly resorts to "flexible" definitions of "public interest", "national" or "strategic" interests to prevent foreign investors from investing and acquiring US firms. The highly publicized and successful US political intervention against the Chinese petroleum company, CNOC's, attempted acquisition of UNOCAL is the most recent example.

Moreover, the efforts of New York Senator Schumer and his congressional allies to slap a 27.5% tariff on imports from China would not reduce the US trade deficit as US importers would turn to other efficient Asian producers and Chinese manufacturers could relocate in adjacent countries. The result would be increased consumer costs, adversely affecting US domestic commerce without creating new jobs for US workers.

The "protected industries" in the US include some of the worst garment sweatshops paying below the minimum wage, some of which can be found in close proximity to Senator Schumer's offices in New York City. The problem is not foreign competition—that should be a given in a free market economy—but becoming efficient, which means investing in high tech and automated production, training, paying highly skilled workers, engineers and designers and providing stable employment so that workers can accumulate the experience and know-how which contributes to greater productivity.

The 1995 Uruguay Round Agreement on Textiles and Clothing (which the US signed) purported to eliminate quotas by January 1, 2005. US textile manufacturers had ten years to upgrade, modernize, and restructure prior to the advent of free trade. Instead they chose to rely on lowering labour cost, subcontracting to sweatshop labour contractors and political payoffs to lobbyists, politicians and labour bosses to impose new restraints on Chinese exports. The US reneged on its agreement to end quotas, pressuring China to limit Chinese exports to the US throughout 2005 and beyond (*Financial Times* Sept. 1, 2005, p. 1).

Current US "quotas" on Chinese exports already affecting textiles, clothing, color televisions, semiconductors, wood furniture, shrimp and steel have only increased the cost to US consumers and domestic sellers and increased profits for US monopoly producers in these same sectors, making them even less competitive. US producers paying monopoly prices to protected domestic manufacturers are hardly likely to be in a position to export and improve the US balance of payments.

The argument of "unfair competition" based on cheap labour is not convincing. The cost of labour is not the decisive factor affecting market competition or trade balances. Many low wage labour countries are not competitive. Many high-wage and high benefit Scandinavian and Low Countries compete successfully in the market relying on quality and specialized products, having abandoned production of labour-intensive consumer items. The resort to moralizing about trade terms especially by anti-union employers who avoid pension and health payments and provide the least time off for vacation and maternity in the Western world is pure cant. The fact is that substantial sectors of the US economy are not competitive given the product lines in which they are engaged, the inferior quality of their goods, the lack of long-term, large-scale investments in upgrading technology and productive organization and the siphoning off of profits to speculative sectors or to offshore subsidiaries.

Hiding between tariff walls, quotas and demagogic "China bashing" is simply an excuse to avoid the harsh discipline of the free market. Facing up to the free market would force the US business and political elite to own up to the fact that we have, in many sectors, a second-rate capitalism directed by a third-rate state.

The Myth of the "China Threat"

Instead of accepting the economic challenge from China and recognizing the need for re-thinking the misallocations of resources and the over-reliance on the paper economy, retrograde business elites and overpaid trade union bosses have joined forces with neo-conservative ideologues in promoting the idea of China as a national security threat which needs to be confronted militarily. The fusion of militarism abroad and protectionism at home has gained many adherents in Congress and in the executive branch—setting the stage for a self-fulfilling prophecy. Faced with increasingly bellicose rhetoric from Washington, China looks eastward toward strengthening its military and economic ties with Russia and Central Asia while diversifying its trade with Asia, Latin America, the Middle East and Africa.

US militant "protectionist militarism" with its confrontational approach to China threatens to block the free market of knowledge and technology. China's dynamic growth is not primarily based on "cheap labour"—it relies on the production of millions of highly trained scientific and professional workers each year. Each year tens of thousands of Chinese students, professors and scientists train abroad—many in the US. Very few US students pursue advanced degrees in science and engineering, with the result that foreign students—including Chinese—are increasingly critical to the US science workforce. In this free flow of ideas and scientists, both China and the US *theoretically* benefit—from a "free market" perspective. But as we have argued the US is opposed to the free market—especially in the free flow of scientific 'know-how'.

The US is doing everything possible to restrict the exchange of scientists, technology and knowledge—by a wide-ranging definition of "national security". Given their military definition of the China challenge, Washington argues that Chinese students and scholars should be restricted in what they study, what they learn as well as their access to technology. Universities, under Pentagon and Department of Commerce ruling, would have to secure special licenses and mark restricted areas within laboratories to prevent foreign students from using supercomputers, semiconductors, lasers and sensors in their research. The Department of Commerce plans to tighten controls in the export of commercial technologies (*Financial Times* Sept. 1, 2005, p. 11). From a free market perspective US export controls to China are self-defeating, lessening exports thus increasing the trade deficit, and have little impact on China's access to technology via Japan, Korea and Europe. In contrast, in July 2005 the European Union signed contracts with China to develop commercial usages of the Galileo satellite navigation system.

From a militarist-protectionist perspective the restrictions on ideas and the free circulation of scientists and students can be seen as part of a campaign of political and perhaps military confrontation and encirclement.

'China bashing' is merely a response to the loss of competitiveness. Nationalist demagogy in a declining global power is a compensatory mechanism for the failure of US capitalism to keep up with the competition—at least from its locus in the US economy.

China's Competitive Advantages

China not only outcompetes sectors of advanced capitalist countries but it competes successfully with low wage nations through the constant application of innovative techniques of production. Moreover, China is increasingly competitive at middle and high-end goods that go beyond consumer durables, garments and electronics. The competitive advantages are derived from the priorities designated by the state and the use of financial mechanisms and incentives. The claim that China "artificially" keeps its currency low thus gaining a competitive advantage is only voiced by the US and some European states. No one in Asia, Latin America, Africa or Oceania is complaining. With many regions of the world, China has a negative balance of payments, so that its overall surplus is much smaller than the China bashers who focus only on US-China bilateral relations would lead us to believe. Japan's global current account surplus is larger than China's by US$ 153 billion to US$ 116 billion

(*Financial Times* Oct. 11, 2005). There are no complaints from Japan, South Korea, India, Brazil, Argentina, Russia or Iran about an undervalued currency. In global terms, Japan and Germany account for 30% of the global current account surplus (228 billion Euros) and China only 8% (US$ 70 billion).

The US trade and budget deficit is exclusively a problem of internal failures: low or negative savings, high speculation, no upgrading of backward or uncompetitive sectors, artificial propping up of uncompetitive state subsidized sectors and large-scale, long-term US investment in productive facilities in China. Out of ignorance or cowardice, US Congressional leaders like Senator Charles Schumer refuse to confront the fact that the US trade deficit is in large part a product of the imbalance between exports by US MNCs located in China selling to the US market over exports from US based manufacturers. For US politicians, it is easier to get re-elected by taking cheap shots at an emerging economic power than to confront China-based US MNCs which finance electoral campaigns.

The US Imperial Threat to China

Throughout history, established global states, which are indebted and dependent on rising new powers, generate politicians who react with irrational resentment and belligerence. The gross failure of the Federal Reserve to contain the irrational exuberance in the paper and speculative economy over the past two decades, its complicity in the growth of unsustainable trade deficits, its outrageous support for tax cuts divorced from any link to the export economy marks the Bank and its Chairman as among the principle culprits in the decay of the US competitive position in the world market.

The danger is that as the US competitive position declines, a coalition of backward industrialists and civilian-militarists will try to compensate by provoking political confrontations and even inventing military threats to justify a military build-up. The politics of confrontation, however, will cause greater harm to the US MNCs than to China. After all it is the US which has imposed political barriers to the entry of Chinese investors in the US, while China has welcomed over 100 billion dollars from the leading US MNCs into the Chinese market. It is China which is financing the US trade deficit by purchasing US Treasury notes of declining worth, sustaining US over-consumption and under-investment.

In contrast to Washington's restrictive policies on Chinese investments in US energy companies, China welcomed large-scale investments by Peabody Energy (the world's largest coal company by sales) in joint venture mines (*Financial Times* Sept. 21, 2005, p. 19).

China is increasingly diversifying its trade and sources of energy. Its trade in Asia surpasses that of the US. China has increased its security links with Russia as a counterweight to the bellicose posturing of the US neo-conservative militarists and liberal democratic "humanitarian" imperialists.

Washington's increasing reliance on rearguard statism, whether in imposing tariffs, quotas, political restrictions on takeover bids, or blocking private investments is doomed to failure. Ultimately the US competitive or non-competitive position in the world market will determine who will be the next economic superpower. The only way for US capitalism to answer the China challenge is to save, invest, innovate, produce and compete in a free market—free of atavistic statism and militarism.

Washington's continued effort to weaken China's export capacity to lower its trade deficit has taken the form of an open-ended crusade. In July 2005, China announced a 2% re-valuation of the renminbi and shifted from a peg against the dollar to a link to a basket of currencies. China promised even greater flexibility over time, to allow its exporters to adjust to the more competitive conditions. The US economy, with all its inefficiencies, could not take advantage of this opportunity and demanded more concessions, a bigger re-valuation and less exports, hoping that state intervention would weaken China's export industries. The escalation of Washington's demands on China is 'open-ended'—one concession granted 'confirms' neo-conservatives in the Bush

Administration that they can secure others, setting the stage eventually for a 'recovery' of US export competitiveness. Even the US Federal Reserve Chairman recognizes that a stronger Chinese currency (or other Asian currencies) will make little difference to the US trade deficit (*Financial Times* Oct. 11, 2005, p. 5). As all G 20 countries meeting in Beijing pointed out the problem is the structural weaknesses in the US.

If we blow away the statist froth, propounded by our free-market economists, we would recognize that what China is demanding is that the US really live up to its free market ideology.

US Treasury Secretary John Snow, driven by the protectionist pressures from a Congress responding to backward sectors of the US economy and civilian militarists in the Executive, endlessly seeks to impose diplomatically what the US economically cannot achieve via the market—a reduction in the US trade deficit. Behind the veneer of diplomacy, Washington threatens a "trade war" via exorbitant tariffs of 27.5% and a hostile propaganda campaign labelling China a "currency manipulator". A "trade war and demonitization" strategy will most likely strengthen the civilian militarists and their campaign of military encirclement and nuclear brinksmanship in the Taiwan Straits. The confrontational strategy will provoke a Chinese defensive response which will lead to major US economic crises—as China unloads its US Treasury Bonds and reallocates its trade surpluses from the US to internal, Asian and European options. Washington will also see a loss of Chinese markets, investment opportunities leading to an attack on the profit margins of major US MNCs in China as Beijing increases its economic exchanges with Asia, Russia and the rest of the world.

If the civilian militarists' war with Iraq heightened the economic deficits and weakened the US competitive position, a neo-conservative confrontation with China will likely precipitate a deep structural crisis and probable collapse of the US economy, as we know it.

Conclusion

US colonial wars, the re-concentration of income in the upper 1% via tax cuts, the relocation of US MNC subsidiaries as overseas exporters to the US rather than exporters from the US, the dominance of the speculative economy (IT, real estate) and the ascendance of import intensive commercial capital over productive capital are the main reasons for the unsustainable US$ 700 billion current account deficit and the US$ 500 billion budget deficit. The speculator-militarist empire builders seek to divert attention from their failed policies by engaging in blatant deception and falsely blaming the 'devious and threatening' Asians, especially the Chinese. A report published in September 2005 by two leading European think tanks totally demolishes this ideological smokescreen. They point out that the US current account deficit grew by US$ 529 billion between 1997 and 2004 but China accounted for only 7% of this rise, compared to 30% for Russia and the Middle East (*Financial Times* Sept. 16, 2005, p. 2). US "blame the Asians" demagogic calls for Asian currency re-valuation would lead to deflation and economic stagnation without solving the US trade deficit. The key to lowering the trade deficit is for the US to engage in structural adjustments. These include re-introducing taxes on the very rich and developing an industrial and monetary policy that promotes local production for export and penalizes speculative investment and overseas relocation. This would increase local savings and investments, lower imports and stimulate exports.

Given the political ascendancy and economic centrality of multinational capital, the major investment banks and financial houses and the extensive web of real estate-construction and mortgage banks along with militarist neo-conservative control of the White House, there is virtually no possibility that US capitalism can rectify, correct or reform its strategic direction.

In the face of the embedded power bloc, which protects non-competitive producers and promotes US relocation of production abroad, the only logical outcome is the militarist-protectionist amalgam which defines US policy today. The backward sectors of US capital, together with the neo-conservative militarists, and the reactionary trade union bureaucracy promote "protectionist nationalism" at home and imperialist wars abroad. The competitive free-market multinational corporations promote overseas market openings but rely on a state, which depends politically on the extensive non-competitive manufacturing and subsidized agricultural sectors and the civilian militarists.

The calls by US economists for China to reform its currency, to accept US quotas on its exports, to retain a highly inferior military defence system while facing US power in the Far East is an attempt to forge a hodgepodge "consensus" between free market manufacturing MNCs and militarist-protectionists. Harmonizing interests between a rising industrial capitalist power like China and a militarist-speculative-commercial power like the US is a difficult chore in the short run and an impossible task in the medium term. China's booming demand for commodities has helped many Third World countries, while US agricultural subsidies and trade constraints have hurt these countries. US military belligerency in the Middle East has alienated the majority of the Arab and Muslim world, and divided Europe and its own population. Germany and Japan have accumulated massive trade surpluses at the expense of US-based exporters. The US ruling elite's resort to militarism in all of its brutal, colonial and invasive forms in Iraq and Afghanistan has exacerbated both the external and internal deficits, while demonstrating the strategic military weakness of an empire predominantly dependent on local satraps and military sepoys to sustain it. The US empire emptied of its domestic manufacturing export sector and relying on speculators and commercial importers (compradors) projects a militarist ideology to shore up the empire. These very forces have substantially weakened the competitive position of the US in relation to China's rising free market technological-industrial power.

The Chinese leaders cannot capitulate to US demands without destabilizing their own rule and the economic model they preside over. Strong capital inflows in 2005 from US, European and Asian speculators are betting on a re-valuation of the renminbi (China's currency), creating conditions for a financial crisis if the Chinese regime recklessly moves toward an unregulated monetary policy. Secondly, the ruling class free-marketeers in command of Chinese policy have gutted the public welfare system in favour of privatization, forcing Chinese workers, employees and shop owners to save to pay for education, housing, health care and retirement and thus have less income for domestic consumption. Chinese savings to pay for basic services limits domestic consumption and forces the Chinese regime to realize profits via exports. Accepting US dictates on reducing exports will destabilize the entire free market model. The elite basis of Chinese rule, in which 5% of the population controls over 50% of all private assets, faces escalating opposition from unemployed workers, exploited peasants and displaced urban and rural dwellers. Between 2001 and 2004 mass protests grew from 4,000 to over 70,000. China needs to create 15 million jobs a year, which requires the GDP to grow at least 8%. The Chinese ruling class believes economic growth will stabilize their rule. Since the growing social inequalities are embedded in the concentration of political-economic power at the top, they can only be changed by socialist movements from below. The rulers' program is to "increase the pie" hoping the trickle down effect will increase consumption and stabilize their rule and privileges. US pressure on China's rulers to increase domestic consumption and decrease exports threaten to undermine domestic class relations and undermine the growth and profit rates. The free-market export-oriented Chinese ruling class, like its US imperial counterpart, is hardly volunteering to sacrifice its class power and privileges to accommodate its economic competitors.

BIBLIOGRAPHY

Financial Times (London) 1990-2006 (March).

Organization for Economic Cooperation and Development (OECD): *Review of Agricultural Policies: China* (Paris, 2005).

China in the Global Economy (Paris, 2005).

Organization for Economic Cooperation and Development (OECD): *Economic Surveys China* (Paris, 2005).

International Monetary Fund, *Recent Trends in the Transfer to Developing Countries* (Washington 2002).

International Monetary Fund, *World Economic Outlook 2001-2005* (Washington 2005).

International Monetary Fund, *International Financial Statistics Yearbook* (Washington DC 2001-2005).

Organization for Economic Cooperation and Development (OECD), *Geographical Distribution of Flows* , (Paris 2003).

Cambridge History of China Vol. 12-15 (Cambridge University Press: London 1981).

Fairbanks, John. *The Great Chinese Revolution 1800-1985*, (Harper Collins: New York 1987).

Petras, James et al. *Empire with Imperialism*, (London: Zed Books 2005).

United Nations Conference on Trade and Development (UNCTAD)—Division of Transnational Corporations, *World Investment Report* 1994, 1998, 2002, 2004. (New York and Geneva).

United Nations Conference on Trade and Development (UNCTAD), *Trade and Development Report (2003)*: New York and Geneva.

US Department of Commerce, *US Direct Investment Abroad*—1994, 1998, 1999, 2001, 2005, (Washington DC).

US Department of Commerce, *Report on China Trade and Investment*, 2005.

World Bank *World Development Report 1997-2005*, Washington DC.

World Bank *Global Development Finance 2002-2004*, Washington DC.

5

Introducing E-government in Bangladesh: Problems and Prospects

SADIK HASAN

ABSTRACT

Use of Information and Communication Technology (ICT) in the government activities has become a common phenomenon in recent times. In the late 1990s, ICT brought in a unique concept—Electronic government (e-government)—in the field of public administration. Since then many far-reaching developments have taken place in the field which tempt the governments of the world to start the 'e-government journey' in the hopes of experiencing efficiency, effectiveness and organizational performance. This paper examines the current status of ICT in Bangladesh by exploring the government initiatives, political commitment, as well as the enthusiasm of the private sector. The paper concludes that the e-government preparation of Bangladesh is still in the primary stage and has not obtained the expected outcomes due to some barriers (technical, infrastructural, etc.). At the end, the paper viewed that may be the progress is slow and may be there is confusion about the means but there is no doubt about what to achieve. A coordinated effort of political leadership, bureaucrats, and private entrepreneurs can really facilitate the desired development in the ICT sector and accelerate the electronic presence of Bangladesh government, i.e. e-government.

Introduction

Use of Information and Communication Technology (ICT) in the government activities has become a common phenomenon in recent years. In the late 1990s, ICT introduced a unique concept—electronic government (e-government)—in the field of public administration. To date, various technologies have been applied to support the unique characteristics of e-government, including electronic data interchange, interactive voice response, voice mail, e-mail, web service delivery, virtual reality and key public infrastructure.[1]

The web and other technologies have shown potential as effective and efficient managerial tools that collect, store, organize and manage voluminous information. The most current information can be uploaded and downloaded on the Internet on a real-time basis. Governments can also transfer funds electronically to governmental agencies or provide information to public employees through an intranet or Internet system. Additionally, governments can perform many routine functions more easily and quickly (i.e. responding to employees' requests for benefits statements). Web technologies also facilitate government links with citizens (for both services and political activities), other governmental agencies and businesses. Government websites can serve as both a communication and a public relations tool for the general public. Information can be shared with and transferred to external stakeholders (businesses, non-profit organizations, interest groups, or the public). In addition, some web technologies, such as interactive bulletin boards, enable governments to encourage public participation in policy-making processes by posting public notices and exchanging ideas with the public. As a consequence, some governments have promoted virtual democracy by encouraging web-based political participation through on-line voting and on-line public forums.[2]

These far-reaching developments in e-government have encouraged governments around the world to establish an on-line presence by publishing statistical information on the Internet. In doing so, they hope to increase efficiency, effectiveness and organizational performance.[3] Countries, irrespective of their developing characteristics, are constantly striving to improve the efficiency and effectiveness of e-government delivery services. They hope that e-government will emerge as a magical antidote to combat corruption, red tape, bureaucratic inefficiency and ineffectiveness, nepotism, cronyism, lack of accountability and transparency.

Bangladesh has joined the race towards adopting e-government. This study examines that effort by addressing the status of ICT in Bangladesh. It analyzes the initiatives of the Bangladesh government, commitment of political leadership, and the enthusiasm of private entrepreneurs to introduce e-government in Bangladesh. It concludes that e-government preparation in Bangladesh is still in its primary stages and has not fulfilled its potential due to technical, infrastructural and political obstacles. A coordinated effort of political leadership, bureaucrats and private entrepreneurs could facilitate the desired development in the ICT sector and accelerate the presence of e-government in Bangladesh.

E-GOVERNMENT: AN OVERVIEW

While still in its early stages of development, a clear definition of e-government has yet to emerge.[4] A recent joint research initiative for the study of e-government sponsored by the United Nations Division for Public Economics and Public Administration and the American Society for Public Administration defined e-government as "utilizing the internet and the world-wide-web for delivering government information and services to citizens."[5] According to the World Bank, e-government refers to governmental use of information technologies (such as Wide Area Networks, the Internet, and mobile computing) that have the ability to transform relations with citizens, businesses, and other agencies of government.[6]

Interest in e-government in general, and in electronic service delivery in particular, is best viewed as a response to the growing fragmentation and complexity of government. It has become fashionable to conceive of government as a set of 'information silos' that establish barriers that inhibit access to information.[7] E-government, at least in the eyes of public service users, promises to dissolve these barriers.[8] This can produce several benefits, including reduced corruption, increased transparency, greater convenience, revenue growth, and empowering people to participate in political processes that affect their lives directly. In short, use of IT in government facilitates an efficient, speedy, and transparent process for disseminating information to the public and other agencies, thus enhancing government administration performance.[9]

In response to this transition in the context of governance, the state, in almost every instance, has taken the necessary initiatives to restructure political and administrative institutions by adopting ICT in order to enhance electronic interaction and service delivery. Today public servants are encouraged and trained to be familiar with the tools and languages of ICT. ICT provides three information processes to promote governance:

(1) **Automation:** Replacing current human-executed processes, which involve accepting, storing, processing, outputting or transmitting information (i.e. the automation of existing clerical functions).

(2) **Informatisation:** Supporting current human-executed information processes, namely supporting current processes of decision-making, communication, and decision implementation.

(3) **Transformation:** Creating new ICT-executed information processes or supporting new human-executed information processes. For example, creating new methods of public service delivery. [10]

For most UN member states, electronic service delivery, or e-government, remains a new and challenging medium. E-government encompasses many applications and incorporates virtually all ICT platforms. The Internet is the most widely recognized and identifiable component driving e-government. A major indicator of a society's openness has become its access to information available on the Internet.[11] Downloading public sector information has become one of the most frequent uses of the Internet. Governments are rapidly embracing the Internet to facilitate an increasing number of transactions, including procurement, tax collection, vehicle registration, and the issuance of permits and licenses. The Internet may well become an ideal medium for many public sector transactions because they are relatively straightforward and require neither physical examination of products nor personal contact.[12]

Information technology also can empower rural people by providing them both access to information and the tools for analyzing it. In agriculture, for example, systems technologies can help farmers in the area of crop management by providing information concerning planting date selection, water use and management, pest and disease control and harvest management. The Land Information System, to cite a specific example, provides information concerning markets, food pricing, imports and exports, tariffs and quotas, underproduction and overproduction as well as information on soil, hydrology and rainfall that support planning activities at various administrative levels.[13] Availability of such information in a timely manner would assist farmers in making decisions that would ensure increases in productivity.

Use of ICT by the government in the education, health care, and environment sectors can also prove beneficial. In education, it can increase literacy rates significantly. Web-based education and e-learning have emerged as handy tools for students in remote rural regions to have access to teachers anywhere in the world. The Digital Revolution also has had a major impact on the delivery of health care. It allows for an efficient exchange of information, such as patient's records and medical diagnosis, between health professionals, which improves the quality of health care. Government can use information technology applications for effective management and monitoring of environmental resources. This would enable authorities to take appropriate actions in case of emergencies. It would also prove helpful in such areas as air and water quality monitoring, pollution warning systems, public environmental information services, and environmental emergency management systems for floods, forest fires and other natural disasters.[14]

In sum, e-government is defined by inter-organizational relationships that promote policy coordination and implementation, and by the delivery of services on-line or through other electronic means to citizens. This includes:

- Developing citizen-centric programmes.
- Promoting and enhancing citizen participation.
- Perfecting on-line service delivery through analysis and evaluation; measuring efficiency and benchmarking against other forms of service delivery.
- Country indexing (performance measurement benchmarking): portal analysis; website analysis.[15]

Discussions concerning electronic governance often produce speculation concerning electronic voting, daily electronic policy referenda, and whether electronically enabled direct democracy will eventually eclipse representative democracy. The subject appears much more conjectural than possible. In the private sector, a business model for electronic service delivery has emerged, but a comparable model of electronic governance has yet to be developed.[16]

CURRENT STATUS OF ICT IN BANGLADESH

ICT is the most popular term in Bangladesh today. Almost every middle-class family owns a computer. Opening up a cyber café, a computer showroom, or a club; publishing a digital magazine; providing Internet service; designing and hosting a website; or participating in computer fairs or web programming contests have all become part of the information technology (IT) culture in Bangladesh. Every daily newspaper and magazine publishes a special weekly supplement containing recent news and discoveries relating to ICT. Numerous IT fairs and workshops are held throughout the year in cities, districts and even in the villages. Noticeably, the young generation of Bangladesh is taking the lead in these IT efforts.[17]

The Computer

The computer was first introduced in Bangladesh in 1964 with the installation of an IBM 1620 computer at the Atomic Energy Commission. Numerous computers were installed in financial institutions simultaneously. In the late 1980s, the printing and publishing industry began using computers and thus played a pioneering role in popularizing the use of personal computers (PCs). PCs gained in popularity in the early 1990s following an adjustment of taxes on an PCs and accessories. Since then, on average, approximately 100,000 PCs are purchased annually. The growth rate of PC sales has averaged approximately 32.44% annually.[18]

The Internet

IT activities started in Bangladesh in 1993 with the introduction of e-mail service using dial-up connections offered by three Internet Service Provider (ISP) companies. On June 4, 1996, Bangladesh tested the Internet (VSAT-based) for the first time. Its high cost, however, limited access to the Internet to business users. The Bangladesh government's decision to deregulate VSAT reduced this cost and opened the door for the general users to access the Internet at a cheap rate. Currently, anyone can browse for one hour by paying US$ 0.50. Broadband Internet is also available for US$ 16 per month. By November 2002, almost sixty-five ISPs were operative in Bangladesh using approximately 1,400 telephone lines.[19] There are almost 200,000 Internet users in Bangladesh, and ten PCs per 100 residents.[20]

Telecommunication Infrastructure

The Bangladesh Telegraph & Telephone Board (BTTB) exercises monopoly control in developing the telecommunication infrastructure of the country. At present, there are 715,000 fixed-line telephone subscribers, 1,381 card phone centers, 630 public call offices, 3,936 international circuits and 21,930 nation-wide dialing circuits in Bangladesh.[21] BTTB has started to build a national structure for high speed Digital Data Network to connect the sixty-four district headquarters. In an effort to reduce the "knowledge gap" between people living in urban and rural areas, the company plans to expand Internet facilities to the Upazilla (sub-district) level by 2006. In addition, BTTB has initiated two new projects—one to install 1,000,000 mobile telephones with Internet access, the other to install

500,000 fixed telephones throughout the country.[22] Bangladesh has already joined the fourteen-nation SEA-ME-WE4 submarine cable consortium to install submarine optical fiber cable that will provide national broadband connectivity with Information Super Highway access, thus enabling all ISPs, both public and private, to have direct access globally.[23]

The last several years have witnessed a tremendous growth in the use of mobile phones in Bangladesh. This is one sector that has expanded very rapidly across a broad spectrum of society; in particular, the business community has been able to satisfy its demand for telephones previously unmet by the BTTB. Indeed, the number of mobile subscribers has almost reached 1,000,000.[24]

Despite this development, numerous limitations in telecommunication infrastructure have hindered IT growth in Bangladesh. The tele-density of Bangladesh stands at only 0.50, quite low in comparison to other underdeveloped countries.[25] Individuals have to wait several years to acquire a telephone connection. Additionally, the existing cable is made of copper that does not transmit information/messages as fast as the fiber optic or other cables. Bandwidth, which is very important in accessing Internet, is between 64 kbs and 2 mbs, but most of the ISPs can use 128 to 256 kbs. Other major limitations, as reported by ISPs, include dependence on BTTB, lack of government assistance, lack of cooperation among the ISPs, and subscriber problems.[26]

IT Companies & E-commerce

Currently in Bangladesh, there are more than 1,000 hardware showrooms and nearly 8,000 IT institutions. More than one hundred companies are involved in software development. Sixteen percent of these firms export their product; ten percent are completely export-oriented. Forty percent sell their software in local markets and forty-eight percent sell their product in both domestic and foreign markets.[27]

Bangladeshi businessmen have already introduced e-commerce, in a limited manner, in Business to Consumer format. Wireless Application Protocol service is also available in Bangladesh allowing for use of the Internet through mobile phones. This has introduced e-commerce to a wide area in Bangladesh. Recently, a US-based Bangladeshi telecommunications engineer introduced a new technology of broadband wireless network suited to the needs of business users in Dhaka, Chittagong and Sylhet.[28] Thus far, there is no law to protect the interest of cyber consumers, though IT professionals and private entrepreneurs are demanding a law that treats different types of software and programmes as intellectual property and provides proper legal actions in case of violation. Expansion of e-commerce in Bangladesh is dependent on the adoption and enforcement of these laws.

IT Education

Bangladesh currently has thirty-one public and private universities as well as four engineering institutes that offer four-year bachelor's degrees in computer science. One hundred thirty-four students are studying computer science in public universities, eighty-four at private universities. There are also some local and foreign IT institutions that offer different types of certificate and diploma courses. National and multinational firms engaged in IT business manage most of those institutions. The government of Bangladesh has already introduced computer-related courses in secondary school, and the higher secondary level so that students can become adept at using computers and IT. This effort to boost the IT revolution has had a positive impact on IT culture in Bangladesh.[29]

Financial & Banking Sector

Commercial and financial institutions such as banks, insurance companies, and private business concerns are also using various means of ICT. Everyday, more websites about Bangladesh are being uploaded on the web. Side-by-side voluntary and service-providing organizations are opening up a web entity everyday. All users primarily rely on computers for word processing, e-mail correspondence, accounting, and Internet browsing. Rates of using computers for maintaining database and payroll, for personal e-mail by employees, and for software application are not negligible either.[30]

Most Bangladeshi banks, both public and private, such as Prime Bank (www.prime-bank.com), Janata Bank (www.janatabank-bd.com) and NCC Bank (www.nccbank-bd.com) have websites containing different types of statistical information. All banks are now computerized, at least at the head office level. Private banks are more computerized than public banks. At present, people can pay their utility bills with their credit/debit cards at any bank in Bangladesh. Some banks provide on-line features that allow customers to check balances and deposits.[31] One survey found that at the branch level 19% of nationalized commercialized banks (NCB), 38% of privatized commercialized banks (PCBs), and 97% of foreign commercialized banks (FCB) are computerized.[32]

Printing, Publications & Multimedia Sector

Different types of entertaining and educational CDs are also being produced here by the Bangladeshi programmers. From the history of our country—our independence and liberation war to fairy-tales for the kids—everything is on the CD now. A number of digital magazines are published every month in Bangladesh in CD-ROM format. Online version of most of the major dailies and magazines are also now available.[33] More than 45 IT magazines and periodicals already exist.[34] Most of these are published both in paper and CD-ROM format; some also publish a web version. There are also some private web portals on Bangladesh, notably, www.bangladeshinfo.com, www.bangladesh.net, www.e-bangla.net, www.bangladesh.cc, www.connect.to/bangladesh, www.techbangla.org, www.webbangladesh.com and www.virtualbangladesh.com.[35]

Government Agencies

Bangladesh has one official government homepage (www.bangladeshgov.org) and some official websites/pages of the different government agencies like Office of the Comptroller and Auditor General (www.cagbd.org), Ministry of Finance (www.gobfinance.org), Bangladesh Bank (www.bangladesh-bank.org), National Board of Revenue (www.nbr-bd.org), Ministry of Science and Information & Communication

Technology (www.most-bd.org) that offer only static information to the user. Legislative branch of the government, the *Jatiya Sangsad* (the parliament) also has a web entity.[36] So far, 5 Ministries and 37 agencies have their own websites.[37] This is less than 10%, and no website provides the facility to access or search in-depth information about a specific topic.

Political Parties

Most political parties in Bangladesh have their own websites. They contain information about their history, philosophy, policy, leadership, political messages, membership in parliament, interviews, and press releases concerning issues and campaigns. These websites provide an option to send feedback and played an important role in the last general election held in October 2001.[38]

POLITICAL WILL OF THE GOVERNMENT OF BANGLADESH

Bangladesh is a country dominated by two rival political parties—the Awami League (AL) and the Bangladesh Nationalist Party (BNP). Power has remained principally in the hands of these two parties since the fall of the military dictator, H.M. Ershad, in 1990. Other parties—the Jatiya Party, Communist Party, Left Front, Bangladesh Jatiya Party, and Jamaat-e-Islami Bangladesh, to name a few—often tip the scales of power in favour of the AL or BNP if either party fails to secure an absolute majority in parliament. In 1991, for example, the BNP obtained the support of Jamaat-e-Islami to assume control of parliament.[39] Five years later, the Jatiya Party and Jatiya Samajtrantik Dol helped the AL secure control of parliament.[40] Most recently, in 2001, the BNP formed a government with the aid of Jamaat-e-Islami, Bangladesh Jatiya Party and other Islamic parties.[41]

Both the AL and BNP have pursued various measures that have influenced the growth of ICT in Bangladesh. Bangladesh received its first offer to link itself to the Information Super Highway in 1988 by connecting itself to a submarine cable.[42] The government, then led by the military dictator, Lieutenant General H.M. Ershad,[43] rejected the offer, fearful that the free flow of information might cause image problems for his illegitimate government by focusing world attention on the repression of opposition parties trying to establish democracy in the country. Additionally, military and civil bureaucrats associated with Ershad's government lacked knowledge about the Internet and the Information Super Highway to encourage its use. Later, in 1994, following the establishment of democracy, the BNP-controlled government received an offer to connect Bangladesh to the Information Super Highway through a submarine cable together with all South Asian countries.[44] After India, Pakistan and Sri Lanka accepted the offer, the BNP leadership rejected it under the pretext of protecting classified state information.[45] Ignorance and doubts expressed by the political leadership concerning the utility of the Internet and ICT probably influenced this decision.

After assuming power in 1996, the AL government took the first important step to activate the ICT sector of Bangladesh. It agreed to connect the country with the Information Super Highway through the Bangladesh Submarine Cable Network project, designated ICT as a thrust sector, established an IT Task Force headed by the Prime Minister herself, and waived taxes on computers and computer accessories.[46] These measures paved the way for rapid computerization and ICT revolution in Bangladesh.

ICT became a vital issue in the October 2001 general election in Bangladesh. Both major parties pledged to do "everything" to advance the ICT sector. The current ruling party, the BNP, issued a thirty-two point manifesto to help secure its victory in the election. The manifesto pledged the BNP government to establish an Internet village with skilled IT experts. It also pledged that telecommunication, including Internet facilities, would be made easier to use, less expensive, multidimensional and widespread. Introduction of mobile phone under BTTB supervision was also promised.[47] BNP's leadership also vowed to prioritize science and information technology. To achieve this, the party promised to establish an IT institute. Additionally, an IT center would be set up in every Upazilla (sub-district) and IT industries would be built throughout the country.[48]

The rival AL party countered with its own twenty-one point election manifesto pledging to alleviate poverty, decentralize administration and encourage the growth of the ICT sector. The AL manifesto also supported the establishment of an IT Village for the betterment of the promising ICT industry as well as the expansion of IT industry and e-commerce in Bangladesh.[49]

With the BNP back in power, Premier Khaleda Zia reaffirmed her government's pledge to enhance the development of the ICT sector. On February 4, 2002, she announced a grant of 10,000 computers for use in the country's primary schools. She also promised to pursue initiatives to establish cyber cafés at the district level for both teachers and students.[50]

TOWARDS E-GOVERNMENT: THE INITIATIVES OF THE GOVERNMENT OF BANGLADESH

Over the last few years, various governments of Bangladesh have undertaken major initiatives towards ushering in Information Technology and its tools for the functioning of government. The emphasis has been on providing better services to citizens and increasing productivity. In an effort to determine the extent of the global e-government landscape, in 2001, the United Nations Division for Public Economics and Public Administration (UNDPEPA) and the American Society for Public Administration (ASPA) conducted a study of the approaches, progress, and commitment of the 191 United Nations member states in adopting e-government. The study tried to determine each country's e-government environment and its capacity to sustain on-line development through a comparative analysis of fundamental information technology indicators and critical human capital measures for each U.N. member state.[51]

In determining what defines an enabling environment, the UNDPEPA/ASPA report analyzed critical factors by benchmarking the core areas endemic to national e-government programmes. The final measure of E-government Index attempts to quantify these factors objectively, and establish a "reference point" for which a country can measure future progress. This index presents a more inclusive and less subjective measure of a country's e-government environment. It examines a country's official on-line presence, evaluates its telecommunications infrastructure, and assesses its human development capacity. The index identifies, underscores and weighs the importance of the requisite conditions that enable a country to sustain an e-government environment thus ensuring that every segment of its population has unconstrained access to timely, useful and relevant information and services.

The UNDPEPA/ASPA survey found that twenty-one countries (11%) had no e-government at all; thirty-two (16.8%) had experienced emerging e-government; sixty-five (34.2%) enhanced e-government; fifty-five (29%) interactive e-government; and seventeen (9%) transactional e-government. None had seamless e-government. Geographically, by region, North America (2.60), Europe (2.01), South America (1.79), and the Middle East (1.76) all registered an index above the global mean (1.62). Asia (1.38), Central America (1.28) and Africa (0.84) fell below the global index. Among individual countries, the United States (3.11) is the current global leader and the only country to register an index above 3.00. The survey placed Bangladesh (0.90) among the countries with a "deficient e-government capacity" where e-government registers a low priority on the policy agenda. The survey, however, noted that Bangladesh recognized the importance of the role technology plays in development and has embarked on e-government programmes representative of its development agendas.[52]

Unfortunately, the survey's findings on Bangladesh are true. The country's private sector has taken the lead in popularizing and diffusing ICT. The government has confined itself to changing the name of the Ministry of Science and Technology to Ministry of Science and Information & Communication Technology, and preparing various plans, such as setting up an IT office in the US and Europe to provide support to private IT companies, expanding IT education across the country, offering cash incentives for further development of software industry, establishing an IT Village/park.[53]

Renaming a ministry probably will not do the ICT sector of the country much good since the responsibilities of the ministry remain the same. Matters related to ICT still come under the control of several ministries. The Ministry of Cultural Affairs, for example, handles copyright law issues. The Finance and Commerce ministries control the importation of computers and accessories. The Ministry of Post and Telecommunication handles matters related to submarine fiber optic cable/ broadband. The Ministry of Commerce supervises the software industry, particularly the export-import of software. And, the Ministry of Education oversees programmes to expand IT education and computerizing educational institutions throughout the country.[54] To bring about the perfect ICT revolution in Bangladesh, each of these functions should be controlled by one ministry.

At present, there is no ICT policy as part of the overall national plan to promote the socio-economic development of the country. There is a draft proposal but the government has not finalized it yet. The private sector has already drafted an IT policy and forwarded it to the government for an updated national policy concerning the future course of IT development.[55] Although there is an IT Task Force to harness and utilize the immense potentialities of information technology for the overall welfare of the country, it met only once in 2001.[56] The highlights of the draft IT policy, which, according to government officials, is one of the friendliest IT policies in the world, includes:

- IT declared as a thrust sector;
- Waiver on all taxes and duties on the importation of computer hardware and software to increase affordability and proliferation of PC use in Bangladesh;
- Tax holiday for software and IT services companies;
- Export over Internet or other electronic media recognized under sales contract or agreement without any need for Letter of Credits;
- Simplified tax-free export earning remittance procedures with 40% retention in foreign currency;

- Special funds allocated by the government for extending collateral free loans to IT entrepreneurs;
- One hundred percent remittance on profit and capital gains for foreign investors without any approval;
- Deregulation of process of acquisition and use of VSAT to facilitate faster, cheaper and higher bandwidth connections and to encourage more widespread Internet use;
- Decision to link the global highway through submarine cable link within two years;
- An initiative to establish an IT village within Dhaka and High Tech Park on the outskirts of the city.[57]

Currently, four government agencies oversee matters related to telecommunication in Bangladesh—the Ministry of Post & Telecommunication, Bangladesh Telegraph & Telephone Board (BTTB), the Ministry of Science and Information Communications Technology and the Bangladesh Telecommunication Regulatory Commission. Lack of coordination between these agencies and ICT entrepreneurs seems to be the root of almost all problems. According to Bangladesh Computer Samity, the association of the computer businessmen, Internet Service Providers' Association, and other IT personalities, lack of farsighted bureaucrats is probably the main hindrance to the growth of ICT in Bangladesh. A recent attempt to tax computers and computer accessories for fiscal year 2002-2003 best exemplifies this problem.[58] The government later withdrew the proposed tax in the face of massive protest.

BTTB monopoly control in developing the telecommunication structure of the country continues to hinder ICT growth in Bangladesh. BTTB has increased the monthly line rent of the telephones used by the ISPs by 667%. It also imposed an extra tariff on ISPs to pay between Takkas 200,000 to 400,000 (US$ 3,600-7,200) per annum depending on bandwidth.[59] A recent BTTB initiative to introduce a "multi-metering" system for local telephone calls is also considered by subscribers and IT professionals to be an expression of bureaucratic bottleneck and technology-skeptic policy.[60] The much-coveted Bangladesh Submarine Cable Network (BSCN) project was supposed to be commissioned by the end of 2002.[61] After a twenty-one month wait, BTTB officially abandoned the BSCN project and decided to join the fourteen nation SEA-ME-WE4 submarine cable consortium.[62]

In other countries, governments have come forward as the principal client of domestic software/hardware industries to stimulate the growth of the ICT sector. The experience in Bangladesh is quite different.[63] Here, one finds only a limited effort to computerize the government agencies.[64] Until now, most official jobs have been done manually. Government officials use the latest model computers with Pentium IV processors as typewriters to compose letters or to play games.[65]

Use of different software in office management or in the decision-making process never occurs in Bangladesh.[66] An attempt to use application software for such purposes would help the local software industry grow and play a vital role in training IT professionals. To be sure, almost all government agencies employ system analysts, programmers, web designers, network and hardware engineers,[67] but these employees spend most of their time installing programmes in the system or troubleshooting. They are not interested in creating new applications for their respective office—not even for personal or commercial use.[68]

There is no recognized IT cell/department in government agencies to supervise websites yet. There also has been no attempt to update existing websites with up-to-date information regularly. Almost every government agency website contains obsolete information, giving a negative impression of the country. Thus far, no website provides the facility to access or search in-depth information about a specific topic or official document. Bangladeshi-owned web portals and commercial websites—even the personal websites—are far better than those of Bangladeshi ministries.[69]

Communications with and within public authorities still depend on telephone and fax. There are few effective electronic communications within government offices.[70] Among the more progressive authorities within the government, the National Board of Revenue is perhaps farther advanced than others. It has undertaken a programme to link up customhouses through an on-line networking system.[71]

ICT has made global trade transactions easier, cheaper, and quicker, but the business community of Bangladesh is still reluctant to pursue electronic trade because existing laws accept only paper documents, signatures, and checks, to verify business activity. As global trade is increasingly dependent on electronic forms, Bangladesh urgently needs a proper law to facilitate electronic commerce and eliminate barriers. Singapore enacted the *Electronic Transactions Act* of 1998, and India recently enacted the *Information Technology Act* of 2000. In Bangladesh, however, a similar law is still at the draft stage.[72]

Conclusion

A country's social, political and economic composition correlates closely with its e-government programme development. There are exceptions, however, as evidenced by several developing and transitioning economies. Key factors such as the status of a country's telecommunications infrastructure, the strength of its human capital, the political will and commitment of its national leadership, and shifting administrative priorities influence how decision makers, policy planners, and public sector managers elect to approach, develop, and implement e-government programmes.[73]

At present, Bangladesh lacks many of the factors necessary to establish e-government. The government continues to struggle in its efforts to provide current information on governmental activities electronically. Not all government agencies possess web identities. To date, Bangladesh Railway is the only government agency that offers electronic service delivery to citizens. That agency has introduced computerized passenger reservation system, thus enabling faster reservation service and less corruption.[74]

Although national leaders seem to possess the political will and commitment to adopt ICT-friendly measures to advance the IT sector and establish e-government, there are still some obstacles to overcome. First, the lack of cooperation and coordination between government agencies and the absence of a national ICT policy have hindered the desired ICT growth in Bangladesh. It is true that there has been an effort to introduce e-governance in a limited range in the ministries by supplying computers and hiring IT professionals in the government agencies under the 'e-governance project' of the Ministry of Science, Information & Communication Technology. But this has done little to encourage ICT growth in Bangladesh.

Second, Internet access is too expensive in Bangladesh compared to Western developed countries. In Bangladesh, the lowest cost to gain Internet access is US$ 0.50 per hour through a dial-up system. Installation of necessary telecommunication facilities for ISP companies is also at the preliminary stage as the country is still not under the full BTTB telecommunication network. A telephone density of 0.50 connections per 100 people is one of the lowest in the world. This compares unfavourably with neighboring countries, namely India (1.0), Nepal (0.5), Pakistan (2.1), Sri Lanka (1.0), and Thailand (2.5). An installation charge of US$ 450 for a new line is also one of the highest in the world (e.g. Pakistan US$ 90, India US$ 60) and the waiting time for a connection is more than a decade.[75] Except for the capital city of Dhaka and the port city Chittagong, a telephone connection remains a pipedream for most Bangladeshis. Even in those cities, problems persist in securing telephone connections, but residents in both areas somehow manage the connections through lobbying, and, sometimes, offering bribes to BTTB officials.

Third, the adult literacy rate in Bangladesh is 51%. Most possess no knowledge in using computers, let alone e-government or electronic service delivery. In a country like Bangladesh, where nearly one-half of the population cannot read and write, this offers little incentive for IT growth.

Fourth, Bangladesh lacks the infrastructural support, e.g. electricity, telephone network. Since only 1.1% of the total population enjoys the use of electricity,[76] use of computers remains beyond the reach of the overwhelmingly majority people in Bangladesh. On average, there is only one PC per

1,000 people in Bangladesh as compared to 585.2 PCs per 1,000 people in the US.[77] Over the last decade, attempts have been made to lay a submarine cable to increase both the speed of overseas data transmission and Internet service in Bangladesh. Yet one still finds a shortage of IT experts in the country to run existing IT initiatives. Most IT institutions, except public universities, are training computer operators instead of computer professionals.

Finally, the tendency of both ruling and opposition parties to politicize everything in Bangladesh has had an adverse effect on the desired growth of ICT initiatives at both the public and private level. As political power changes hands between the two major parties in Bangladesh, the bitter rivalry between the BNP and AL often results in the abandonment of policies pursued by the previous government. This feature of the country's political culture has stymied efforts to promote the IT sector in Bangladesh.

Despite all of the confusion and frustration associated with ICT initiatives in Bangladesh, e-government is becoming a fact in the lives of the citizens of that country. Perhaps progress is slow and there is confusion about the means to achieve this, but there is no doubt about the goal of attaining e-government. A coordinated effort by political leaders, bureaucrats, and private entrepreneurs is critical to facilitate the growth of the ICT sector, and, hence, the socioeconomic development of Bangladesh.

NOTES

1. M. Jae Moon, "The Evolution of E-government among Municipalities: Rhetoric or Reality?" *Public Administration Review* 62, No. 4 (July 2002): 424. The term "key public infrastructure" refers to the web-based organizations of the government that provide the facility of web-based political participation of citizens/stakeholders through sophisticated interface and interoperable technologies (i.e. chat rooms).
2. *Ibid.*, 425.
3. Jim Melitski, "The World of E-government and E-governance," http://www.aspanet.org/e-government/melitski (April 20, 2003): 1.
4. Ian Holliday, "Building E-government in East and Southeast Asia: Regional Rhetoric and National (In)Action," *Public Administration and Development* 22:4 (October 2002): 324.

5. United Nations Division for Public Economics and Public Administration/American Society for Public Administration (UNDPEPA/ASPA), *Benchmarking E-government: A Global Perspective: Assessing the Progress of UN Member States,* (Washington D.C.: United Nations Division for Public Economics and Public Administration & American Society for Public Administration, 2002): 1.
6. The World Bank Group, "E-government Definition". http://www1.worldbank.org/publicsector/egov/definition.htm (20 April 2003): 1.
7. L. Byrne, *Information Age Government: Delivering the Blair Revolution* (London: Fabian Society, 1997), 6, quoted in Christine Bellamy, "From Automation to Knowledge Management: Modernizing British Government with ICTs," *International Review of Administrative Sciences* 68:2 (June 2002): 215.
8. Bellamy, "From Automation to Knowledge Management," 215.
9. Government of Karnataka, "E-governance"; http://www.bangaloreit.com/html/egovern/egovern.htm (20 April 2003): 2.
10. Richard Heeks, "Understanding e-Governance for Development," *Information Technology in Developing Countries* 11:3 (December 2001): 13.
11. UNDPEPA/ASPA, *Benchmarking E-government,* 5.
12. Sandford Borins, "On the Frontiers of Electronic Governance: A Report on the United States and Canada," *International Review of Administrative Sciences* 68:2 (June 2002): 200.
13. Nagesh Kumar, and Alka Chadha, "Exploiting the Potential of Information and Communication Technologies for Development in South Asia," *South Asian Survey* 9:2 (July 2002): 206.
14. *Ibid.*
15. UNDPEPA/ASPA, *Benchmarking E-government,* 54.
16. Borins, "On the Frontiers of Electronic Governance," 205.
17. Sadik Hasan, "Prospects of IT in Bangladesh: The Case of Election Pledges of the Major Political Parties," *Bangladesh Journal of Resources & Development* 1:1 (December 2002): 119.
18. Shakhawat Alam, "Electronic Government," *eBiz Magazine*, April 4, 2003: 28.
19. Hasan, "Prospects of IT in Bangladesh," 120.
20. UNDPEPA/ASPA, *Benchmarking E-government,* 69.
21. Badrul Hoque, "ICT for Bridging Digital Divide—Bangladesh Perspective," *Daily Star World Telecommunications Day Supplement* (Dhaka), May 17, 2002: p. 23.

22. Bangladesh Telegraph & Telephone Board, "Homepage of the Bangladesh Telegraph & Telephone Board"; http://www.bttb.net/index.htm, September 20, 2003: 3.
23. "Bangladesh Joins the SEA-ME-WE4," *The Daily Star* (Dhaka), April 25, 2002: 16.
24. Mustak Hossain, "Mobile Telephony: PBTL to Expand Network," *Daily Star World Telecommunication Day Supplement* (Dhaka), May 17, 2002: 22.
25. Hoque, "ICT for Bridging Digital Divide—Bangladesh Perspective," 23.
26. "Grameen Fiber Optic Network: Pipeline of Possibilities," *eBiz Magazine*, March 7, 2003: 24.
27. Farhana Mili, "Information Super Highway & IT Bazaar: The Position of Bangladesh," *Daily Janakantha Periodical*, September 7, 2001: 16.
28. "Broadband Wireless Network Introduced," *The Daily Star* (Dhaka), February 1, 2002: 8.
29. Hasan, "Prospects of IT in Bangladesh," 121.
30. Bangladesh Computer Samity & The Asia Foundation, "*Base Line Survey on IT Sector of Bangladesh*," (Dhaka: Bangladesh Computer Samity & Asia Foundation, 2002): p. 5.
31. Sadik Hasan, "E-government: Is Bangladesh Ready?" *Social Science Review The Dhaka University Studies Part-D* 20:1, June 2003:181.
32. Alam, "Electronic Government," 36.
33. Hasan, "E-government," 182.
34. Mili, "Information Super Highway & IT Bazaar," 18.
35. Hasan, "Prospects of IT in Bangladesh," 119-26.
36. Hasan, "E-government," 182.
37. Government of Bangladesh, "Official Homepage of the Government of Bangladesh," http://www.bangladeshgov.org/index.htm, September 20, 2003: 2.
38. Alam, "Electronic Government," 38.
39. Bangladesh Election Commission, *Report on Election Activities: Parliament Election 1991* (Dhaka: Government of Bangladesh, 1991): 2.
40. Bangladesh Election Commission, *Statistical Report on 7th Jatiya Sangsad Election* (Dhaka: Government of Bangladesh, 1996): 4.
41. Bangladesh Nationalist Party, "BNP as Government" http://www.bnpbd.com/index.html, September 18, 2003: 2.
42. Mili, "Information Super Highway & IT Bazaar," 18.
43. Lawrence Ziring, *Bangladesh: From Mujib to Ershad: An Interpretive Study* (Dhaka: The University Press Limited, 1994): 153.

44. Mili, "Information Super Highway & IT Bazaar," 18.
45. Alam, "Electronic Government," 38.
46. Hasan, "Prospects of IT in Bangladesh," 122.
47. *Ibid.*
48. "BNP Announces Election Manifesto: Law & Order, Corruption Top Priority," *The Daily Star* (Dhaka), September 8, 2001: 1.
49. "Awami League Announces 21-pt Election Manifesto: Accent on Poverty Alleviation," *The Daily Star* (Dhaka), September 10, 2001: 1.
50. "Khaleda to the Nation," *The Daily Prothom Alo* (Dhaka), February 5, 2002: 1.
51. UNDPEPA/ASPA, *Benchmarking E-government,* 28.
52. *Ibid.*
53. Hasan, "E-government," 181.
54. Acting Secretary of the Ministry of Science and Information & Communication Technology, interview by author, tape recording, Dhaka, Bangladesh, April 10, 2003.
55. "Proposed ICT Policy of IT Professionals," *The Daily Jugantor* (Dhaka), February 5, 2002: p. 3.
56. Kanak Sarwar, "Information Technology & Bangladesh," *The Daily Janakantha Periodical* (Dhaka), April 22, 2002: 4.
57. M. Zafar Iqbal, "Present IT Status of Bangladesh," *Bangladesh TechTransfer 2000*, April 28, 2000: 2.
58. "Saifur to Tax Computers," *The Daily Star* (Dhaka), June 7, 2002: 1.
59. "ISPs to Pay Extra Tariff," *The Daily Star* (Dhaka), February 1, 2001: 16.
60. "Multi-metering System from July 1," *The Daily Star* (Dhaka), June 25, 2002: 16.
61. "BSCN Project," *The Daily Star* (Dhaka), December 30, 2001: 16.
62. "BTTB Dropped the BSCN Project," *The Daily Star* (Dhaka), April 25, 2002: 1.
63. Hasan, "E-government," 182.
64. Alam, "Electronic Government," 40.
65. Bangladesh Computer Samity & The Asia Foundation, *Base Line Survey on IT Sector of Bangladesh*, 25.
66. Alam, "Electronic Government," 40.
67. Secretary of Ministry of Science and Information & Communication Technology, interview by Pratap Saha, *e-biz Magazine*, March 19, 2003: 38.
68. Hasan, "E-government," 182.

69. Hasan, "Prospects of IT in Bangladesh," 122.
70. Alam, "Electronic Government," 40.
71. Atiur Rahman and Taifur Rahman, "Cyber Connectivity: Are we moving in the right direction?" *The Daily Star 11th Anniversary Supplement 2002* (Dhaka), February 13, 2002: 27.
72. "No ICT Policy Yet," *The Daily Star* (Dhaka), May 15, 2002: 16.
73. UNDPEPA/ASPA, *Benchmarking E-government*, 2.
74. Deputy General Manager (Public Relations) of Bangladesh Railway, interview by author, tape recording, Dhaka, Bangladesh, April 13, 2003.
75. Bangladesh Center for Advanced Studies & The World Bank, *Bangladesh 2020: A Long-run Perspective Study* (Dhaka: The University Press Limited, 1999): 97.
76. Bangladesh Bureau of Statistics, *Statistical Pocketbook of Bangladesh 2000* (Dhaka: Government of Bangladesh, 2002): 222.
77. UNDPEPA/ASPA, *Benchmarking E-government*, 33.

6

Global Disorder: An Important Agenda for 21st Century Population Studies

BERTIL EGERÖ

ABSTRACT

Poor underprivileged countries face a long period of high population increase, while poverty and natural resource limits provide growing constraints to the management of population increase. Demography appears increasingly to turn to the study of populations well underway in the fertility transition. The "development optimism" implied in this shift needs to be set against the evidence of rapidly growing inequalities, between and within countries. The question needs to be raised whether fertility reductions will reach replacement levels everywhere.

Das Gupta's recent contribution on the role of institutional and socio-political change for the demographic transition appears to offer a very viable framework for further research on historical Europe as well as current non-European states. However, it needs to be extended in the direction given by Castells' theories on the process of social exclusion in the information age in order to incorporate situations where fertility stabilises well over replacement level. The social implications of such a scenario are a challenge to both science and politics.

1. Demography and Population Matters in the Future of Humanity

Demography is in some countries a branch of statistics. In others it might have a place of its own in the context of social sciences, engaged in scientific theorising not only on methods but also on the substance of its matter. Irrespective of such differences, as a science demography appears virtually everywhere to develop in a dialectic relation to government and politics—demographers are often called in to give support both to politicians and to planners. How demographers handle the delicate balance between autonomous critical science and policy-serving applied science has varied over time and given distinct marks on its articulation among other social sciences.

Ever since the days of Thomas Malthus, demographers have in varying degrees concerned themselves with the destiny of humankind. Discourses on over-population are to a great deal carried out by demographers. Rarely would one hear a demographer object to being associated with that type of exercise in his/her profession. But, as Joel Cohen has shown (Cohen, 1996), population and sustainability issues are among the most complex issues on the agenda today, requiring the contributions of a broad range of scientists in order to be discussed intelligently.

Malthus' works were temporarily overtaken by the momentum of industrialisation and global expansion, both of which appeared to invalidate his theses. Whatever the historical viability of his theses on population, he contributed to pinning the population/resources issue firmly on the agenda of the 20th century. By then, the globalisation process—which had only started during Malthus' formative years—had matured, and the slave trade had been replaced by colonial economic domination in an increasingly globalised European economy that was rapidly extending over the world with new means of communication. While Malthus generally contextualised his demographic dynamics with the nation, the 20th century Western demographers looked at the whole world. And they discovered that the "great demographic transition", which had been a demographic push on 19th century European economies comparable to that of its counterpart in East Asia in the late 20th century, was starting up in the colonies, but in forms that promised to be even greater.

Today, the world population is four times its size in 1900 and more than twice its size in 1950. All serious projections show the same thing; that the increase will continue for several decades, and that neither the time of levelling out nor the maximum population size can be predicted with any degree of certainty. This historically unique population increase is still modest compared to the speed of the simultaneous growth in production of commodities, international transport, movements of people and average material consumption. The multiplier effect of these two—the number of people and the material impacts of the average person—is already so heavy that global climate and weather conditions are changing. Local ecosystem change is observed all over the globe, and food support systems begin to show visible signs of their limits.

These developments have led to an almost universal consensus that a halt to further population increase is necessary—a consensus that is compounded by a whole series of other difficult questions such as whose child-bearing to contain, contain by what means, etc., the answers to which tend to clash with human rights and demands for individual freedom.

2. The Demographic Transition, Demography and Today's World

Human history continually repeats the same paradox; a growing historical understanding of what social and economic change is about, and an ever-present tendency to bypass that understanding in attempts to steer such development through policy. This was the case of the "socialist experiments" unfolding within the decolonisation process and which aimed at constructing a state of the workers even where there was no working class (Egerö, 1990). This was—and in part still is—the case of the "population industry" (Demeny, 1988) which, by about the time the theoretical groundwork was made on the Demographic Transition, took shape in the search for ways to modify the very transition itself by means of policy. While in relation to Europe the demographic transition was seen as an integral part of a great historical shift affecting all aspects of society, in relation to the colonies its progression was deemed necessary to address through "social engineering" or policies and practices through the state.

If there is one central finding of the ambitious European Fertility Project of the 1960s,[1] it is the realisation of how complex the demographic transition is as a process. Judging from the way the findings were summarised by Ansley Coale (1974), it produced more of a framework for further research than any clarification of the mechanisms behind the process.[2] The strength of the "bypass" tendency of state power holders is well demonstrated by the very fact that such insights were never systematically brought to bear on the "population industry" and its strategies for demographic change in non-European societies.

It could certainly be argued that colonisation itself was such an extreme case of external influence that nothing like the organic dynamics of change in institutions and society in Europe was ever possible. Warren Thomson's (1946) note about "the Malthusian dilemma of all colonialism" may even have served to reinforce this tendency.[3] In addition, as the early formulations of the demographic transition had paid much theoretical attention to possible links between mortality falls and fertility declines, the absence of any such trends in the colonies/postcolonial states cast a shade of doubt over the demographic transition as such, at least in its general theoretical value (Chesnais, 1992, p. 2).

The strong engagement of the "population industry" (which included many demographers) in the issue of policy-driven fertility reduction in poor non-European countries was driven by a mixture of motives, not all of them scientifically sound. The result was that in respect of "Third World demography", much of the scientific integrity and rigour got lost, and the science took on a character of support to policy, or a "policy science". The process is well described in a range of contributions (see e.g. Demeny, 1988; Grimes, 1998; Hodgson, 1983; Hodgson, 1988). The only field of demography that systematically gained during this period was methods development; from techniques for measurement and estimation to models for approximation or simulation of reality. In all other respects, the science came to suffer.

By engaging in research guided by already formulated official policies, demography came to be marginalised by social scientists engaged in defending the value of autonomy of science. By accepting the officially sanctioned means to implement policy—influencing individuals rather than changing structures and conditions—as the limits to research, "Third World demography" lost touch with the structural and power-related dimensions—centre/periphery and dependency relations, cultural imperialism, etc.—that preoccupied their colleagues in social science and could have opened the door for a vital reconsideration of theories on the demographic transition.[4]

Today, when over twenty of the so-called less developed countries or LDC have a fertility close to replacement level and many of the others are understood to be well on their way in that direction, the growing convergence in country demographic profiles in the world (Wilson, 2001) appears to move demography in two directions. One is a return to the technical sphere, as it was phrased by George McNicoll (1992, pp. 3-4):

> "Demographers themselves seem to have reached a rough consensus that trends in vital events are progressing as they should, confirming their expectations and justifying the advice they have proffered to officialdom. In a familiar disciplinary trajectory, their attention is now taken up with technical issues—complex and, for those with that specialized taste, rewarding—leaving the public face of the field one of dull routine."

The other is a growing interest in the demographic transition, which brings more dialogue with other social sciences, and a gradual convergence in the discourses of demographers specialised on the North and the South, respectively.

Anthologies and monographs on the fertility part of the transition have grown in number through at least the 1990s. Interdisciplinary collaboration is increasingly common, and the questions asked are likely to produce much more interesting interpretations. Obviously, some inertia is present not only in population change itself but equally in the articulations of the science[5] and insufficient attention is still paid to important aspects of the fertility trends, which may cause unexpected surprises in the near future. I will return to some of these further down.

3. Taking Stock of Current Trends

3.1 *Recent theoretical contributions on the demographic transition*

The theoretical framework developed to encompass the European experience, the theory of demographic transition, was formulated in the 1940s and 1950s. Subsequent research on the patterns and correlations of the transition exposed a range of local variations, between countries and even more between regions or local areas. In some localities, fertility decline even preceded mortality decline. Susan Greenhalgh, in a review of fertility theory, adds to the critique of the classical transition theory. She refers to Kertzer and Hogan's studies in northern Italy, which:

> "...corroborate the European Project's finding that fertility decline does not follow changes in such indexes of modernization as literacy, women's work, or female autonomy. But they go beyond the European Project to demonstrate what it does follow: Alterations in the value of children in the class-specific family economy. Political developments, such as the adoption of laws making school attendance compulsory and restricting child labour in factories, were crucial instigators of fertility change, underscoring the importance of political and legal forces that lie outside the purview of conventional theory."
>
> (Greenhalgh 1990: 85f)

Later in the same article, she refers to research in the Sicily which confirms the above and "suggests that fertility transitions may best be construed as products of changes in class-specific opportunity structures in response to transformations of global and regional economies...the adoption of contraception may be an eminently political process, both reflecting and exacerbating power differentials between the sexes and classes" (Greenhalgh, 1990, p.98).

The legal and political changes Greenhalgh refers to are in themselves reflections of external processes, which influence the political processes in a given country. Can such dimensions be incorporated in theories on the demographic transition?

Painstaking historical research by Monica Das Gupta (1998) has demonstrated that in India, local communities in historical times have responded to changing economic conditions with temporary fertility adjustments similar to those in historical Europe. Dyson (1996) offers evidence of fertility declines in South Asia which started well before any substantial economic modernisation or introduction of modern contraception (for other examples, see the evidence of early fertility declines in Argentina and Uruguay in Guzmán et al., 1996).

Wilson's (2001) more recent review of what he calls the growing demographic convergence in the world reconfirms the need to go beyond either economic development or special policy inputs in the search for understandings. Presumably well aware of the state of pervasive poverty, high levels of illiteracy and gender inequities in many regions, he states: "...it is clear that social and demographic change has progressed far more rapidly than economic development." However, in terms of what kinds of social change are relevant for the process, we may only have reached the understanding that "...there are many demographic transitions, each driven by a combination of forces that are...institutionally, culturally and temporally specific" (Greenhalgh, 1990, p. 88).

In terms of their individual forms, the inter-relation between fertility and mortality dynamics, and their time-shape, there are bound to be many demographic transitions. This in itself does not preclude the workings of common factors, if not on the whole process so perhaps on the start. Dyson (1998)—see below—underlines the mortality transition as the basic and necessary condition for any fertility decline. And mortality declines are in themselves expressions of social change whose causes may also be related to reproduction.

This appears to be the position of Das Gupta (1999), in a contribution to the demographic transition debate which is groundbreaking in that it subsumes the European and non-European transitions under a common framework. "It may well be that both socio-economic development and fertility transition are driven by the same gamut of institutional changes," she proposes (p. 2), and focuses her search for these changes at the general level of diffusion of ideas. The point of departure is the variation in timing and speed of fertility changes in Indian states such as Punjab, Kerala, Tamil Nadu and Maharashtra. The development experiences of these states are radically different. For instance, while Kerala's record of social development can be linked to the beginnings of fertility decline already in the 1940s, the same early timing has been demonstrated for Punjab, "almost a quarter of a century before the spread of education and the extension of the health and family planning programme" (p. 6).

Das Gupta's conclusion is, that "whether states have placed greater emphasis on economic development or on social development is of far less consequence than whether they have placed emphasis on development at all" (p.9). The search for factors behind such differences brings her to the main shifts in socio-political institutions and order. The 19th and 20th century transformations marked a shift from hierarchical relations where power rested in local and national elites which "provided [their underlings with] some measure of insurance while severely circumscribing individual mobility." Embedded in this relation was a lack of sense of alternatives and choice. The change to a modern state was also a completely different relation to the citizen, "creating both the possibility and the incentive for [the latter] to improve one's own situation" (p. 15).

Das Gupta outlines two further steps in government/citizen relations: the establishment of modern governance, and the openings for "participatory processes of local governance."[6] That more participatory local governance—by sharpening people's perception of the connection between their own actions and their well-being—is conducive to more rapid fertility decline fits with a variety of evidence from Asia.

Finally, Das Gupta outlines relations between technological change and fertility change. Modern contraceptive methods is one case, modern mass media another. The way canal irrigation in colonial northern India brought people out of a total dependence on "the vagaries of nature", and nurtured a perception that they could work to shape their lives also in other ways, is another relation which fits into Das Gupta's overall perspective on the importance of "development as such."

'Development' should be expected to correlate positively with mortality declines. Without making any direct reference to the debate about the role of mortality decline, Das Gupta proposes that institutional change may drive different types of socio-economic development. In this interpretation, 'development' and fertility decline are associated with each other while not necessarily sequential in nature. "Thus, for example, we should not be surprised to find fertility declining when levels of mortality are still relatively high or when standards of living are still quite low, as has empirically been the case in large parts of the world" (p. 21).

3.2 *Current realities: unfinished demographic transition among growing poor strata*

Effective instruments are nowadays available for monitoring change in parameters of vital rates in a sufficient number of countries for the United Nations to be able to revise its global "world population prospects" (WPP) every second year. Particular attention has been given to the trends in average fertility, both in empirical surveys and in the UN work.[7]

The 2000 WPP demonstrates the current state of "mobility of countries" down the scale towards low fertility: 21 LDC countries have a fertility at or below replacement level, while the majority of the remaining 122 LDC countries have levels below 5 children per woman.

Wilson (2001, p. 167) interprets the trend as one of growing demographic convergence in the word. He summarises: "A large majority of the world's population is (or soon will be) demographically 'modern' by any definition." The WPP prefers to emphasise the opposite, namely growing signs of polarisation in the world: "Particularly rapid growth is expected among the group of countries classified as least developed. Their population is expected to nearly triple between 2000 and 2050..."; among those, 16 countries "...exhibit sustained high fertility...for which there is either no recent evidence about fertility trends or the available evidence does not indicate the onset of a fertility reduction" (*Idem*, p. v; 7). In respect of the latter group of countries, the 1998 WPP was too optimistic about incipient fertility declines, and population estimates have been adjusted upwards in the 2000 WPP.

The WPP records another trend, so far poorly recognised in scientific reviews of fertility trends. For two South Asian countries regarded as well into the fertility transition, India and Bangladesh, there are clear signs of a stabilisation in fertility levels during the 1990s. In Bangladesh for instance, TFR remains at 3.3-3.4 right through the decade (BDHS, 2000).[8] There are no simple explanations available for this new trend. For instance, both educational enrolment and prevalence of contraceptive use have gone up during the decade. An as yet untested hypothesis is that family size has reached levels that are commensurate with average desired number of children.

Current instances of powerful constraints to a fertility fall to replacement level are not hard to find. Some Arab states and other countries where conservative traits of Islam dominate are a good case. There are countries in sub-Saharan Africa whose exclusion from development in conditions of political stability sharply reduce the probability that urban-based social movements towards smaller families will spread broadly over the country. Not least in the latter context, anything remotely similar to universal access to contraceptives would seem out of the question. A highly likely scenario is that, even where fertility declines are initiated, the demographic transition will remain unfinished among growing poor strata.

These types of fertility trends are insufficiently covered both in fertility theories and in empirical work on fertility declines. Perhaps the implicit and never tested assumption inherited from the first formulations of the demographic transition, that fertility will fall to replacement level, still has an impact on our thinking? For the group of 'more developed countries', this assumption has proved untenable—with few exceptions—fertility has continued to fall well below 2, and a bottom level of 1-1.5 appears more likely. For less developed countries, family systems and living conditions may well generate other bottom levels, different for different countries and regions.[9]

3.3 *Widening differences, further impoverishment*

> "Face reality. Think the unthinkable. Be intellectually honest and politically realistic about what is happening to the overwhelming majority of people in Third World countries. With a very few exceptions, development has not come. Nor is it going to. The necessary investment will not be available. Modern technology cannot provide the jobs. And the environment cannot take the strain. Most countries are not in the process of becoming Newly Industrialized Countries (NICs), but Non-viable National Economies (NNEs)."
>
> "What then is to be done? The wealth of nations agenda must be replaced by a survival of nations agenda. To prevent increasing disorders, many countries will have to abandon dreams of development and adopt instead a policy of national survival based on the search for water, food and energy security and the stabilization of their populations." (quote from launching text to Oswaldo de Rivero, 2001)

Despite much evidence to the contrary, an overwhelming tendency in population/development analysis, including writings about the demographic transition, is to assume that poorer regions and countries will catch up, or get out of their poverty traps, within a foreseeable future.[10] UN projections assume further mortality declines, temporarily affected only by AIDS. Further improvements in living standards and national incomes must be an implicit assumption behind projections that give modern contraception a key role in people's switch to smaller families. So well entrenched is this thinking, that Tim Dyson (1998), reviewing an anthology on the fertility transition, feels compelled to remind his colleagues that without the mortality transition there would be no fertility transition to talk about.

The Human Development Report, published annually by UNDP, has regularly reported on another trend: that of increasing polarisation between the poor and the rich, of economic stagnation in poor countries, of lack of improvements in living standards for poor communities. Concrete demonstrations of this trend are given in Sutcliffe (2001), a concise summary of many dimensions of the growing global inequalities. Several of the poorest countries of the world are now hit by AIDS, an epidemic that has begun to cut into the most valuable asset of any nation, its young adults. To search for policies of survival might not be entirely wrong as an advice.

Population increase is part of the poverty issue. Reviewing the links between poverty and environment, Ekbom and Bojö (1999, p.13) argue that whether population increase induces negative or positive environmental change "is ultimately and fundamentally driven by the overall policy framework." Rather than to embark on fertility-reducing programmes, they recommend that "underlying policy and market failures should be scrutinised and corrected first and foremost." It is an old wisdom, and still so difficult to turn into action. The global economic development seems to work against this advice.

In a bold analysis of both macro and micro-trends in the world today, Manuel Castells (2000) uses unconventional language to communicate his findings. The way globalisation works, by excluding segments of economies and societies, people and territories may gradually shift into "a position of structural irrelevance. This widespread, multiform process of social exclusion leads to the constitution of what I call, taking the liberty of a cosmic metaphor, the *black holes of international capitalism*. These are regions of society from which, statistically speaking, there is no escape from the pain and destruction inflicted on the human condition for those who, in one way or another, enter these social landscapes" (p. 165, italics author's). Together, these black holes of social exclusion make up a Fourth World, which "comprises large areas of the globe, such as much of sub-Saharan Africa, and impoverished rural areas of Latin America and Asia. But it is also present in literally every country, and every city, in this new geography of social exclusion" (p. 168).

Castells' description would stand to gain from modification in the direction of introducing degrees of social exclusion, or inclusion, around the world. Still, his metaphor is valuable as a guiding perspective for the analysis of current trends and relations. It certainly supports the views already referred to, which hold that in some areas and countries policies of survival is a more apt challenge than policies of development.

4. An Agenda for 21st Century Population Studies: Continued Population Increase under Social Exclusion and Poverty

Demographic dynamics will play out differently in the three worlds of the 21st century. More developed countries are moving into a state of sustained population decline. Less developed countries have to handle long periods of continued population increase, generally linked to the ageing of their populations. The Fourth World concept epitomises those areas where fertility is unlikely to drop to replacement levels, i.e. whose population increase remains an integral part of the future.

The West is firmly into a process of reinforcing its walls against mass immigration. This process is continually reinforced by the growing economic and social gaps between the West and the majority of the less developed countries. Even if such barriers would not be there, the level of migration required to balance, or even substantially reduce, rates of population increase in poor regions is simply too high to be either theoretically or practically an alternative.

In 1990, the former head of the UN Population Division Léon Tabah (1990) presented to a meeting of the OECD Development Assistance Committee (DAC) his views on the prospects of population development in the world. He pointed at many unrealistic assumptions behind international population projections, and demanded a greater realism in order for the world community to meet the challenges of continued population increase in poor areas. His plea appears to have gone unheeded.

Of the numerous agenda that have preoccupied demographers and population experts over the past fifty years, one that needs renewed emphasis in the new century is reflection and analysis over the demographic transition. Dyson (1998) has labelled it "a global phenomenon, and arguably the most important turn of events of our time." His statement carries weight not least in terms of what is requested from the science of population studies.

Das Gupta's exploration of the role of institutions and broad socio-political change offers a potentially very fruitful framework for new country-studies, blending political economy with demography. It is tempting to consider whether by introducing a dimension of social differentiation, including exclusion, a reference could be found to Castells' 'black holes' analysis. Although Castells himself does not refer to social classes, Greenhalgh's focus on "class-specific opportunity structures" appears fit to his way of reasoning, and indeed to much of the differential patterns of reproduction seen in countries and regions today.

The prospect of a combination of slow development and above-replacement fertility in many parts of the poor regions of the planet presents a serious challenge of growing global disorder to both science and politics. To develop a science devoted to exposing the demographic and social implications of global polarisation and exclusion—perhaps a new version of the "Concerned Demography" of the late 20th century—is certain to become a key task for the demographers of the 21st century.

NOTES

1. The European Fertility Project aimed at exploring the causes of fertility decline in Europe. A wide range of statistical data was organised so as to permit spatial analysis untied by national borders. Nevertheless, statistical analysis failed to confirm the significance of any of the 'traditional' causes such as religion, education or urbanisation.

2. Coale (1974) summarized the findings in three points: a) fertility must be within the calculus of conscious choice; b) reduced fertility must be advantageous; c) effective techniques of fertility reduction must be available.
3. Thompson (1946) showed how the colonial powers by introducing modern preventive and sanitary medicine created special conditions for mortality declines, without addressing the conditions behind high levels of child-bearing.
4. In 1984, Nathan Keyfitz compared demography with the other, more expansion-oriented social sciences. He found that (quoted in McNicoll 1992:24): "Far from being imperialistic, [demography] has withdrawn from its borders and left a no man's land which other disciplines have infiltrated." In a foreword to the same book, Maximo Livi-Bacci complained: "[O]ur discipline, after several decades of very rapid growth, of increasing specialization and technical sophistication, [runs] the risk of isolating itself, of becoming more a technique than a science...." (*Idem*: 26).
5. A recent publication by the US National Research Council (NRS 2000, ch. 3) upholds the view that modern contraception has been "the dominant proximal force" behind post-war fertility declines, a view that is modified in later passages of the text. A similar pattern of reasoning is found in an influential study of fertility decline in Bangladesh (Cleland et al., 1994), where initial statements about the significant role of family planning are replaced with admissions that they mainly serve to speed up a change initiated by other forces.
6. As Das Gupta (1999) rightly points out, the latter is not necessarily part of national democracy.
7. In the 1970s, European and American demographers elaborated a standardised fertility survey called The World Fertility Survey that was run in many low-income countries. It was later replaced by so-called Demographic and Health Surveys, which are run intermittently in different countries of the South. The data from the DHS rounds are available for secondary analysis, and the DHS vital rates estimates dominate the database for estimations of population trends. The UN WPP contains projections based on three different fertility projections while only one mortality projection is used.
8. WPP 2000 mentions Nigeria as a third country where this pattern is estimated. The different adjustments made in the 2000 version due to such observations result in higher 2050 projections than two years earlier. A period of downward adjustments from one WPP version to the next might now be over.
9. Paul Demeny is reported to have written: "The idea of a trend towards a stationary population might be justifiable from a normative point of

view, but it lacks theoretical, empirical and historical support." (Quoted in Tabah 1990).

10. Taken from the launching text of Oswaldo de Rivero, *The Myth of Development—The Non-Viable Economies of the 21st Century*, Zed Books 2001.

REFERENCES

BDHS 2000. *Bangladesh Demographic and Health Survey 1999-2000, Preliminary Report*, NIPORT et al., Dhaka.

Castells, Manuel. 2000. *End of Millenium*, Blackwell Second Edition.

Chesnais, Jean-Claude. 1992. *The Demographic Transition: Stages, Patterns, and Economic Implications*. Clarendon Press.

Cleland, John. et al. 1994. "The Determinants of Reproductive Change in Bangladesh: Success in a Challenging Environment," World Bank Regional and Sectorial Studies.

Coale, Ansley. 1974. "The Demographic Transition," in "The Population Debate: Dimensions and Perspectives," Papers of the World Population Conference in Bucharest, Vol. 1.

Cohen, Joel. 1995. *How Many People Can the World Support?*, W.W. Norton & Co.

Das Gupta, Monica. 1998. "Fertility Decline in Punjab, India: Parallels with Historical Europe," in Martine, George, Monica Das Gupta and Lincoln C. Chen, (eds.), *Reproductive Change in India and Brazil*, Oxford University Press, pp. 65-96.

Das Gupta, Monica. 1999. "Liberté, Egalité, Fraternité: Exploring the Role of Governance in Fertility Decline", *The Journal of Development Studies*, 35, June 5, 1999, pp. 1-25.

Demeny, Paul. 1988. "Social Science and Policy," *Population and Development Review* 14, September 3, 1988, pp. 451-79.

de Rivero, Oswaldo. 2001. *The Myth of Development—The Non-Viable Economies of the 21st Century*, Zed Books.

Dyson, Tim. 1998. Review of Jones, G.W. et al., *The Continuing Demographic Transition*, in *Population and Development Review* 24, December 4, 1998, pp. 863-68.

Egerö, Bertil. 1990. *Mozambique—A Dream Undone: The Political Economy of Democracy 1975-84*. Scandinavian Institute of African Studies, Uppsala.

Ekbom, Anders and Jan Bojö. 1999. *Poverty and Environment: Evidence of Links and Integration into the Country Assistance Strategy Process*. Discussion Paper No. 4, Environment Group, Africa Region, The World Bank, January 1999.

Friedlander, Dov, Barbara S. Kun and Sharon Segal. 1999. "The Demographic Transition Then and Now: Processes, Perspectives, and Analyses," *Journal of Family History*, 4, October 4, 1999, pp. 493-533.

Greenhalgh, Susan. 1990. "Toward a Political Economy of Fertility: Anthropological Contributions," *Population and Development Review* 16, March 1, 1990, pp. 85-101.

Grimes, Seamus. 1998. "From population control to 'reproductive rights': ideological influences in population policy," *Third World Quarterly* 19, 3, pp. 375-93.

Guzmán, J. Miguel et al. 1996. *The Fertility Transition in Latin America,* Clarendon Press, Oxford.

Hodgson, Dennis. 1988. "Orthodoxy and Revisionism in American Demography", *Population and Development Review* 14, December 4, 1988, pp. 541-69.

McNicoll, George. 1992. *The Agenda of Population Studies: A Commentary and a Complaint.* Working Papers No. 42, The Population Council, New York.

Sutcliffe, Bob. 2001. *100 Ways of Seeing an Unequal World*, Zed Books.

Tabah, Leon. 1990, "The Population of the World—A Look Ahead," paper given to a DAC meeting on Population and Development, Paris 19-20 April.

US National Research Council (NRS) 2000, *Beyond Six Billion: Forecasting the World's Population,* National Academy Press.

Thompson, Warren. 1946. *Population and Peace in the Pacific.* University of Chicago Press.

Wilson, Chris. 2001. "On the Scale of Global Demographic Convergence 1950-2000," *Population and Development Review* 27, March 1, 2001.

WPP 2000, *World Population Prospects: The 2000 Revision, Highlights,* UN Population Division, February 28, 2001.

7

Culture and Civilisation for Human Development Perspectives in India on the Gandhian Path

RANA P.B. SINGH

ABSTRACT

The overall perspective of development in India presents a complex scene. Certainly it needs to be viewed in various perspectives and spatial contexts. Of course, in span of time the share of rural poor has recorded a tendency of decrease since 1951, yet the absolute number is too high; in 1994 it was 257.3 million. The rural masses also suffer by high disparity in terns of wages, allocation of money, infrastructural facilities like health and education in comparison to their counterpart urban. The increasing trend of deficit economy, continuous loss in share in foreign trade, increasing foreign debt, devaluation of currency and associated factors are among the major hindrances to India's development. At the other end India is presently facing the crises of parliamentary democracy, political pollution and constant loss of moral ethics. We certainly need moral education and cultural awakening, rooted in its indigenous base together coping with the pace of modern technology and culture of consumerism. The message of Mahatma Gandhi has already paved the path of sustainable and holistic path of human development.

Introduction

In spite of tremendous scientific-technological innovations and their application in the name of development, humankind today faces a crisis at several levels. The main idea of 'progress and development' has been conceived in the light of the positivistic-reductionist, empiricist and anthropocentric enterprise introduced in Europe in the seventeenth century. However, the alternative worldview of interconnectedness and holism is considered more relevant today. Modern science, like new physics, is recapitulating in many ways the ancient spiritual worldview of integral living. In the light of such shifts, the idea of 'development' also needs to be reassessed, rethought and reoriented.

The sacred worldview is a unitary principle of cosmic interconnectedness in search of universal order and meaning of existence—ecological cosmology. Is it possible to discern any sense of sacred in the 'alternative development' strategy? Eco-friendly development is a strategy that emphasises the integration and promotion of environmental sustainability by reorienting lifestyles, transforming technology to suit the socio-economic and indigenous systems of resource use and local habitat, maximising employment opportunities through a structural shift in occupational structure, and stimulating a 'trickle down' process to ensure socio-spatial equity. The world is full of objects and ideologies which 'we do not notice, either because we are not interested in them or because we are not equipped to see them' (Paden, 1992: 7). We take into account what currently concerns us, and avoid matters that have deeper values and that may have application in the distant future. Remember, the present makes the future and also interlinks with the past. Interpretation is sometimes connected with scientific viewpoints of causal explanation; nevertheless, it is also associated with the humanistic explanation of meanings where stands the sense of sacredness.

Like two sources of knowledge—the 'indirect' notion of understanding and imagination, and the direct one related to sensibility and perception—'development' is also to be purveyed in the light of non-sensuous and sensuous sources, and these might be seen as complementary. This ideology has a presuppositional bias. Each culture has some of its own distinctiveness but also commonality with others. One cannot presume that any one culture is complete and to be adopted by or superimposed upon others. Certainly, we need a thorough diagnosis of the sick culture, instead of always prescribing and using different means, measures and medicines for recovery in the frame of 'trial and error'. Let us understand the total spectrum of disordering.

In the process of development since independence in 1947, we have encouraged cultures of consumerism, inequality, exploitation of natural resources, falling human values, immorality, social injustice and insecurity, loss of mutual cohesiveness, individualism and self-centredness, materialism, violence, environmental pollution, loss of tribal and traditional lifestyles, unemployment, and so on. In a television programme (on the DD1 National channel, 12 Feb. 1998 at 10.30 pm), the leader of an environmental awareness movement, Ms Medha Patekar, argued for national co-ordination between public movements with an activist political consciousness and made an appeal for all political parties to replace their fostering of and fawning upon a political leader with a spiritual concept of human development and national integrity. Generally, conventional development is occurring only within the purview of economics, and we have reached the point where the freedom of society and our economic independence are in danger. Rural artisans, tribal culture, women and poor labourers have lost their status and roles in running the societal base and maintaining communal harmony. Natural and environmental settings have been ruined by the encroachment of the modern pace of development programmes like big dams, heavy industries and urban sprawl. The victim families are now living, in slums and refugee camps or are wandering from one place to another in the hope of rehabilitation and a better life.

I do not want to write as an expert or scholar, but as a citizen of my culture and era, i.e. what India is at present, what roots it sustains and how it is trying to make its future.

This is a narration of the intense 'inside' story—the never-ending political story—which I shall explain by an analogy based on the great epic, the *Ramayana* (cf. Singh, 1999a: 56-57):

On the orders of (king) Lord Rama, his brother Lakshmana paid a visit to the demon Ravana who was mortally wounded by Rama and was passing the last breath of his life. Ravana was the greatest scholar of the science of diplomacy and government. Lakshmana begged Ravana to teach him some of the key lessons of handling diplomacy and the smooth running of government.

Ravana suggested, "whatever system of government—democratic or dictatorship is imposed is immaterial; but how you expose it, is a matter of serious concern. Make the public fool in such a way that the public are always confused. And whenever some groups raise their voices against it, convince them that you are trying to integrate the varying ideologies together; and form a Commission to formulate this plan. Continue this at least for five consecutive years. Afterwards take time for reviewing and assessing progress; again make further plans and propagate assurances for the next five years. Take care that the public in no way learns which form of government is operating. This way you will succeed to rule this great country of India forever. Remember that this culture has a deep sense of faith in the future, hope and tolerance! Take heed of this sense and rule them."

Soon afterwards the demon, Ravana, died. Since then Rama is the *President* and Lakshmana is the *Prime Minister* of India in different faces and in different dresses.

Towards Development and Rethinking

The concept of 'development' has been based on the role of science and technology in the service of humankind with a view to controlling nature and the cosmic order. This needs reorientation—a paradigm shift. The political scientist Kothari (1990: 34) suggests: "This must give place to the original purpose of science, namely seeking to understand the mysteries of nature with a deep sense of humanity and wonder." However, it does not mean that humanity must sacrifice all the structures developed in the process of evolution and development. There is a need for *re*-evaluation and *re*-orientation in the light of historical roots wherein lies the moral sense of development. Let us make general consciousness and awareness interlink with the concept of sanctifying the Earth and with community development. If there should be a moral imperative for sustainable development, we need a sense of sanctity about the Earth (Ibid., 33).

Rethinking development involves a shift from the present-day development crisis to the ethical march. A new ethic—value and faith systems—is required for humankind to live in harmony with the natural world on which we depend for survival and well-being. The rethinking should be based on the foundational value—the reasoning that underlies the ethical sense. Important ethical systems are based essentially on a foundational value, which for Gandhi was *ahimsa* (non-violence, which he interpreted as 'firmness in the truth'), for Schweitzer reverence for life, and for Aldo Leopold the sacredness of land (cf. Skolimowski, 1990: 98).

The Gandhian view of non-violence, vegetarianism and *karma* (right action) is based on the idea of the total spiritual interconnectedness of all life, of the divine within all life. The essence of divinity exists in all life forms; all these should therefore be treated in the light of harmonious community life. Divinity is a deep sense of realisation of the power of interconnectedness with nature. All natural phenomena are, therefore, divine, sacred and of equal value. As human beings, we have to take the main responsibilities towards nature through a moral-ethical-religious approach. Gandhian thought is more relevant today and well suited to the soul and society of India. It is only possible if the controllers and legislators of development strategies are conscious of 'Self-realisation' (*svachetana*). This is different from the Western concept of 'ego-realisation'. The concept of 'Self-realisation' is known in the history of philosophy under various names, like 'the universal self', 'the absolute', 'the *atman*', etc.; however, it is not 'self-centred'. This concept is the assumption of a capacity for self-determination, a capacity for realising potentialities (see Naess, 1989: 85,141).

One has to realise that 'the living Earth has a right to life, and that right is the primary moral argument for sustainable life' (Kothari, 1990: 32). We need to make development sustainable, both environmentally and culturally. In this way, development also has a dimension of faith and reverence. However, ethical and moral pollution by materialism and consumerism is replacing the old value systems, which supported sustainability. Alas, this tendency of pollution is constantly threatening the sense of culture and even the identity of humankind (Singh, 1996: 103).

In the Indian psyche, there are two image-views of society: (i) the very rich, who are considered to be like earthly gods as a result of their good *karma* in the past, and are perceived as happy people by others, and (ii) the rest, who are poor, always trying to experience some pleasure through monetary gain. The first group donate a lot of money in the name of gods and to make their shelters (temples), while the second group worship there and always pray to the gods living there to be kind enough to bless them with wealth. Even the kingdom of God is controlled by rich and powerful humans. The power is mostly derived from money, with the further support of political power. 'Since money is everything, everything is to be done for money' is currently accepted as the social norm. Moreover, all the ethical norms are defined through the power of money. This is an absolute practice of materialism and its modern offshoot of consumerism. If someone slips down from the track, society labels it corruption and 'taking the wrong path'. However, remember that philosopher A.W. Watts (1962: 58) says: "For in this world nothing is wrong, nothing is even stupid. The sense of wrong is simply failure to see where something fits into a pattern."

The institutions involved in development at state or central level are reduced to the function of accounting for the allocation of funds between different government agencies, and they play only a small role in genuinely integrating the process of development (Gadgil and Guha, 1996: 48). This issue is concerned more with political and personal interest, which is practised on priority level at the place of national development. Small is beautiful is not always good; nor are 'big projects' always bad; rather these are a matter of context and regional suitability. It is a tyranny that in 'India the indigenous is sometimes the foreign, and the foreign is sometimes the indigenous' (Larson, 1995: 144). We have left far behind the ethical domain of the Earth as the mother who nourishes us and whom we have to take care of; this is fully narrated in the *Prithvi Sukta* (Hymn to the Earth) of the *Atharva Veda,* a c. fifteenth century BCE text. Instead, in many respects we have accepted the Christian ideology of an exploitative and materialistic view of the Earth as resource. This is now part of our culture, and it has become difficult to escape from. Over time, by the process of development, the masses of Indian society have accepted corruption, inflation and rising prices, and social evils like the dowry and caste systems as part of their life and culture. Every Indian criticises them; nevertheless, we are part of it and are responsible for making them flourish.

India: The Savage Scene

The mass majority of Indian people are worried about inflation and drastic price increases. We're unsure as to whether we'll be able to purchase the food or clothing that we need next year! Uncertain whether we'll be able to get enough resources to sustain and survive the speedy increase of population in the near future? Disturbed about the incompetence, dishonesty, hypocrisy and hegemony of political leaders. Distressed about the kind of cultural and physical environments our children will have to live in when they grow up. If we think about such things, certainly we share the concerns of many hundred millions of Indians. Everyday things are going badly for the rural masses, struggling peasants, and the lower middle class, and they all sense this. Above all, this culture has a deep sense of faith in the future, hope, and tolerance! Politicians take heed of this fact and are successful in ruling them (see Singh, Rana, 1999: 57). A folk proverb says, "if all roads are blocked, involvement in politics is the best strategy in India as it can ensure your future in terms of economic prosperity. Even winning only one election will guarantee your future" (Singh and Singh, 2002: 66, also cf. Singh, 2000). This is proved by the salary-cum-pension scheme for the whole life, as recently passed by the parliament for those who has wined the election even only once; the monthly stipend given is Rs. 30,000 (i.e. about US$ 630).

Ecologists Ehrlich and Ehrlich's (1974: 119) remark about India serves as a warning:

> Whether we like it or not, the fate of some countries—India, for example—is largely sealed. While an awakening within India coupled with imaginative and compassionate aid from other nations might help cushion its collapse, no human agency is likely to prevent the disaster. A run of miraculously good weather might delay it—perhaps for a decade, maybe even to the end of the century—but the train of events leading to the dissolution of India as a viable nation is already in motion.

Mesarovic and Pestel (1974: 80) have narrated the drastic situation in India by quoting Tarzie Vittachi, the Executive Secretary of World Population Year of the UNO: "To cope with the population increase, India needs to build 1000 new school-rooms every day from now on for the next twenty years, 1000 new hospital wards every day from now on for the next twenty years, and 10,000 houses every day from now on the next twenty years." Further, a delay in implementation of an effective population policy will result in calamity, starvation, malnutrition, etc. and lead to total chaos and social crisis. We've already reached the critical stage of urgency on two fronts: unprecedented growth of population, and speedy loss of moral values (i.e. *mental pollution*).

Agarwal's (1991: 83) conclusion is a plain reality and a challenge to our conscience; she says:

> After three and half decades of state-directed development, India continues to be characterised by high levels of poverty and economic equality. Over the

> past two decades in particular, the pursuit of primarily growth-oriented policies, without due consideration of distribution aspects and structural reform, has resulted in its own contradictions. Agricultural stagnation in several parts of the country, and rapid degradation of natural resource base will ultimately constrain long-term agricultural growth rates. A continuing large population under poverty, and a deteriorating physical, social, and political environment will be the other consequences. More than ever before there is a need to ask: Development for whom? Development in terms of what? And, most important, development how?

Development, not to be defined as goals or results, is in fact after all a process of growth, not an object. It cannot be pointed at in a physical way, like a table, for the sake of explication; rather it must be purveyed with respect to a changing scenario of growth, human satisfaction, comfort, peace and harmonious relationship among human beings. Growth for growth's sake in the sense of ever increasing numbers and larger size simply cannot continue forever, and also cannot provide a sustainable and stable solution in the long run. Democracy is also one of the paths of development.

The Scenario and the Roots

At some point in the present era, Indian culture lost its traditional sense of social harmony and community. *Dharma* (moral order, *not* religious dogma), which was the root of the culture, is now threatened by politically vested interests under the umbrella of secularism. Religion is currently used as a tool for 'secular democracy' with the support of 'secularisation of religious ideas'. The Indologist G. Larson (1995: x) opines that the post-independence 'secular state of India' is to a 'significant degree a forward-caste neo-Hindu state, or, in other words, that the "secular state" in the Indian context has a number of religious aspects and may even represent in some respects a religious entity'. The philosopher S. Radhakrishnan (1956: vii-viii), who was the second President of India, argued that the Indian idea of secularism 'does not mean irreligion or atheism or even material comforts. It proclaims that it lays stress on universality of spiritual values which may be attained in a variety of ways. ...This is the meaning of a secular conception of the state though it is not generally understood.' In maintaining secular democracy, the Hindu sense of tolerance, a living tradition, 'has contributed vitally. ...More important, is the attitude of "live and let live" toward all manifestations of religious diversity' (Smith, 1993: 149). According to a newspaper report (*Aj*, 8 June 1997: 6), the central government provides a subsidy of Rs. 400 million (US$ 11.4 million) to Muslims for the annual Hajj (pilgrimage) to Mecca, and additionally it grants a sum of Rs. 930 million (US$ 26.6 million) for the arrangement of air and land transportation. For no other religious group are such provisions made. Would this be called a policy of 'religious secularism'? This is an example of satisfying a group (a so-called minority!) for electoral populism. At present the scene is different—more complex, together with crises and chaos. Of course, the majority of people still have a sense of hope for a miracle in the near future (Singh, 1999a: 59).

India has its own history of contrasts—ecological, religious, linguistic, historical, political and eco-psychological. At present, India is divided into thirty-five states, embracing 190 religious groups with 1,652 languages and dialects in twelve language families with twenty-four different scripts, and 3,742 castes and sub-castes further grouped into 4,635 communities. Before becoming a British colony, the country had never been a united sovereign state; instead, it had been an amalgam of various independent republics. Historically, successive invaders (e.g. the Huns, Turks, Kushans, Mughals) became part of this culture, and Hindu society accepted them all. It was only the British who rarely tried to be part of this culture and sought to remain aloof. The Hindu sense of tolerance was used as a tool to empower them, as it is the very material form from which the Indian character is formed (cf. Segal, 1965: 33). The Hindu religion teaches a renunciation of worldly goods and preaches against materialism and consumerism. This spirit serves as a great source of strength in achieving sustainable development.

However, it would be alarming if this spirit were to turn into fundamentalism (cf. Dwivedi, 1990: 211).

When the British colonies in Asia and Africa became independent from the late 1940s onwards, they looked firmly away from their past and, towards the future. India received independence from the British Empire on 15 August 1947. Since then, it has regarded the colonial past as best forgotten, a history of exploitation and humiliation that had left its people poor. Attention has been paid to economic development and prosperity, the benefits of which can supposedly be passed on to the poor masses. Strategies and plans were made to solve the then development problems through assessing the resource potential and spatial gaps. Following a socialist pattern of society under the leadership of Jawaharlal Nehru, the first Prime Minister of the Indian republic, people from widely diverging interests and ideologies like Gandhians, Western-style socialists, communists, capitalist industrialists and others started working together and finally supported a central planning framework. This resulted in the formation of the Planning Commission of India, which introduced a series of Five-Year Plans, the first of which, covered the period 1950-55. With a view to promoting central and state planning linkages, the National Development Council was set up in 1952. Currently, under the IXth Five-Year Plan (1997-2002) these development programmes are in progress. Until the Vth Plan (1974-79), more emphasis was laid on the national economy, eliminating poverty and promoting self-reliance, but in the following Plans the focus was changed with a view to benefiting the then government's policies and its romantic propaganda. A poet in the poets' assembly exclaimed about such plans (*Aj*, 13 June 1997: 3):

> There is everything in the new proposals
> To sell this country at the rate of salt.

The greatest loss recorded in India during the colonial period was the loss of our old ethic of eco-justice, which refers to the sanctity of life and cosmic interconnectedness (ecological cosmology), which extends to the sense of global family or universal brotherhood *(vasudhaiva kutumbakam)*. This ethic helped society to maintain an order between *dharma* (moral code of conduct) and *karma* (right action). In the course of acculturation, the ideology of materialism, consumerism and individualism— which was always proscribed in traditional Hindu thought—has been accepted by contemporary society. At the other extreme—and perhaps in consequence—the movement of revival of ancient cultural values is being turned to fundamentalism by some groups. The old principle of *satyameva jayate* (only truth triumphs) is now replaced by *arthameva jayate* (only wealth triumphs). The foreign cultural domination of India during the last 700 years and the influence of imported culture have played a major role in this form of transformation (Dwivedi, 1990: 210).

The country is currently facing a cultural crisis in most of its sectors. As a consequence of the progress of development, the rich are becoming richer and the poor poorer. It is a common complaint that whatever good ideas one has are highlighted in India's files of planning programmes, but the most crucial problem we face is non-implementation. The cultural and ethical crises that the country faces today are more dangerous than any other pollution. The good, age-old cultural traditions are not being followed, nor are the ills of the present tradition being solved. The culture of individualism, consumerism and sordid love for materialistic gain is part of our lifeworld. The political environment is facing the more critical scenario of cultural downfall, immorality and lack of national identity. Currently, the Indian political scene is structured by the scandalisation of the political system, the criminalisation of politics, the politicisation of criminals, and the amoralisation of political behaviour. In common talk people say, "Cash, Crime, Corruption, Communality and Casteism are the fundamental weapons for political victory in India" (cf. Singh and Singh, 1981: 65). Segal's (1965: 309) advocacy is a warning: Will India have an *Indian Government* ruthless enough to rule in the interest of the still-silent masses? And if it will not, how much longer will the masses stay silent? How can this 'political environment' be cleaned? How is the problem of 'moral pollution' to be solved? Where has our philosophy of *karma* (right action) and *dharma* (right duty) gone? This is difficult to answer. Is it really a democracy that has to be regulated *of* the people, *by* the people and *for* the people? This is now replaced by the practice of 'off' the people, 'bye' the people and 'far' from the people.

Indian politicians operate in a manner similar to the Orwellian view of betrayal. Orwell's paraphrased statement (1945: 11) will help us to understand the situation:

> Never listen when they tell you that *politicians* and the *people* have a common interest, that the prosperity of the one is the prosperity of the others. It is all lies. A *politician* serves the interests of no creature except himself. And among us *people* let there be perfect unity; perfect comradeship in the struggle. All *politicians* are enemies. All people are comrades.

Politicians are successful in dividing the social psyche in terms of rich *vs* poor, owners *vs* labourers, high *vs* low castes, religious groupings, and so on. The policies of reservation and economic support for a section of society create conflict in the society due to discrepancies in their operation. In this process, politicians gain enhanced electoral support. There is at least hope for perfect unity among the various sects, sections and sectors of society. The policy of 'divide and rule' has taken root in the political environment. Larson (1995: 288) says:

> That India has made almost no progress in developing a uniform code and that it continues routinely to extend the system of 'reservations' even though such reservations were to cease ten years after independence (provides) further evidence of the politics of a nation without 'citizens'.

There is little hope that the polluted political environment will be cleaned and made more humane in the near future. Before any treatment of the sick culture and sick economy of India, a sympathetic diagnosis is necessary at all levels. During the late 1930s, the national poet, Maithilisaran Gupta, lamented: "Let this educational system be dead as it is only for jobs!" Currently, there are 203 universities and 9,700 postgraduate colleges; however, this has been a great challenge for our education, which has left no place for ethical values and human service. Those who control power pontificate to others, while in their own life they Practise something else. 'Corruption, like sacrifice, starts at the top and, percolating down, colours the whole society' (Segal, 1995: 288). Bribery—or what is delicately called 'grease money'—is now so much rooted in the official functioning that without it nothing could move in the right direction. The rapid expansion of economic liberalisation and the commercialisation of politics are the crucial factors making corruption more intense.

Over a history covering over two hundred years of colonial hegemony of Britain, and mismanaged governance during the last fifty years after independence in 1947, India has lost its traditional resource base, industry and economic status. Liberalisation, strict agreements with agencies like the IMF and the World Bank on their own conditions and own terms, the increase of an open market system, the constant devaluation of Indian currency against the Dollar, and several such related causes depressed the Indian economy far beyond what is easy to cope with and solve. In the new economic policy passed in 1991 by the Congress Party Government, with no regards to the consequences, the structural adjustments as proposed by the World Bank have been accepted, and in different ways also followed by the successive governments.

Even after nearly sixty years of independence, the common people in India feel that they are suppressed by the present 'New-Anglicised Indian rulers' (modern politicians and bureaucrats). Following the colonial policy of 'divide and rule', these rulers have also succeeded in segregating Indian society into various hierarchical sections of castes, cults, communities, religious sects and regions. Political culture is really, at present, a form of hypocrisy. In the name of Gandhian moralist thought, seminars and meetings are organised and declarations are made to follow the path shown by him. However, in practice nobody follows. False and 'dummy' celebrations are performed in which self-praise and big shows are the common scenes. In Orwellian thought, this is an example of 'doublethink'.

Some people say 'the British exploited India for the sake of their own country, but the present Indian rulers are exploiting us for individual gain; we are relieved from the British slavery, but in no way could we liberate ourselves from the "new" slavery imposed upon us by the political system after independence'. In British India, it was said that 'every Indian is born in debt and dies in debt'. In 1970, India's foreign debt was US$ 7,940 million, i.e. Rs. 110.5 per person; it reached US$ 106.7 billion in 1997, i.e. Rs. 4,210.5 (US$112.3) per person (Bose, 1997: 52). The profit from such international debt accrues to some individuals and institutions, both at home and abroad, but every citizen has to bear a share of the burden. Budget deficits and escalating prices to consumers are the norm. Under the tough conditions of the IMF, India is bound to take loans, which are further misused by a particular section for their own profit. Ultimately, that burden of indebtedness falls on the common people.

In the name of development for depressed classes (*dalits*), the policy of reservation (22.5 per cent of all jobs) was introduced in the early 1950s through the initiatives of B.R. Ambedkar (1891-1956), the leader of the untouchables and India's first Law Minister. According to Article 334 of the Indian Constitution, this reservation was to be for ten years only. However, in 1960, 1970, 1980 and 1990 the time limit was routinely extended for an additional ten years, mostly to serve the vested interest of politicians for the sake of electoral support. In 1990, the Mandal Commission recommended an additional 27 per cent of reservations for OBCs (other backward castes). Thus, in total, 49.5 per cent of reservations have been approved by the Central Government. This policy and the idea of social justice are used as political tools. Comparing the statistics of employment by caste in 1935 and 1982, Khushwant Singh (1990: 19) concluded that 3.5 per cent of India's Brahmin community (the highest caste in the hierarchy) holds between 36 and 63 per cent of all the plum jobs available in the country. Out of sixteen Indian Prime Ministers during the period 1947-98, eleven have been Brahmins. Of course, under the reservation policies the people from the downtrodden classes are given opportunities even without the required qualification and merit. The upper-caste elites always complain about such an imposition. They suggest that the reservation policy should be applied only to education and scientific training, and that merit should be given priority in job selection. This is the way that, over time, the depressed classes should be upgraded. Through the misuse of reservation policy a great mass of unqualified engineers, doctors, administrators and even scientists (so-called!) are now part of the system by which the path of India's future development is to be made. One has to appreciate the level of tolerance of Indian people, who believe that this is the era of falsehood (*kali yuga),* where anything is possible. They say: wait for the new light; don't cry! This way the country is continuing on the path of development in the hope of miracle and charisma! There may be total collapse, or a completely new world!

In the early phases of development after independence, the strategy to eradicate poverty was in line with capitalistic views—more production and more benefits. The consequences were more economic disparity, social gaps, and an increase of mass poverty. In statistical terms, it is easy to explain that the ratio of poor people has a tendency of decline, however the absolute mass has constantly been increasing. According to the National Sample Survey and Planning Commission, in 1984-85 an average Indian family of 5 members spending Rs. 6,400 annually was considered poor. This means a per capita expenditure of Rs. 106.67 (i.e. Rs. 6,400/5-members/12 months) formed the poverty line index. If the 1960-61 price value is assumed as 100, then a comparable figure for 1984-85 comes to 521; it means the purchasing capacity of Rs. 100 in 1960-61 has declined Rs. 20.47 when compared with 1984-85. With several revisions and adjustments, the poverty line is defined. In 1993-94, the per capita expenditure of Rs. 235 per month in the rural areas and Rs. 310 in urban areas was defined as the upper limit of the poverty line. With respect to price rises and purchasing power, this scale is revised accordingly. In a regional perspective, with the exception of the two southern states of Kerala and Karnataka, all the states have recorded an increase in poverty since the 1980s, and in the richer states like Punjab, Haryana and Gujarat, the rate of increase was more apparent than the Indian average. The total number of poor people in India (326.6 million) is equal to the total population of the U.K. and the U.S.A. together (i.e. 327 million in 1997). Specifically, since 1991 the country is becoming an economic slave. This has a direct relationship with the growing masses of the poor; keep in mind that 36.8 per cent of the population (326.6 million) lives below the poverty line. The majority of these people do not even get basic meals at least two times a day. Moreover, 66 per cent of children below 5 years suffer from malnutrition, and infant mortality is at 65 per 1000 live births. This is a tragic situation and stands as a shame to humanity and the present democracy.

It is a great dilemma that even after nearly sixty years of independence, the Indian Government is unable to fix the minimum daily wage for the 25 per cent of the labour force at the bottom—those living below the poverty line, mostly agricultural labourers and their dependants. Does India have no resources, no economic capacity, or no development strategy for the solution of such a tragic situation? One example can be used to explain India's potentiality and requirements. Based on a National Sample Survey in 1993-94, it was estimated that a subsidy of at least Rs. 2,750 for rural poor and Rs. 3,175 for urban poor was required to improve conditions for those living below the poverty line. By this scale the total money required would have been:

— **Rural poor** : 257.3 million × Rs. 2,750 = Rs. 707.6 billion;

— **Urban poor** : 69.3 million × Rs. 3,175 = Rs. 220.0 billion.

This way to be out of poverty required a total sum of Rs. 927.6 billion, which was about 5 per cent of the total Gross National Product (see Singh, Jasbir, 1999: 12). But no single strategy was prepared to solve this tragedy. This simple calculation supports the idea that only strong political desire, ethical viewpoints, transformation of resources and their rational allocation, and a suitable strategy would have solved this problem. Lack of economic resources is not the basic problem in this context.

According to the last census of India (1991), 74.3 per cent of the total 844 million inhabitants lived in rural areas, and 37.7 per cent represent the working population. The economy of the country is grouped into three sectors: (i) primary sector (farming, forestry, fishing, livestock and mining), (ii) secondary (industry and manufacturing), and (iii) tertiary (transport and communication, administration, and services). Their growth rates during 1950-1996 were 2.66, 5.6 and 5.1 per cent, respectively. Moreover, the primary sector's share in gross domestic product fell from 56.45 per cent in 1950-51 to 28.75 per cent in 1995-96. For the poor, lentils have been the major source of food protein; their share of daily food intake was 16.1 per cent in 1950-51, but this had declined to 7.1 per cent in 1995-96. Even at present, about 40 per cent of the people (mostly living in rural areas) do not have an adequate food intake (cf. Bose, 1997: 29). In rural India, 34 per cent of families are still absolutely landless; with additional landless labourers, this reaches 39.5 per cent. When marginal landholders are included, the figure comes close to 58 per cent; together they possess less than 6 per cent of arable land (1992 data). Conversely, the top 5.3 per cent of landlords account for 40.17 per cent of total holdings. Even today, around 200 million people engaged in agriculture have no work for about 100 days per year (*Ibid.*, 43). During the period 1981-91, the percentage of cultivators decreased from 41.58 to 38.75 per cent and the share of agricultural labourers increased from 24.94 to 26.15 per cent. It is sad to notice that land reforms over much of the country since independence have failed.

This has encouraged leftist movements, beginning with the communist-led peasant revolts of Telangana in the 1940s and continuing at present with several armed organisations such as the Naxalites and similar extreme left movements among the tribal and poor landless farmers. The British land policy of high taxation, converting agricultural land into a commodity, creating a large class of tenant farmers, encouraging local chieftains to control the land and its products, and related factors promoted a substantial degree of autonomy and control by the landlords (*zamindars*). This resulted in the development of a two-ladder social class—the masters, omnivores, and the servants, dispossessed. The government policy of boosting agricultural production in limited areas like the northern states of Haryana and Punjab, with the support of conservative landlords, left the masses of people in the Indian countryside impoverished, while on the other side a new class of omnivore was created from among the large and medium-sized landholders of the areas of 'Green Revolution' agriculture (Gadgil and Guha, 1995: 66). This lopsided agricultural development has had a series of environmental consequences e.g. waterlogging of over-irrigated lands, depletion of soil fertility, pesticide pollution, nitrate pollution of aquifers, and so on. Moreover, vast areas of India's countryside are left out of enhancement programmes. It is rightly said that 'Forty years of planned development has created an India in which islands of prosperity peep out of a sea of poverty (*Ibid.*, 34).

Since independence, about 3,000 big multipurpose dams have been built; consequently, about 3 million villagers, mostly poor tribal people, have been displaced, and the majority of them still live like refugees. After they move off their land, abandoning their livelihood and culture, they are forced to survive in new ways, which they had never imagined. The authorities closed their development files on these projects by providing meagre compensation for the losses that these people suffered. The benefits of large dams have accrued primarily to the industrialists and urban dwellers in general. The largest and the most controversial hydroelectric and irrigation complex, based on 30 major, 135 medium and 3,000 minor dams, and to be built over fifty years on the Narmada River in western India, was started in 1987 at an estimated cost of US$ 5 billion. The World Bank is the largest source of funds for this project. The dams will displace 200,000 people, submerge 2,000 sq. km of fertile land and 1,500 km of prime teak and *sal* forest, and eliminate historic sites and rare wildlife. Thanks to the anti-dam movement by local and tribal people, referred to as India's first nation-wide environmental protest, under the leadership of Ms Medha Patekar, the project has now become an issue of debate and dispute, and ultimately the work is not progressing optimally as proposed by the donor institution. In the light of uncertainty over government policies, rising pressure from the anti-dam movement and rejection of the major conditions proposed, the World Bank recently withdrew its support for this project. Internationally, the World Bank is having to rethink its policies, juxtaposing its role as a commercial 'development' institution with international demands for a greener and more socially aware lending body.

Under the impact of structural adjustments and the pre-conditions of getting loans from the international agencies, like the World Bank, the country is speedily marching towards deficit economy. In 1950-51 the deficit was only Rs. 20 million, i.e. 0.3 per cent—indicating relatively a balanced trend, but by 1997-98 it reached to Rs. 236.44 billion, i.e. 17.3 per cent. The situation was worst in 1960-61 and in 1980-81 when deficit had crossed 40 per cent. In the world trade the share of India is constant since 1970, i.e. only 0.6 per cent. In the export of tea, spices and sugar India is constantly loosing its share in world trade. The only increase recorded has been under coffee, and pearls and stones. This tendency is a clear indication of economic downfall at several frontiers (Singh and Singh, 2002: 69, and also cf. Singh and Singh, 2004).

Through the process of capitalist globalisation, the Group of Seven (G-7) countries (the USA, Canada, Japan, the UK, Germany, France and Italy) promote a system of greater dependency on foreign loans and investments, the main sources of which are the World Bank and the IMF. Through the pressure of their terms and conditions, the receiving nation is bound to satisfy their objectives (cf. Farmer, 1993: 145-146). Foreign companies and investments are now rapidly and easily capturing the Indian market while replacing the indigenous system, and behind the scenes they are also influencing the political system to gain favour. India's foreign trade deficit of US$ 1 billion in 1960-61 reached US$ 9.5 billion in 1990-91. This resulted in major changes to economic policies under the pressure of the World Bank. Moreover, to try to clear the foreign deficit, another loan was taken from the World Bank, ultimately creating a further economic threat. Consequently,

India has to devalue its currency from time to time to suit the bank's conditions. It is charged that "international debt has accelerated the rate of extraction and conversion of natural resources to enable the country to meet its external financial obligations" (Reed, 1992: 143). The multinational companies of the G-7 countries and the World Bank are also promoting structural adjustment, mostly with the aim of securing their capital and gaining more profit on investment through the system of devaluing the Indian currency[1], promoting an open market and checking the nationalisation process. In the absence of (adequate) social objectives in adjustment programmes, structural adjustment has failed at different levels (cf. Reed 1992: 36-40).

In recent years, many non-governmental organisations (NGOs) and voluntary organisations have been established with specific objectives, primarily to try and activate local groups to play a watchdog role in preventing further ecological deterioration and to canvass public opinion in general for their active participation in development programmes. Self-help and self-reliance have been at the core of such programmes. NGOs are highly diverse organisations, are engaged in various activities and operate at a variety of scales. As watchdogs on the activities of governments, they play a key role in sustainable development, which perhaps governments themselves are unable to. The World Bank is also now encouraging alliances with NGOs which have traditionally been vociferous opponents of the World Bank, although of course the money granted is transacted through government channels. However, again the omnivores are slowly capturing the NGOs, through which they can extend their capital. Many NGOs are now being established in order to receive money from abroad. Initially, they follow their objectives, but over time the NGOs are mostly used for personal economic benefits. There are currently around ten thousand NGOs in the country. (This observation is based on various Indian newspaper reports during 1997-98. Through visits to and close interaction with the areas where NGOs are running their projects, one could gain such an impression.) Here the issue of moral ethics comes into being. If one lacks the sense of service as moral duty, no system can achieve its basic goals. There is a need for an attached system that may serve the role of watchdog in preventing NGOs from betraying their constitutions and objectives. This is also an example of cultural-downfall, where economic gain is the end.

Crisis in Indian Democracy

Democracy is accepted as the most desirable form of government and management. This form of government relies on the idea of an 'open' society as a pre-requisite, a society where every person has the basic right to exercise power and influence. *Democracy* would be taken into account in at least three broad senses: *political*, through forms of active participation congruent with cultural preferences; *economic*, providing the right of all those engaged in the process of production to influence that process, keeping in mind the need for an adequate level of production; and *social*, providing absolute access to all forms of social security (see Tinbergen, 1976: 72).

The political scientist Kothari (1987: 404) describes resultant scene in contemporary Indian politics:

> Together, both the technocratic and the 'fundamentalist' perversions have rendered the Indian State into a no man's land, a playground for corruption, criminalisation, and terror for the mass of people and a cynical withdrawal from the political process on the part of urban elite and the upper and middle classes in general. The result is large-scale de-politicisation and a tendency to leave matters to a few dominant individuals and their authorised agents.

More than a decade ago Kothari (1987: 413) stated that "the new alignment of forces is likely to be conceived less in terms of political coalition-making or the consolidation of a social coalition, and more in terms of a simple and straight forward manager-cum-Mafia-cum-police *raj* (-rule)". This is proved to be a reality in contemporary India, the state of Bihar, of course, being the worst example (cf. Biswas, 1996). Indian politicians always pursue power in order to rule the country, instead of pursuing policy to make the country and people prosperous and happy.

It has been the bad luck of Indian democracy that no coalition government has completed its tenure. The leading party, Congress Party, which ruled India for thirty-nine years in the nearly sixty-year period after independence, has played a central role as catalyst by falling out of the coalition government six times. During its rule, the Congress Party government has given "the business community the means by which to hold the Congress part to ransom. The richer and more powerful the business community becomes, the richer and more powerful it demands to be, and greater are the resources with which it is able to pursue its demands" (Segal, 1965: 303). The second major party at national level is the BJP (Bhartiya Janata Party). The Congress Party is a gathering of imperialists, while BJP comprise conservative nationalists. Both follow the line of capitalist economy and both promote liberalisation and globalisation, ignoring the interests of the poor masses of the country. Both of these national parties are dominated by a majority of Brahmins (elite-rich), feudal and neo-feudal. There is no strong Third-Stream approach in politics. Moreover, the Congress Party and the BJP both formed a united front to oppose the growth of Third-Stream that would be a party of rural poor, downtrodden and backward people. However, the Third-Stream movement is already coming up, and of course shifting to extremist positions. The sixteenth Prime Minister of India, Mr. A.B. Bajpayee formed a government in alliance with eighteen other political parties on 19 March, 1998. Their ideologies differ greatly; for the sake of power they all take shelter under one umbrella.

According to the Election Commission the cost of General Election is increasing. The September-October 1999 elections cost over Rs. 12 billion, i.e. Rs. 12 per person, in public funds, an amount that the people of India never expected, nor were prepared for. There are 600 electoral constituencies, consisting of about 600 million voters, and in each of the constituencies there were three major political candidates and several secondary candidates. In this context, let us view the economics of elections (see Joshi 1999). On average, each of the 3 major candidates spent Rs. 10 million, and other secondary candidates Rs. 20 million altogether, thus we see that per constituency the expenditure might be (Rs. 10 million × 3) + Rs. 20 million, i.e. Rs. 50 million. For all 600 constituencies this could amount to Rs. 30,000 million, which also includes the major share of black funding. In total, the election expenditure amounted to Rs. 50/per voter (Rs. 30,000 million/ 600 million voters) per political candidate, and an additional Rs. 20/per voter (Rs. 12,000 million/600 million voters) by the Union Government. Elections are used as a process to get black money transferred into white money. This money laundering is done to answer public demands and the demands for vested interests on the part of political leaders! One may call it a liberalisation of the open market for black money—should we call this an economic achievement?

The basic difficulty of the contemporary materialistic-scientific culture is a constant loss of value-dynamics in human society. When cultural values are lost, culture will die. If there is no ethical sense behind progress or prosperity, an ethical dead-end will not be far behind. Democracy is not only a form of government; it is also a way of life, a code of cultural values. But when it loses its public conscience and is used as hypocritical tool for obtaining power, it becomes a tool by which by any ways, by any means, and at any cost politicians gain the support of the innocent masses. In India, less than half the electorate cast their vote, of which about twenty-five per cent is forged balloting, and even that share is divided into regional parties. This process results in no single party attaining the required status to form a government. Coalition becomes the only strategy through which people from different ideologies, backgrounds, and interests form a government, of course knowing all the while that the government will never complete its 5-year tenure. Gandhi warned politicians about the social and political evils of which they become part!

The Ideological Search: Gandhi vs. Nehru

Mahatma Gandhi (1869-1948) and Jawaharlal Nehru (1889-1964) were more responsible than any other persons for influencing the Indian psyche and the society for mass awareness towards an independence movement, and the basic framework of the philosophy of development. Committed to non-violence (*ahimsa*) and self-realisation (*svachetana*), Gandhi wanted to solve India's problems from the perspective of individual conversion and with the ideology that 'every man has an equal right for the necessities of life even as birds and beasts there' (Segal 1965: 186). In pre-partition India, his vision was represented by 'religionisation of the political', directly related to the ultimate meaning and significance of human existence. However, in independent India his successor, Nehru, transformed it into a 'politicisation of the religious', referring to the tasks of political mobilisation and acquisition of power (Larson 1995: 199). Gandhi advocated doing the right thing at the right time through seer participation. According to him, the 'right thing' is a moral order (*dharma*) operated by right action (*karma*). Gandhi's emphasis upon self-realisation and rules of conduct and virtues is essential for spiritual life and also for the maintenance of the social order. For him 'right' comes only through the realisation. of truth: he said "God is the means and Truth is the end". Truth and non-violence 'appear to him to be the same thing or different aspects of one and the same thing, and he uses these words almost interchangeably' (Nehru, 1960: 279).

During the pre-independence period, Gandhi had attempted a public awareness movement through his walking tour, *padayatra*. The march was to spread the message of communal harmony and realisation of society's problems related to poverty and inequality. His disciple, Vinoba Bhave, continued this march to persuade landlords to donate land to the landless. In many areas it was successful; however, examples of donating rough and wasteland were also recorded. This shows the lack of a conscience to support the poor.

Gandhi's successor, Nehru, was his apparent antithesis and wanted mechanised agriculture and rapid urban-industrial growth as the route to development. Segal (1965: 308) remarks that:

> Nehru never wished to be a tyrant, but he became one—not a great one but a petty one, and not through will but through vacillation. He reigned but did not rule, he commanded but did not conduct, he arbitrated where he should have resolved. ...He despised corruption and recognised its dangers, but he sat by, silent, while political colleagues, and even relatives, openly engaged in it.

The contrasts and contexts between Gandhi and Nehru can be summarised in Table 1. Gandhi fought throughout his life to restore the old ethical values and for the revival of cultural identity. However, his successors and politicians interpreted him in their own way for their own benefit. In this way, the seed of self-interest, polluted political environment and sordid love for power was planted.

TABLE 1. Gandhi and Nehru

Context	*M.K. Gandhi*	*J.L. Nehru*
Social organisation	Indian village	Urban society
Industrial growth	Handicraft, small level	Heavy industries
Change	Individual, attitudinal	Social and economic
Democratic frame	Moral democracy	Social democracy
Ideology towards non-violence	Indigenous alternative to class war	Marxian instrument of struggle

Until his death in 1964, Nehru had been Prime Minister of India; he 'was wrapped in visions of the future so tightly that he lost sight of the disorder and dismay everywhere around him' (*Ibid.*, 309). With Gandhi's assassination in 1948, and the deaths of the leading voices of alternative models, Subhas Chandra Bose in 1945 and V.B. Patel in 1950, Nehru was free to develop his own ideas and rule the country according to his own consensus. Nehru's daughter, Indira Gandhi, using the populist rhetoric of 'removing poverty', became Prime Minister in 1971. Of course, she destroyed the boss structure of the Old Congress Party, but she failed to replace it with an effective system. In 1984, Mrs Gandhi was assassinated, and following the 'dynastic succession' her airline pilot son, Rajiv Gandhi, was given the prime ministership. He was defeated in the general election in 1989, and was also assassinated, in 1991. By his death dynastic rule was ended. The lineage of father (Nehru), daughter (Indira Gandhi) and grandson (Rajiv Gandhi) held the prime ministership of India for thirty-nine years in the fifty-year period after independence. No leading party has ruled at the centre for a longer period since 1989, except from March 1991 to May 1996 (cf. Larson, 1995: 228). After the downfall of Narasimha Rao's Congress government in May 1996, Mr Bajpayee (Bharatiya Janata Party, BJP) succeeded as Prime Minister, but for only thirteen days. He had been replaced for one year (1996-97) by Mr Devegouda, who was nominated by the United Front, an alliance of fourteen political parties having different ideologies, and with the support of the Congress Party, which pressed to replace the Prime Minister. That is how on 21 April 1997 I.K. Gujral took over the chair, replacing Mr Devegouda. Great political chaos was created by the Congress Party, which withdrew its support for the government. Therefore on 4 December 1997, the president of India dissolved Parliament and imposed an unexpected burden of parliamentary elections (February-March 1998).

The government at the centre represents a combination of contrasting ideologies and varying ambitions of the politicians who are gathered under one umbrella to enjoy the lust of power. On 19 March 1998, a new BJP government was formed in alliance with nineteen other political parties. Mr Bajpayee returned as the sixteenth Prime Minister of independent India. Factionalism is the chief characteristic of Indian politics at central, state and regional levels. Tricks like electoral populism, emotional blackmailing of voters, manoeuvring and bargaining for support are commonly used by politicians to get a seat in the government—enjoying its fruits of power, influence and affluence. It has now reached its worst stage—every day some new scam or scandal is recorded. According to a newspaper survey, during the 1948-97 period the sum of major reported scams and scandals in India was around Rs. 20,428.7 billion (i.e. US$ 544.77 billion)—that is Rs. 21,503.8 (US$ 573.4) per person (cf. *Amar Ujala*, a daily newspaper from Allahabad,

4 February 1998: 7). In all these cases, politicians and ministers from the central and state governments were indicted.

In the 1998-99 Union Budget, the Indian Government increased its allocation to the departments of Atomic Energy and Space Research by Rs. 13.66 billion in order to promote defence and nuclear power. This increase is more than five times higher than that for health, over 52 per cent higher than that for the central education vote, and over 72 per cent higher than the increased allocation for rural employment and poverty alleviation *(The Hindustan Times,* 9 June 1998: 22). So, the world's second most populous country, while propagating its ideology of 'truth and global peace', is in reality involved in a nuclear arms race, as evidenced by its nuclear test explosions on 11 May 1998—ironically the Buddha's birthday. After all, the Buddha enunciated his philosophy of compassion, peace and brotherhood to the world in the sixth century BCE. This reminds one of the statements by the former Prime Minister, late Indira Gandhi, in 1981 that the cost of building an intercontinental ballistic missile (ICBM) was equal to that of building 340,000 primary schools, or 65,000 health care centres (*Ibid.*). It was Indira Gandhi who ordered India's first atomic test, on 18 May 1974. These nuclear tests represent a kind of insanity that in no way promotes national prosperity but instead enlists the support of the poor masses through emotional blackmail for purposes of making India a nuclear power and thereby entering an ongoing struggle for hegemony through weapons build-up and terrorism. Yet it is the poor who ultimately bear the principal costs through their inability to meet their basic needs. Hence the rich become richer and the poor poorer—a development strategy devoid of sensitivity to moral ethics or brotherhood.

Gandhi on Moral Passion

In the late 1940s, the term 'development' was not in currency as it is today. Gandhi had, therefore, used the term 'progress' for a holistic form of human development, more with respect to ethics and cosmic integrity. He said, "by economic progress we mean material advancement without limit, and by real progress we mean moral progress, which again, is the same thing as progress of the permanent elements in us" (*The Collected Works of Mahatma Gandhi* (*WMG*), vol. 87: 249). He never made an academic contribution to 'development', instead he pleaded for an organised effort to change the ruling paradigm and move towards a superhuman stage. The Gandhian idea of development is based on the foundational ethics of *ahimsa* (non-violence, which he interpreted as 'firmness in the truth'). Perhaps Gandhi's most important influence has been on the black civil rights movement in the USA led by Martin Luther King.

In the cosmic-moral organisation, faith is the path of spirituality, and spirituality in its true sense is the spirit of proper action. This sense has a direct relationship with society and social life. Those who believe that their way of life and spirituality are different are ignorant of cosmic interconnectivity and its harmonic functioning. *Mahatma* Gandhi (1869-1948) has suggested "Seven Social Sins" which are to be avoided (see Singh, Ramji, 1999b: 6). Of course, these are ideals, but they are more relevant in the present era of desperation and could easily be accepted. Gandhi reminds us that no one can escape from one sin and be part of the other. The "*Seven Social Sins*" according to Gandhi (cf. Singh, 2006: 107) are:

(i) *Consumption without conscience*: The means and symbols of consumption are the 3Ps, i.e. property, power and prestige. Without conscience or moral responsibility, consumption always turns to evil, in other words, eating food is consumption, but without conscience it leads to sickness; similarly, sex is a biological gift, but without conscience it turns to disorder. Consumerism is one of the basic root causes of social conflict.

(ii) *Knowledge without character*: Knowledge is power, but without morality it is hypocrisy. With a lack of morality knowledge becomes a heavy burden on humanity.

(iii) *Wealth without labour*: In the modern era, wealth is the highest symbol of projecting the level of personality and status. The ideology that 'Money is everything, so everything is just for money', is now part of the culture.

This promotes the tendency of the 'rich becoming richer and the poor becoming poorer'. Accumulation of wealth by all possible means is the path to success for the majority of people. These rich people never realise their social responsibility; this leads to social crisis.

(iv) *Business without morality*: According to the philosophy of welfare economics, the basis of economic success is morality. However, at present, 'morality' has no place in business. The proverb that 'everything is fair in love and war' is also applicable to business. The speedy encroachment and expansion of industries on our fertile land is one example. Gandhi said, "Economics that hurt the moral well-being of an individual or a nation are immoral and, therefore, sinful" (*WMG*, vol. 13: 317, also cf. *WMG*, vol. 75: 158)

(v) *Religious duty without sacrifice*: Compassion, service, sacrifice, and altruism are the basic rules of *dharma* (religious-moral duty). Lacking the sense of sacrifice promotes individualism, egocentricity and selfishness. Serving the poor is service to God.

(vi) *Science without human sense*: Science has both the power of creation and destruction; its nature depends the way in which it is used by man. Misconception of science as tool and technique for the use of resources has promoted the philosophy of consumerism, which finally resulted in environmental disorder, pollution and loss of peaceful life. The misuse of power of government with the support of science converges into satanic actions that will finally destroy the world. This power has promoted inhumane behaviour, desperation and cultural crisis. Today, we have reached the stage where science becomes the master of mankind instead of its assistant. Remember science is the means, but the end is the human kindness!

(vii) *Politics without principles*: Politics without principle is the cause of the global crisis. Whatever direction and ways concerning science, international relation or trade, war, education and ideological acceptance one proposes or selects are motivated by politics. And if it follows the track of immoral principle it destroys the social harmony. Gandhi has emphasised the need of spirituality as the first step of politics and governance.

The idea of brotherhood, in a sense the global family, is not new. It has full description in the Vedic literature (ca. 15th century BCE). This has now become special idea to our times as a pre-condition for survival. How many of our politicians realise this! Generally they use the tool of "emotional blackmailing" to win elections. Law is never used as tool, rather as a process through which institutions and ethics go hand in hand with the process of human thought and always-keeping pace to cope with the changes in time and international perspective. However, those have the power, political or economic, they interpret and practice it in their own way for their own benefit, satisfaction, or vested interest.

Whenever the ethical code of society is lost, civilisation will end. In such a situation, a cultural tradition is unable to find a balance between the needs and expectations of society, and that is how it fails to illuminate a path of revolution. In this way, the road to growth and development comes to dead-end. Gandhi proposed a philosophy of revival and peace; he called it *Sarvodaya* ("well-being for all"). Whenever personal welfare (*sva-*) is enhanced to the level of human existence (*sarva-*), this is the cultural code of *Sarvodaya*. History has proved that the alternative to war and conflict is *ahimsa* ("non-violence"), i.e. peaceful agitation, creating mass awareness of cultural unity. There are two ideas inherent in the philosophy of *Sarvodaya* (see Singh, Ramji, 1999a: 6):

(i) *Democracy is a lifestyle*: Democracy is not only a way of governance, it is also a way of life. Gandhi has warned that a process of dialogue and criticism must always be maintained between the public and military powers. The continuing trend towards loss of public awareness is a sign of the decline of democracy. The speedy increase of interference by police, Mafia, the military, and capitalists, and their protection by politicians for their own vested interests, indicate that 'democracy is in danger', that it has neither scope nor future in India. Now, government rule on the basis of majority is also an illusion. Under the ideology of decentralisation, bureaucrats and politicians try to please their own people within various parties by awarding them government positions. The only motive considered is that of who would be more helpful in future elections in terms of donating money and manoeuvring the electorate.

(ii) *Machines also have a cultural value*: The use of *machines* (a product of science) also has a cultural value. The application of science, or its tool, the machine, depends on human intention. Science is like a machine, the effects of whose use depends upon the attitude and motives of the person who has control over it. In fact, we have crossed far beyond the limit of science, and left far behind the culture of humanity and ecological cosmology. One may expect that machines can help improve welfare, well-being, scarcity of needs, and also support human emotions, feelings and brotherhood. Machines help humanity in two ways: improving our lives and enhancing our minds. If science is only for the sake of science, humanity is in danger. The path on which science is presently marching will lead to a great dissolution. Cultural values are imposed upon machines by human beings (*WMG*, vol. 25: 251-252).

Gandhi's view of non-violence, *ahimsa*, vegetarianism and *karma* (right action) is based on the idea of the total spiritual interconnectedness and divinity of life as form of ultimate human development. All natural phenomena are, therefore, divine, sacred and of equal value. As human beings, we have to take the main responsibilities towards nature through a moral-ethical-religious approach—perhaps this is the only approach to human development. His theory of *ahimsa* was not strict like a sectarian rule; he said: "whoever believes in *ahimsa* will engage himself in occupations that involve the least possible violence."

Committed to non-violence (*ahimsa*) and self-realisation (*svachetana*), Gandhi wanted to solve India's problems from the perspective of individual conversion and with the ideology that 'every man has an equal right for the necessities of life even as birds and beasts'. According to him, the 'right thing' is a moral order (*dharma*) operated by right action (*karma*). Gandhi's emphasis upon self-realisation and rules of conduct and virtues is essential for spiritual life and also for the maintenance of the social order. Gandhi warned politicians about the social and political evils of which they become part!

Gandhi said, "every human being has a right to live and, therefore, to find the wherewithal to feed himself and where necessary to clothe and house himself" (*WMG*, vol.38: 197). He said, "there's enough in the world to meet the needs of everyone but there's not enough to meet the greed of everyone". If every little village became self-sufficient then one would have an ideal set of life. Therefore he did not advocate macro-economic policy. All villages should become self-sufficient. It must work from the bottom upwards and not the top down (cf. Singh, 2006: 108-109).

Remember what Fritjof Capra (1983: 324) says:

> More than any other social species we engage in collective thinking, and in doing so we create a world of culture and values that becomes an integral part of our natural environment. Thus biological and cultural characteristics of human nature cannot be separated.

True knowledge always enlightens integral thoughts of ecological cosmology. Storing information is not knowledge. Knowledge is wisdom gained in a deeper quest in the service of humankind. Lovelock's (1995: xvi) statement that "Modern science has become as professional as the advertising industry" needs to be changed and adapted for humanity. He further (*Ibid.*, 13) and eloquently stated that the future of mankind depends much more upon a proper relationship with mother earth than with the never-ending drama of human interest.

Basic and Moral Education

In spite of several programmes designed to check the speedy growth of population, India has not been able to reach its optimal goal. In 1986, a new educational policy was formed based on a realisation that only moral education and conscience would help in this context. This new policy has proposed a "programme of action" which would emphasise the cultural recognition of the "small family"—*ham do, hamare do* ("we are two: husband and wife, and we have two: a son, a daughter"). Population-education is also given due consideration to promote "family planning and family welfare" programmes. Population-education is a form of moral education promoting awareness of the basic realities of population problems and their consequences on lifestyle, development, and the ongoing daily situations we have to face, as well as the broader perspectives of the interrelation between population and ecological order. The three main objectives are: (i) to inform of the consequences of high population, (ii) to examine the impact of increasing population on development, human life, and the natural environment, and (iii) to create awareness and realisation of the consequences of population growth and a strategy for checking and reducing the same, while simultaneously promoting the "small family".

Population education is an impartial part of moral education which itself is directly associated with the formation of human values such as compassion, sympathy, moral duty, simple living with high ideals, respectability and reverence, honesty, devotion to work, welfare and kindness, brotherhood, and mutual unity. In Indian thought this is called *dharma* ("moral duty"). Moral education has been misused and misinterpreted by politicians in the frame of secularism, secularist democracy and secular education. Keep in mind that India is a multi-religious country, forming a mosaic, which together makes a cultural-whole. Moral education is in no way related to a religious idea, rather it is a process, an internal dialogue, a mental transformation towards realising universalism, global brotherhood and ecological cosmology. In many respects, the present educational system is failing in the face of a mass awakening for human service. The situation with regards to primary level education is more crucial.

It has been obvious that during the four decades following independence, the literacy growth was very poor. One of the major obstacles has been socialist planning that emphasised spending volumes rather than productivity, and has had disastrous results for education as well as other fields (Aiyar, 1999: 14). During 1951-91, India spent 3.8 per cent of its GDP on education, but achieved a 52 per cent literacy rate (1991), while in China Mao spent only 2.5 per cent of GDP but achieved 85 per cent literacy. Traditionally, educational funds were misspent in two ways in India. First, disproportionate amounts went to higher education, and secondly, mostly in the Hindi heartland (Uttar Pradesh and Bihar).

Based on their case study of Uttar Pradesh, (U.P.), Dreze and Gazdar (1996: 86) concluded that educational backwardness primarily reflects the *combined effects* of (i) the state's failure to provide adequate schooling facilities, and (ii) social norms and practices that have been detrimental to the widespread utilisation of available facilities. They (*Ibid.*, 87) have further added: "the system of governmental schools has been comprehensively corrupted. The failure of the schooling system in combination with persistent inequalities of class, and gender, has kept even the most elementary achievements out of reach of large sections of the population". The situation in Bihar is beyond imagination; the state is well known for its corruption, scandals, political manoeuvring, caste and class war, non-payment of salaries to employees, bribery, and so on, i.e. for a type of barbarian society where chaos is accepted as way of life—a *jungle raj*! The state of Bihar is distinctly different from the usual accounts hitherto on corruption, the criminalisation of politics, domination of the society by the Mafia, carnage, casteism, and insolent bureaucracy, etc. that the State conjures up in popular mind (cf. Biswas, 1996).

In two other ways one can see pitfalls in the education budget: first that it is not sufficient, and second that the categorical allotment is not structured. In some states, teachers' salaries swallow 99 per cent of the education budget, leaving nothing for aids or training. Aiyar (1999: 14) states that "Training was useless where no teaching materials were available, so teachers lack motivation. Rapacious politicians often diverted sums earmarked for education". He rightly suggests "In this milieu, doubling the education budget (as proposed by former Prime Minister Narasimha Rao) would simply have doubled the waste. The most urgent need was institutional reform to spend money more productively". The District Primary Education Programme (DPEP), a Central Government initiative in 1994 supported by foreign donors, has been successful and now spread to fourteen states. Under DPEP, the Central Government provides 85 per cent of the funding for extra educational efforts focussed on districts with the lowest literacy and gender disparities.

From Rethinking to Remaking

It seems certain that, as *Homo sapiens,* we should face the physical realities of the world, but also as human beings we should fulfil our psychological and spiritual needs. Only with a proper balance in the fight of the situation will we guarantee a happy and creative future for the ecological worldview. It is simple to be happy, but difficult to be simple! Above all, the country is in pursuit of a great social revolution—a revolution of mass consciousness to fight against corruption and the evils of society, to establish the symbols of honesty and working culture. In the recent past, we have lost the demarcation line of existence between right and wrong, moral and immoral, and also the realisation of the basic *dharma* (right action). This resulted in our acceptance of honesty as a psychic disease. The politicians and the bureaucrats are mainly responsible for creating this situation, but who will now remove it? A great social revolution with *svachetana* (Self-realisation) is suggested as the only strategy! However, again the basic problem is still unanswered. How is it to be implemented?

The core issues and conditions for an alternative, sustainable, development as identified by the World Commission on Environment and Development (1987) are population and development, food security, biodiversity and ecosystems, energy, industry, and the urban challenge. However, for direction and implementation, changes in thinking and motivation are a prerequisite. It is the people who *do* development, not the government, and therefore real development is ultimately a local activity and is generated by ethical issues. The neo-Marxist approach regards inequality as the major hindrance to development, and the latter is not possible within the existing world system. As in other developing countries, India's most crucial problem is a mass of absolute poverty, which is more dangerous than any other pollution! The present political and economic system is unable to solve the problems. Of course, no one can suggest a blueprint for eco-friendly development in the future; however, this does not mean that there is no prospect of a peaceful future.

Concerning the context of theoretical debate and perspective in India, postcolonialism is assumed to be a Eurocentric construct, post-traditionalism is too naive and postmodernism is yet more moral-idealist thought. At least some postmodern views of development convey a clear sense of moral duty or commitment (for a detailed critique and evaluation, see Simon, 1999). Being part of the Indian grassroots, I support the sentiments of Lehmann (1997: 577): "expert hegemony in which the poor of the world are turned into labouratory specimens, endlessly classified, catalogued and manipulated by a supremely arrogant and power-hungry professional community...who survey the globe from an air-conditioned panopticon." Above all, we have to cultivate the sense of self-realisation and the will to become directly involved to help the poor. Theory is the tool and practice is the result of inner quest; we need an integrated unity between them.

A system of moral education based on age-old ethics (religion, in the sense of moral duty) and the use of indigenous methods needs to be promoted. Alas, this requires the strengthening of grassroots democracy based on reconstituting society into more homogeneous units. Proposals for a 'multi-religious state' (like biodiversity) are not a new idea. At the time of independence, C. Rajgopalachari (1959: 83, cited in Smith, 1963: 151) proposed the idea in this way:

> And if India's government is to be an institution integrated with her people's lives, if it is to be a true democracy and not a superimposed Western institution staged in Indian dress, religion must have an important and recognised place in it, with impartiality and equal reverence for all the creeds and denominations prevailing in India.

Larson (1995: 294) advocates: "Perhaps this old idea from the time of independence, dismissed at the time as being naive and unworkable, should be given a renewed hearing as India approaches the half century mark of her independence." It is a sad point in intellectual history that "after Independence, when the Indian ruling class modelled itself on its departed counterpart, any emphasis on the 'flories of ancient India' came slowly to be viewed as an act of Hindu fundamentalism" (Chakrabarti, 1997: 2). Further, in the light of metaphysical grounding in Indian thought, Deutsch (1989: 265) suggests that:

> we might yet find a way to bring our scientific understanding of nature's organic complexity into an integral harmony with a spiritual understanding of reality's simplicity. The *Gita* (IV, 18) states laconically: "He who sees inaction in action and action in inaction, he is wise among men, he does all action harmoniously."

In fact,

> Morally we ought, as best we can, to allow the living world, and the entities thereof, in their diversity, to thrive in richness, harmony and balance. In all things we must ask whether our actions are conducive to, or at least compatible with, the fullness and well-being of life.
>
> (Johnson, 1991: 288)

Gadgil and Guha (1995: 124) propose an alternative development paradigm flowing out of 'conservative-liberal-socialism' and marching towards eco-friendly alternative development, which has the following elements:

1. Active public participation in democracy and bureaucracy at the various levels of power and transaction of resources.
2. The management of natural resources should substantially be devolved to the local population, taking into account the traditional (also indigenous) knowledge and sensitivity to sustainability in the frame of 'existence-maintenance-continuity'.
3. Decentralisation and mobilisation of resources and appropriate technology with the support of wider and more active public involvement.
4. Promotion of a more equitable society in its regional setting compatible with its natural and social/ historical background or 'heritage ecology' (cf. Singh, 1995).
5. Realise that the Indian experience, with its corrupt, inefficient and wasteful bureaucratic apparatus, is thoroughly discredited; the private and voluntary sectors (e.g. NGOs) are relatively much better and should be promoted in the service of society.
6. Economic enterprises should not be selected on the basis of appropriate scale, but rather on their validity, rationality and regional suitability.
7. The sense of tolerance and acceptability should be replaced by a deep sense of awareness and self-realisation (*svachetana*) in the context of reviving age-old ethics in the context of eco-justice, what Skolimowski (1990: 102) calls *reverential* development, where reverence, frugality and eco-justice form the minimal core of intrinsic values for right conservation and sustainable development.
8. Government policy should be integrated with the people's lives and ideologies, i.e. the morality, ethics and faith (*dharma*), and should not be a superimposed, Western institution staged in Indian dress, but have religious faith with impartiality and equal reverence for all that the early leaders like Rajagopalachari and Radhakrishnan had provoked during the 1950s.

It seems that by mobilising politicians and bureaucrats to adopt a more holistic view of the global ecosystem and by demanding the maintenance of deep human issues, many of the intricacies and obstacles can be addressed. The need for spiritually-oriented education should also be accepted as an alternative strategy drawing upon India's rich variety of indigenous spiritual and cultural heritages. Like the Gaian concept of 'the alive Earth', the realisation of the sense of deep connectedness is the concern of deep ecology. One of the most sacred ancient texts, dated c. 2000 BCE, the *Rig Veda* (X.18.11) mentions a funerary hymn honouring the mother Earth (cf. Singh, 1995: 192):

> Heave thyself, Earth
> nor press thee downward heavily:
> afford him easy access
> gently tending him.
> Earth, as mother wraps her skirt
> About her child, so cover him

Following the ecological notion that everything is interconnected, ecological awareness leads to the ethical question of finding an inner guide for right action, right thought and sustainability. Devereux (1996: 16) says that: "It is our fate, not the fate of the planet, that is in question. We have to save ourselves. We need stewardship for our species. Rather than thinking of healing the Earth, we should be looking to the Earth to heal us."

Remember also that modern education has alienated humankind from the cosmic integrity because most of it is imparted in closed buildings and labouratories (Asopa, 1994: 87). Carl Jung has acknowledged spirituality as an integral aspect of human nature and a vital force in human life (Capra, 1983: 406). Capra (*Ibid.*, xix) feels that spirituality in its ultimate nature will lead to profound changes in our social and political structures. He further adds that: "we find a profound state of world-wide crisis. ...It is a crisis of intellectual, moral, and spiritual dimensions; a crisis of a scale and urgency unprecedented in recorded human history" (*Ibid.*, 1).

Schroeder (1996: 305) believes that by broadening our worldview it is possible for us to take the spiritual values of nature seriously without abandoning our scientific heritage. Let us promote the attitude to humankind (say moral ethic) by balancing and reconciling the rational-scientific and the intuitive-spiritual viewpoints in ourselves and our society. Ethics is a technique of the soul and a seeking to understand a deeper nature of things, especially why we should behave in one particular way rather than another (Skolimowski, 1990: 97).

Does economic growth lead to development in India or other countries with a long tradition of particular value systems? Can this be called holistic or sustainable development? Certainly not! Development denotes progress and improvement in the quality of life and human peace. In a deep sense, this kind of development can be achieved only by a balanced integration at various levels in all spheres, including economic, social, cultural, scientific and technological, and moral and spiritual values. We need an integrated framework of sustainable development that combines contemporary ethical imperatives with traditional ethical codes; it should attempt to serve all people of all cultures, and promote the establishment of a place between humankind and nature (*Ibid.*, 103). The fact that it may be difficult to implement in practice in no way negates its importance and desirability (*Ibid.*, 102). Mass awakening, what Gandhi exemplified by his *satyagraha* movement, is 'the perfect example of how one could confront an unjust and uncaring, though extremely superior power' (Dwivedi, 1990: 211). In contemporary India, the Bishnois (a small community in Rajasthan, western India, who practise a religion of environmental conservation), Chipko (the movement to hug trees to keep them from being cut down for industrial uses, started in 1974 by Sundar Lal Bahuguna) and Appiko (the Chipko movement in Karnataka, south India, begun in 1983) people are engaged in a kind of 'forest *satyagraha*' today. Of course, it is a hard task for those from that society, but not impossible. The Hindu view of cyclic incarnation has immediate consequences for conservation, moral ethics and respect for harmonious life, because all lifeforms have essentially the same soul (*atman*) which passes in cyclic form from one life form to another, thus completing 8,400,000 species (Palmer, 1990: 53).

Following the analogy of the Buddhist 'middle path', India has to strike a balance between its deeply rooted value system to generate a cultural ethic in the service of national identity and to cope with the influx of postmodernist and postcolonial pressure, especially the techno-economic-ethical threat coming from the West. A synthesis between conservative 'moral imperative', liberal 'democratic capitalism' and 'socialist pattern of equity and empowerment' may be taken as an alternative development strategy. Moreover, regardless of the question of which path of development should in fact be followed, the government has to realise that in future the open-market economy and liberalisation would also have dangerous effects on the country's progress in respect of its resources, management and culture. A journalist has written provocatively:

> The neo-liberal policies, called 'structural adjustment', would not benefit the poor in the short or long run. The whole logic of adjustment is to transfer resources from non-tradable to tradable, unorganised to organised, poor to rich. This is how the 'free' market works—free to morality, equity, justice or concern for the poor.
>
> (Bidwai, 1997:12)

Let the Indian tradition of tolerating, assimilating and synthesising diverse strands flourish in making India a nation of brotherhood, peace and prosperity with equity.

> Since the roots of *ecological* trouble are so largely religious, the remedy must also be essentially religious, whether we call it that or not. We must rethink and refeel our nature and destiny.
>
> (White, 1967:1207)

Ethical value is the moral force in the sustainable existence, progress, maintenance and continuance of human beings. Gandhi's life and work do hold possible implications for postmodern approaches to the environment, mostly based on his principles of *ahimsa* and *aparigraha* (non-possession). He said:

> I must confess that I do not draw a sharp or any distinction between economics and ethics. Economics that hurt the moral well-being of an individual or a nation are immoral and, therefore, sinful.
>
> (Gandhi, 1959: 33-34)

His theory of *ahimsa* was not strict like a sectarian rule; he said: "whoever believes in *ahimsa will* engage himself in occupations that involve the least possible violence" (*Ibid.*, 35).

Without any political propaganda, Acharya Tulsi's Anuvrat Movement has been promoting the process of self-purification and self-control, in many ways akin to Gandhianism, since 1949. In support of this movement, Radhakrishnan (quoted in Chapple, 1993: 62) said:

> A civilised human being must be free from greed, vanity, passion, anger. Civilisations decline if there is a coarsening of moral fibre, if there is a callousness of heart. ... It requires strict adherence to the principles of good life.

For Raine (1997: 7, 11) India is not a country; it is a state of mind, which gives birth to beauty and embodies the spirit:

> the treasury of spiritual knowledge and practice is beyond doubt India's greatest resource. And it may be that our bankrupt materialism has brought us in the West to a point where we recognise our own need to relearn what our full humanity entails.
>
> (*Ibid.*, 11).

Let us hope for such breakthroughs in India's cultural development. The root of the Indian mindset is Hinduism, a mindset that possesses the inherent roots of tolerance, secularism, and adaptability in keeping with changing socio-economic conditions at global level. Says Bakker (1999: 10), "For the inhabitants of India it (*Hinduism*) is much more than that; the development of Hinduism does not take example by the bloody history that joins the three great Semitic religions". Gandhian thought of *ahimsa* has shown us the right path on which to proceed (cf. Singh, Rana, 1999a: 57). Think universally, see globally, but act locally. This is an appeal for cosmic vision, global humanism, and self-realisation (see Singh, 1999b for details). Should we call it 'human development'?

The spectres of global warming, lack of water through deforestation, and continued depletion of natural resources and diversity on Earth, are some of the results of 'unsustainable development' and economic growth. Should we not follow the path of Gandhi? He corrected himself over and over in his striving for moral-spiritual perfection while doing his best to reform existing institutions and social practices. He wrote in 1932, "I do not accept defeat but hope, with God's grace, to melt the stoniest heart and, therefore, continually strive to perfect myself" (*WMG*, vol. 50: 451).

We are slowly realising that reducing poverty or moving towards sustainable development is not just an economic or a technical problem, or of acquiring greater financial inputs—all these are important but achieving these goals also needs an inner awakening, an inner transformation of man—a path already paved by Gandhi. If we ignore Gandhi "we ignore him at our own peril" what once Martin Luther King said.

Acknowledgements

I personally express my gratitude to David Simon, who put forward so many constructive criticisms and also kindly thoroughly edited and polished the English. Our friend, (late) Anders Närman, too has been supportive in the development of this essay in several ways at different stages. This essay is a tribute to both of them.

NOTE:

1. The value of the *Indian Currency* was Rs. 7.11 to the US dollar in 1970 but declined to around Rs. 42.00 in mid-1998, [in early 2003 was Rs. 50, and in fell down to Rs. 45.50 in early 2006].

REFERENCES

Agrawal, Bina (ed.) 1998. *Structures of Patriarchy*. Kali for Women, Delhi.

Aiyar, Swaminathan S.A. 1999. "Institutional Change Spurs Literacy Breakthrough." *The Sunday Times of India* (New Delhi), 23 May: p. 14.

Asopa, S.K. 1994. "Environmental Ethics: a Hindu Perspective," in, Misra *et al.* (eds.) *op. cit.*: 69-89.

Bakker, Hans T. 1999. *The Hindu Religion and War.* 13pp. Institute of Indian Studies, University of Groningen. (a lecture).

Bidwai, P. 1997. "Rich Village, Poor Village. Neo-liberal Policies have Hurt Rural India and its Poor." *The Times of India: Sunday Times*, Delhi, 12 January: 12.

Biswas, A.K. 1996. *Understanding Bihar.* Blumoon Books, New Delhi.

Bose, A.N. 1997. "India in the 50th Year of Independence: Economic Situation. What happened?" What would be? *Samayika Varta* a Hindi quarterly. 21 July-September: 20-59.

Capra, Fritjof. 1983. *The Turning Point.* Flamingo, London.

Chakrabarti, Dilip K. 1997. *Colonial Indology. Socio-politics of the Ancient Indian Past.* Munshiram Manoharlal Publishers, Delhi.

Chapple, C.K. 1993. *Non-Violence to Animals, Earth, and Self in Asian Traditions.* SUNY Press, Albany, NY.

Deutsch, E. 1989. "A Metaphysical Grounding for Natural Reverence: East-West," in, Callicott, J.B. and Ames, R.T. (eds.). *Nature in Asian Traditions of Thought.* SUNY Press, Albany, NY: 259-265.

Devereux, Paul 1996. *Re-Visioning the Earth. A Fireside Book.* Simon & Schuster, New York.

Dreze, Jean and Hazdar, Haris. 1996. "Uttar Pradesh: the Burden of Inertia," in, Sen and Dreze, (ed.) *Indian Development, op. cit.*: 33-128.

Dwivedi, O.P. 1990. "Satyagraha for Conservation: Awakening the Spirit of Hinduism," in, Engel and Engel (eds.) *op. cit.*: 201-212.

Ehrlichs, Paul and Enne. 1974. *The End of Affluence. A Bluprint for your Future.* Ballantine Books, New York.

Elliott, J.A. 1994. *An Introduction to Sustainable Development.* Routledge, London.

Engel, J.R. and Engel, J.G. (eds.). 1990. *Ethics of Environment and Development.* University of Arizona Press, Tucson.

Farmer, B.H. 1993. *An Introduction to South Asia.* 2nd (edn.). Routledge, London.

Gadgil, M. and Guha, R. 1995. *Ecology and Equity: The Use and Abuse of Nature in Contemporary India.* Routledge, London.

Gandhi, M.K. 1959. *My Socialism.* Navajivan Publishing House, Ahmedabad.

Gandhi, M.K. *The Collected Works of Mahatma Gandhi*, 100 vols. (Publication Division, Ministry of Information and Broadcasting, Govt. of India, New Delhi: 1958-1994).

Johnson, L.E. 1991. *A Morally Deep World.* Cambridge University Press, Cambridge.

Joshi, Jagadish. 1999. "The Basic Mystery of Democracy." *Aj* (a Hindi daily from Varanasi), 20 May: p. 6.

Kothari, Rajni. 1987. *Politics and the People.* vol. II. Ajanta Publications, Delhi.

Kothari, Rajni. 1990. "Environment, Technology and Ethics," in, Engel and Engel (eds.) *op. cit.*: 27-35.

Larson, Gerald J. 1995. *India's Agony Over Religion.* SUNY Press, Albany, NY.

Lehmann, D. 1997. "An Opportunity Lost: Escobar's Deconstruction of Development." *Journal of Development Studies,* 33 4.: 568-578.

Lovelock, James 1995. *The Ages of Gaia.* W.W. Norton, New York.

Mesarovic, Mihajlo and Pestel, Eduard. 1974. *Mankind at the Turning Point.* New American Library, New York.

Misra, R.P. *et al.,* (eds.) 1994. *Environment, Development and Education.* Heritage Publishers, New Delhi.

Naess, A. 1989. *Ecology, Community and Lifestyle. Outline of Ecosophy.* Cambridge University Press, Cambridge.

Nehru, J.L. 1960. *The Discovery of India.* Oxford University Press, Delhi. Reprinted.

Orwell, G. 1945. *Animal Farm.* Secker & Warburg, London.

Paden, W.L. 1992. *Interpreting the Sacred.* Beacon Press, Boston, Mass.

Palmer, M. 1990. "The Encounter of Religion and Conservation," in, Engel and Engel (eds.) op. *cit.*: 50-62.

Radhakrishnan, S. 1956. "Introduction," in, S. Abid Hussain, (ed.) *The National Culture of India.* Jaico, Bombay: vii-viii.

Raine, K. 1997. All roads lead to India, *Resurgence* 183 July/August., 711.

Rajgopalachari, C. 1959. "The Place of Religion in Future India," in, *Message of India.* Government of India, New Delhi, vol. 1: 83; cited in Smith 1963:151.

Reed, D. (ed.) 1992. *Structural Adjustment and the Environment.* Earthscan, London.

Schroeder, H.W. 1996. "Spirit of the Forest," in, Swan and Swan (eds.) *op. cit.*: 294-306.

Segal, Ronald. 1965. *The Crisis of India.* Penguin, Harmondsworth. Reprinted in India: Jaico, Bombay, 1968.

Sen, Amartya. 1996. "Radical Needs and Modern Reforms," in, Sen and Dreze, (eds.) *Indian Development, op. cit.*: 1-32.

Sen, Amartya and Dreze, Jean, (eds.) 1996. *Indian Development: Selected Regional Perspectives,* Oxford University Press, Delhi.

Simon, David. 1999. "Development Revisited," in, *Development as Theory and Practice,* David Simon & Anders Närman (eds.) *op. cit.*: pp. 17-54.

Simon, David and Närman, Anders, (eds.) 1999. *Development as Theory and Practice.* Longman, London.

Singh, Jasbir. 1999. "Poverty of Common Masses in India: Reasons and Solutions." *Samayika Varta* (a weekly from Delhi), 22 (no. 5, February): 9-14.

Singh, Khuswant. 1990. "Brahmin Power," *Sunday* (23-29 December): 19.

Singh, Ramji. 1999a. "Global Crisis and the Philosophy of Sarvodaya." *Aj* (a Hindi daily from Varanasi), 1 April: p. 6.

Singh, Ramji. 1999b. "Seven Social Sins." *Aj* (a Hindi daily from Varanasi), 15 April: p. 6.

Singh, Rana P.B. 1995. "Heritage Ecology and Caring for the Earth," *National Geographical Journal of India* 41 (2): 191-218.

Singh, Rana P.B. 1996. "The Ganga River and the Spirit of Sustainability in Hinduism," in, Swan and Swan (eds.) *op. cit.*: 86-197.

Singh, Rana P.B. 1999a. "Rethinking Development in India: Perspective, Crisis and Prospects," in, David Simon & Anders Närman (eds.) *Development as Theory and Practice, op. cit.*: pp. 55-75.

Singh, Rana P.B. 1999b. "Ethical Values and Spirit of Sustainability in Indian thought," in, F.J. Coasta, *et al.* (eds.) *Geographic Inquiry at the Beginning of New Millennium.* Westview Press, Boulder, Colo.

Singh, Rana P.B. 2000. "Development Crisis in India: From Scenario to Rethinking," *Annals of the National Association of Geographers, India* (New Delhi), 20 (1): 69-86.

Singh, Rana P.B. 2006. "Mohandas (Mahatma) Gandhi (1869-1948);" in, David Simon, (ed.) *Fifty Key Thinkers on Development.* Routledge Key Guides Series. Routledge, Taylor & Francis Group, London and New York: pp. 106-111.

Singh, Rana P.B. and Singh, R.B. 1981. *Changing Frontiers of Indian Village Ecology.* National Geographical Society of India, Varanasi, Research Publication No. 27.

Singh, Rana P.B. and Singh, Ravi S. 2002. "Development Crisis in India: Scenario and Ideology," in, *Towards a New Regional and Local Development Research Agenda,* (eds.) Anders Närman and Kamal Karunanayake; Dept. of Geography, Göteborg University (Sweden), Series B, No. 100, and CDS, University of Kelaniya, Sri Lanka No. 1: pp. 65-78.

Singh, Ravi S and Singh, Rana P.B. 2004. "Development Crisis in India: From Scenario to Re-thinking." *South Asian Affairs* (ISSN: 1349-8851), Vol. 1, No. 1, 2004: pp. 12-30.

Skolimowski, H. 1990. "Reverence for Life," in, Engel and Engel (eds.) *op. cit.:* 97-107.

Smith, D.E. 1963. *India as a Secular State*. Princeton University Press, Princeton, NJ.

Swan, Jim and Swan, Roberta, (eds.) 1996. *Dialogues with the Living Earth*. Quest Books, Wheaton, IL.

Tinbergen, Jan. 1976. (Coordinator). *RIO. Reshaping the International Order*. New American Library, New York.

Watts, A.W. 1962. *The Joyous Cosmology*. Random House, New York.

White, Jr. Lyne 1967. "The Historical Roots of our Ecological Crises." *Science* 155, 10 March: 1203-1207.

World Commission on Environment and Development 1987. *Our Common Future*. Oxford University Press, New York.

The World Bank 1999. *World Development Report. Knowledge for Development*. New York: Oxford University Press for the World Bank.

8

Need for E-governance and E-government to Sustain the Development in India

DILIP ROY

EXECUTIVE SUMMARY

The process of economic development in India has gone through multiple phases, viz. the phase of initiation, the phase of control, the phase of slow decontrol and the phase of flexibility and reform. The current phase of reform works on four principles identified as liberalization, privatization, globalization and stabilization. The outcomes are of mixed type. Basic intention was to uplift the standard of living, provide best inputs, best technology and adequate capital to firms to meet the external challenges from competitors. Though the industrial growth rate has become 8% on an average with overall growth rate reaching the new height of 5% and foreign investment is also increasing in line, yet the fiscal deficit is showing an irregular behavior. The overall performance studied in terms of Human Development Index (HDI) is also not satisfactory. As per the HDI, 2005, India has a rank of 127 amongst 177 countries of the world.

To ensure an all-out progress, political, institutional and cultural issues should be taken into development thinking and informational reforms, technological reforms and operational reforms are needed for strengthening India's attempt towards global leadership. In this context role of governance becomes very important. It is the crisis of governance that can be identified as the primary cause of underdevelopment and poverty. So, superior governance should be the key objective of all development plans. And one should consider dual plans of development by tracing upon development economics and development administration. Development economics addresses issues like capacity building, efficient resource utilization, and development administration calls for legal adherence, accountability and transparency.

Quicker the use of modern technologies, better will be the country's economic and administrative developments. In fact, the adoption of modern governance technologies can act as a catalyst to reform work. A mere shift in policy can hardly give rise to economic benefits.

To change the slow and timid administrative structure electronic media can be of much use. Continuous role-play by the people of our democratic nation may become a reality now, provided careful attempts are made in this direction. Here comes the concept and need of E-governance that aims at direct participation of the true representatives of the government in the administrative and economic activities of the government.

An in-between-stage of this process of transformation to E-governance is E-government. It provides government services and disseminates information through electronic media. Being a transient state, the scope of E-government is constrained in nature in comparison to the same of E-governance but the resource requirement will be less.

Installation of E-government may be classified according to four types. *Innovative Leader* is the one, which provides more than half of the facilities required to run a fully matured on-line government. *Visionary follower* offer large number of on-line services but the degree of sophistication is moderate. *Steady achiever* provides large number of on-line services but their level of service and mode of delivery are not full-grown. *Platform Builders* are basically initiators and thinkers and not active developers.

Government - to - Citizen (G2C), Government - to - Business (G2B), Government-to-Employee (G2E) and Government-to-Government (G2G) are different types of E-government that one may like to install. Installation should not be an impulsive one. It should be innovative in nature where experts from different disciplines may work together to decide about the changes. Zero level model, critical flow model, comparative analysis model, interactive service model and evolutionary model can be of use for administrative reforms.

Government of India has an integrated plan to employ a system of E-government and E-governance. Ministry of Information Technology has taken initiative and providing a common agenda to other ministries. Progress is reasonable with central government offices, state governments and district offices taking active role. Activities like election, treasury, land and land records, land acquisition, motor vehicles have been placed under e-network. But more reforms are to be undertaken to support the economic development

Introduction to Developmental Phases

The process of economic development in India changed its track over years leading to different phases of economic development. The first phase of economic development is the phase of initiation that started from the beginning of the first five-year plan and came to an end in the mid sixties. It was marked with resource-based approach that admitted inability of the government to operate in every field of economic activity and decided to play positive roles where state's participation was most needed. Basically, the approach was to identify the market failures and absence of markets and to use public sector to fill up the gaps in the economy. During the first phase, the average rate of growth of Gross Domestic Product at factor cost was recorded as 4.2% per year.

The second phase started from the middle of the sixties and continued up to the end of seventies. It was aimed at handling the negative impacts of food crisis due to drought in

1966, global oil crisis in 1971, etc. The basic approach was to suppress market responses and control the economy through government's intervention and state's participation in a highly rigid manner. *The Monopolies and Restrictive Practices Act* and the *Foreign Exchange Regulation Act*, to mention a few, were brought in force to keep control over the private sector, and licensing and controls were made instrumental for shaping the path of agricultural exports, industrial investment and imports. There was nationalization of banking and insurance sectors. The public sector activities were extended to enter into the field of consumer goods. The importance of agriculture was re-recognized and the introduction of the "Green Revolution" programme took place to become self-sufficient. Though the government was able to successfully manage the drought problem and the macro-economic imbalances created by the oil shock, yet this second phase experienced a slow rate of growth with an average rate of growth as 3.5% per year. The economic studies have revealed that the productivity of capital, measured in terms of average ICOR of the economy, dropped to 2.6 against 4.7 of the earlier phase. Thus, the decline in productivity of capital was about 45%.

The third phase of development began around 1979-80 and continued up to 1990-91. This phase was marked by slow de-control of the economy in recognition of the government and public sector failures and case-by-case withdrawal of industrial control of earlier phase. For example, the cement and aluminium industries were de-licensed, the scopes for expansion were re-ensured for large industrial groups, imports of capital goods were made procedurally easier. In view of these re-orientations, the average rate of growth of GDP increased to 4.9% per year during 1979-80 to 1990-91.

The current phase of economic development is the phase of liberalization, privatization, globalization and stabilization. It is a phase of flexibility and reform, a deviation from normative approach. Balance of Payments crises of early and mid 1991, along with an increase in the fiscal deficit, that made the macro-economic condition a prey of external shocks, suddenly led to this new economic policy. This reform phase has aimed at improved efficiency and high quality of production. It also admits that firms must be provided with best inputs, best technology and adequate capital to meet the external challenge from competitors. As a result, the industrial growth rate has become 8% on an average with overall growth rate reaching the new height of 5%. Foreign investment is also ascending at a remarkable space. Fiscal deficit, however, is showing an out of control state and needs close monitoring. The performance measured in terms of Human Development Index (HDI) is also not satisfactory. As per the HDI, 2005, India has a rank of 127 amongst 177 countries studied therein.

In order to make the success story free of blemishes and sustainable over a long period, one has to go beyond the economic reforms. The development should be aimed at in integral way by taking into consideration political, institutional and cultural issues into development thinking (see Stiglitz, 1998). Simultaneously, informational reforms, technological reforms and operational reforms are needed for strengthening India's march towards global leadership.

An Invitation to Economic Governance

Questions raised on suitability of conventional economic thinking have drawn the attention of the planners to the role of governance. Crisis of governance has been identified by many as the primary cause of underdevelopment and poverty. They consider superior governance as the key objective of all development plans. In this process two new concerns have assumed priority of the day. These are known as development economics and development administration. Development administration calls for a replacement of bureaucratic administration to increase the scope of work and reach the end state with ease and efficiency. Under its meritocratic fold, there will be no political pressure on economic policies, no corruption in public dealings, no intention of unwanted interference. It has been observed that developed states provide good governance and good governance is a catalyst that transforms grasping states into developed states. Thus, development and governance are the two sides of the same coin. And very rightly,

World Bank defines governance as "the manner in which power is exercised in the management of a country's economic and social resources for development". Management of economic resources addresses issues like capacity building, efficient resource utilization, and management of social resources calls for legal adherence, accountability and transparency. However, structure of operation may vary. Person and Tabellini (2000) are of the opinion that governance structure varies from one state to another as it depends on the ability to support the execution of a given transaction.

UNDP has been working on a two-stream agenda for governance. One stream emphasizes on participation of citizens in the decision-making process to uphold human rights and ensure democratic philosophy, while the other deals with outcomes in terms of policies, capacities and institutional arrangements to upgrade the socio-economic condition in the country without making large-scale expenditure by the government. In both the streams, the nature of inflow and outflow matters a lot. Therefore, let us have a preview of the prevailing information technology before addressing the desired structure of governance. Economic development goes hand in hand with technological development development is a precondition for economic and social upliftment.

Accelerating Role of Technological Factor

In strategic analysis and planning one may observe that for macro-environmental analysis technology is having an important role (see Jauch and Glueck, 1988, Hills and Jones, 1992) having significant impacts on business units, government and other non-government organizations. It is an integrated and organized knowledge, which is systematically used for achieving operational efficiency. In fact, technology is the major determinant of the business advantages of a country. It has contributed, in the past, to the remarkable growth in business in the developed countries and has provided them with distinctive competence and competitive advantages needed for making any strategic move (David, 1989). Business units of developed countries have tactfully induced changes from the stages of invention and innovation to the stage of diffusion. As a result, over the last decade economies of those countries have flourished at the cost of poorer nations. They have been able to achieve a very high productivity, which is an important measure of operational efficiency in production. In the context of globalization and global competition, one cannot afford to lag behind in terms of productivity. So, it is important for us to be aware of and avail the benefits of technological changes to keep pace with the rapid growth in productivity and discrete changes in product life cycle curves of the present era.

In the management parlance, we often refer the mother earth as a global village. Different locations are easily accessible. Different cultures are getting intermingled. Different activities have become subsystems of an overall system. If we examine carefully, we are bound to realize that it is the advancement in information technology that has redefined the globe as a small village. In the past, distance between two countries was a major factor for determining the degree of close cooperation and trade. But now the distance constraint does no longer exist even for a common man of any technologically advanced country. Globalization is a logical end state of this situation. Some countries have established close links among themselves adding to their ability to compete more effectively in the global market than others who prefer to shy away from oneness.

For a developing country like ours there are both positive and negative aspects of globalization. But whenever there is fire there is smoke. Fire provides the opportunity. Smoke brings forth the threat. Our objective should be to avail the opportunities without any further delay and neutralize the threats by following an accommodative posture through long drawn strategic planning exercise. In view of the delayed start in the process of our administrative development proactive posture is out of our reach now. Defensive or reactive responses (Carroll, 1978) will fan the flames of threats by complicating the environment further and weakening the internal capabilities. Delayed reaction may even convert an opportunity into a threat seeking significantly higher level of investment for embracing corrective measures. We may therefore conclude that quicker is the espousal of modern technologies, better will be the country's economic development and administrative status in the globe. It is through adoption of modern governance technologies, that globalization can be favourably nurtured; a mere change in policy framework cannot alone lead to reaping of the economic benefits. If due to timid administrative structure globalization fails to usher the rosy way, one cannot wrongly jump to a conclusion that liberalization be pushed back and global opportunities be ignored.

E-government and E-governance

The political philosophy of India is democracy that upholds freedom of speech. This freedom in its best spirit must welcome the participation principle and not a mere free exercise of electoral right. Since the people elect the government in our country we may consider the same as a formal representative of the people. It should not work with a tunnelled vision of a political group but widen its fold to embrace all and work for the development of the people through economic, socio political and cultural progress. In view of the principle of participation, people must play a major role in running the government and not wait for the next election to express themselves. While elections are periodic, people's role-play is not. It should be continuous and positive. This continuous role-play is no longer a hypothetical concept. A few decades back this concept was unimplementable. But the emergence of electronic media for communication can make implementation possible. So, continuous role-play has every scope to become a reality now, provided careful attempts are made in this direction. There comes the concept and need of E-governance that aims at direct participation of the true representatives of the government in the administrative and economic activities of the government.

E-governance is not restricted to participation in activities like policy-making and planning only. It also encompasses the concept of citizen-to-citizen communication. This E-governance concept is the ideal form of a meritocratic configuration where administration imbeds and appreciates competence in the structural set up and encourages transparency, accountability, responsibility and competitive mutualism. However, in view of the present limited participation, switching over from the same to a fully developed E-governance system is not a walk in the park. This entire process of transformation needs meticulously drawn planning, supported by adequate mobilization and continuous development of human and other resources and a cultural change.

An in-between-stage of this process of transformation is known as the E-government form of administration. It is aimed at providing government services and disseminating information through electronic media. Being a transient state, the scope of E-government is constrained in nature in comparison to the that of E-governance. But compared to the existing system of governance, E-government is one step higher. For a developing country like ours, it is easier to switch over to E-government form of administration than to a completely grown up E-governance form. This is so because the government has multiple roles to play along multiple dimensions but has limited resources.

Switching over to E-government may also be conceived as a multistage task and can be introduced in a phased manner. Identification of domains of change and assignment of priorities along the different dimensions of administrative development assume importance due to resource constraints. Government is a creator of new economic activities. It is the protector of existing domestic firms. It is the developer of business units and markets and is a bulk consumer of finished goods. It is the maker of economic plans to indicate the direction of economic, social, political and cultural movement. Also, the legal structure for operation of business houses is being framed by the government. Another emerging role of a government is to provide information to cater to the economic and transactional needs of the people. Being a representative of the people it must be fully accountable to them for all its offers. These offers should be made in an efficient, effective and timely manner so that cost is minimum but facilities are maximum and response is immediate. Conceptually, E-government, in self-service mode can make it possible to offer uninterrupted services, services for twenty-four hours a day, seven days a week, and fifty-two weeks a year. A common form of man and paper-based government can hardly handle time and space problems and offer service at this level.

In this context, one may refer to a few cases from countries where E-government is in full swing. In U.S.A., the Federal Revenue Agency has observed the benefits of electronic submission of tax returns. In-depth study has revealed that those who file tax returns by electronic media are happier than those who submit through print media. Because of the electronic processing, which is fast and accurate, on-line submission can result in refund of excess payments in nearly three weeks. Nearly double of that time is required for the same processing under paper submission. And the most important aspect is all these benefits accrue out of no additional charge. It has further been estimated that the cost of on-line processing is very less, almost one-fourth of the cost of paper processing. Keeping in mind the cost break up, we may remark that the cost of delivery of services for all types of governments eats away a significant proportion of the state exchequer. So, a reduction in processing cost by three-fourths will have long lasting positive effects on the overall financial strength of the state. Funding of developmental projects will be easier and flexibility in operation will be more due to those cost savings. Renewal of vehicle registration by on-line mode has also been found more effective and less costly. Cost saving is nearly three-fourth as realized from USA experience.

There is no surprise that these findings are not country-specific. Experience of Singapore government is also in consistency with time saving and cost-saving experiences. Previously, it was a tough task to get an import or export license in Singapore. Formalities were many. An applicant had to fill up twenty-one forms for obtaining such a license. So many forms were meant for generation of data at different related offices and keeping cross-informational records. Processing time was obviously on the higher side, not less than three weeks. Electronic processing of on-line submitted form needs only one submission and the processing time has unbelievably come down to fifteen seconds. This is because all the government offices have been made interconnected. Even the updating work has become extremely simplified. Under the electronic information dissemination scheme as soon as the user changes a data item by typing it on his/her desk that information reaches postal department, policy department, trade department, etc. within a fraction of a second. And if Singapore government can ensure such a speed of service with a less cost, there is no reason why others can't repeat the same feat.

A Call for Attitudinal Change

Gone are the days when people used to refer to government in terms of laws and regulations; in terms of instructions and orders and at the most in terms of types of services. Under the changed scenario, people, throughout the global village want to talk not in terms of systems, structures and services only, but in terms of their best performances also. In this era of competition with barriers getting dismantled like a house of cards, nowhere people are satisfied with a mere service. They are conscious about the global value to price benchmarks. They are demanding for the best return from their investments and even more. An optimum service in a transparent and accountable manner is the claim of the day.

The type of E-government varies according to type of responsibility, levels of response and postures and different issues of immediate interest. According to Jupp (2001) there are four classes into which E-governments can be clustered. He classified twenty-two countries into these four classes. According to Jupp, *Innovative Leaders* are those countries that have provided at least half of the facilities required to run a fully matured on-line government. They have portals along the length and breadth of the country. A citizen can have single point touch with the government for services and deliveries. In management terms we may refer them as proactive in nature and positive in selection of issues. E-government in United States is a befitting example of innovative leader.

Visionary followers offer large number of on-line services but the degree of sophistication is moderate and not the ideal.

They are positive in the selection of issues to be addressed under electronic access. But they are still planners in installation of facilities. E-government prevailing in United Kingdom may be considered as an example of visionary follower.

Steady achievers also provide large number of on-line services but their level of service and mode of delivery are not full-grown. Scopes for maturity are definite. It is the positive zeal that may help them to go for further improvement in future. Negative orientation may block the progress of administrative evolution. A good example of a steady achiever is E-government of France.

Platform builders provide limited number of on-line services. They are basically initiators and thinkers and not active developers. A good example of a platform builder is E-government of Japan.

There can be many other ways of classifying the E-government system. One such classification system is a classification that borrows ideas from the E-commerce concept. Depending on the nature of the delivery system one can install different classes of participation such as Government-to-Citizen (G2C), Government-to-Business (G2B), Government-to-Employee (G2E) and Government-to-Government (G2G) classes. To improve the G2C activities one has to identify the issues of importance by observing the needs of citizens over time. Processing bottlenecks, wastage of time and energy and limitations of the scope, if carefully studied, can pinpoint weaknesses of the structure and system and give shape towards better governance through greater interaction. G2C that allows downloading of forms, on-line submission of information, forwarding of electronic receipts and the convenience of continuous access can upgrade the level of development along with the benefits of time and cost reduction. In India most of the government offices are having decentralized structure. Regional offices enjoy the power of making end-decisions. For example, Regional Passport Office can issue and renew passports, regional income tax offices can deal with tax returns, refunds and discrepancies. But this structural flexibility is of no use in view of the outdated concept of file keeping, maintenance of hard copy and slow processing system. Style and skill of staff and the processing modalities in different government offices need to be rationalized to appreciate the interconnections among super-ordinate goal, structure, system, style, skill, staff and strategy as described in 7-S McKinsey model. And solution lies with E-government of G2C type.

This interconnection is more relevant for G2B form of administration, and an appreciation of it can vastly improve business-government interaction. It is this interaction that can make the opening up of the economy more functional. We have already stated that government is the protector, developer, planner and end user of many business activities. So, executive machineries are having different roles to play; a positive role and an intimate role. The New Economic Policy (NEP) of the government of India made a deliberate attempt to induce freshness in the market place, appreciate competition-led quality improvement, generate innovative ideas and reduce hurdles on the way. But procedural bureaucracy is still remaining a stumbling block. It is negatively affecting the purpose of liberalization, which aims at providing freedom in the choice of industry and generation of profit. The requirement of licensing has been nearly withdrawn. Automatic approval of a cent per cent exporting unit has been ensured. But all these policies carry meaning only when bottlenecks are removed during business operation. Privatization policy may reap results only when business receives a cordial help not only at the time of entry but also during the day-to-day operation. Globalization via acceptance of membership in the World Trade Organization (WTO) has opened global market for Indian products. But this measure along with other measures like lowering of custom duties, smoothening the way for direct foreign investment are not good enough to ensure attractiveness in the Indian business scenario. To make the Indian economy business friendly installation of a G2B system is a must. Otherwise opening up of the economy may lead to chaos without enjoying the benefits in time and in volume. The most applauding action taken so far by the government of India is the introduction of electronic fund transfers. But many more actions need to be taken to develop an environment of economic opportunity and operational efficiency.

Directing, interacting, developing and sharing of information with the employees are parts of human resource management. Human resource is the human capital that an organization makes use of. It is made of intellectual capital, social capital, emotional capital and spiritual capital. Without a defined structure for close and quick interaction with the employees, no government can accomplish governance of high standard. So, for the government employees, G2E is the emerging concept of importance. As an example, let us consider an employee in the front office who needs to handle queries. He must be very informative. To remain aware of the situation he may find it easier to handle queries if he has electronic connection with the back office. Especially for distant employees, G2E removes the feeling of becoming isolated and neglected by providing with the electronic company of the members of the head office. Even distant training and conference may take place to boost the morale of employees. As attention increases performance increases too, as revealed from the Hawthorne experiment. Thus, G2E is a must for fool-proof administrative development. It is the employer-employee relationship, which is at the heart of an organization. If relationship is good, optimum efficiency cannot remain out of reach. If relationship is not good, even a set of efficient hands may put up a non-performing show in the organization. Thus, G2E, has become a cry of the day for our country.

G2G is an orientation towards electronic communication and electronic dealings with governments within and outside the national boundaries. State and central governments can work together without sitting together and resolve the controversial issues in an affable environment. The present era demands for quick and close dialogue; demands for cooperation and clear understanding about each other. Especially when resource constraints are active, it is necessary to work together for moving forward. In this current era, time and information have been earmarked as the two most crucial resources.

Government, being at the top of the policy-making level, cannot afford to ignore the worth of these two resources. Within the fold of G2G we would like to have fast electronic interaction between Government departments too. To ensure efficiency at the apex level one has to induce efficiency at the lower and grass roots levels. There must be improved workflow between government departments and it is the modern information technology that has great potentiality for improving workflow among departments located in far off places.

Further, dual systems like C2G, B2G and E2G can increase reciprocity in the electronic-governance and strengthen the system and its structure.

Some Additional Remarks

We have so far stressed upon the benefits of E-governance and E-government. But there are cases where benefits turn out as costs due to impulsive installation of E-government and E-governance. Recognition of multifaceted activities is needed. But consideration of multiple faces may complicate the nature of the E-government. Also, it will be difficult to define the interacting environment. Sufficient time should be allocated to developers and planners to carry out systematic, adequate and in-depth analysis to frame the parameters of environmental requirements and to undertake careful diagnosis to ascertain the significance of changes in those parameters. This does not mean that we prefer to have a time-consuming long-drawn pre-work during this process of designing E-government and E-governance systems. We basically like to suggest that innovative behavior should rule over impulsive behavior to understand the minimum requirement of analysis and diagnosis.

What mostly has been installed in many governmental systems is stagnant bureaucracy. As a result, system is crowded with risk aversive planners who do not lend ear to listen to environmental changes. Limited interaction and static reaction with the environment may lead to a separation of the government from its environment. In order to achieve the developmental objectives, a public system has to be adaptive in nature, should carry out in-depth study on internal and external entities, make use of modern computing, storing and disseminating facilities, and prefer creative ideas for forward march without chaos and loss of energy.

If needed, experts from different disciplines may be grouped together to assess and react to environmental changes. Also, the main thrust of operation should be decentralization to handle the environmental dynamicity, if any. If the environment is not very dynamic, a centralized system may work. If adequate measures for transparency, accountability and justice are not taken at the appropriate time, flow of global investment cannot be smooth. Without sufficient inflow of capital, development process will retardate leading to a more weak and vulnerable economy. With a weak information and economic base government has to swim upstream in vain. Late awareness about the global changes may eat away the capabilities, needed to avail the future opportunities and neutralize the threats, due to an unmanageable scarcity of technology, infrastructure and zeal.

About Some Models for E-government/E-governance

Anandkumar and Jeyakumar (2002) have indicated a few models that have been proposed in the recent past. It is quite likely that many more are going to be reported in near future. These models differ in their scope, coverage and extent of sophistication. The basic model is the zero-level model. It is also known as the Broadcasting model or Dissemination model. The underlying objective of this model is to ensure that governmental procedures, rules and regulations be available within an extended domain. To widen the domain, domain experts mostly use ICT and convergent media. A broadcasting model ensures online information on laws and regulations, post with names and addresses of local, regional and national contact persons.

Critical-flow model is the next level model. It makes a selective dissemination by scanning the use value of each and every information, identifying the users who critically need the information and then disseminating that critical information to those identified users. The basic idea behind selective dissemination is to lessen the information burden of the users and trim down their scanning time, reduce the work of the disseminating system. However, incurring higher cost in the beginning for designing a complicated processing system can ensure all these benefits. For example, research results in different fields may not be of immediate use for all researchers. In that case, only those who are directly interested in a specific topic may be provided with information on the academic advancements in that area. Users may be classified according to degree of interest. Some users may be interested in summary type information, others may be interested in detailed study. Similar will be the case for study reports, enquiry reports and white papers.

A few other types of models are also available. One such model is E-advocacy model. It is also referred as Lobbying model because the basic objective herein is to form virtual buddies to work in favour of a group of individuals forming a major societal segment or the entire society. Formation of such buddies comes into existence only when there exists a common platform that shares some specific values and concepts. These buddies may play a positive and leading role in e-governance by drawing the attention of the government to the limitations and ill-effects of governmental policies on the society or societal segments. They can mount pressure on the policy makers and compel the executive wings to recognize their views while planning and implementing developmental programmes. Virtual bodies are in fact in operation to protect human rights and cry foul in case of gender discrimination and atrocities to women.

The Comparative analysis model aims at providing specialized knowledge to users for developing a high knowledge based society. To do so it makes use of available information, integrates different isolated data, dresses and analyzes them to derive specific conclusions. The knowledge that it provides shows the path for accomplishment of developmental goals and related targets. For example, Human Development Report (HDR) of UNDP is an upshot of a comparative analysis model. In the HDR, the nature and extent of country-wise development are described in terms of Human Development Index (HDI).

Policy recommendations are also being made in terms of HDI. This index number is calculated based on country-wise statistical data. Based on Life expectancy, Adult literacy, Combined enrolment ratio and Per capita real GDP($) (PPP) four key indices are calculated taking into consideration minima and maxima values, wherever the minima and maxima are meaningful and available. Once the deprivation indices are calculated to measure the relative deviation from the desirable states then these indices are combined with equal weightage to arrive at the overall index number of human development by subtracting the average of the deprivation indices from one.

Interactive service model is another important variant of the E-governance models. It is basically a two-way interaction; a combination of G2C and C2G models. The objective behind the two-way flow is to allow participation of people in the governance process by informing them about the future policy-plans and seeking their reactions. In this sense it can alternatively be referred as a G2C2G model. Issues that may initially be covered are matters related to revenue collection, payment, submission of returns, procurements, etc. In its ideal form there should be interaction among the citizens too. Thus the model can reach the pinnacle if it is of the type G2C-C2C-C2G. Attempts have been initiated in some districts of our country to develop a system that is close in spirit to G2C2G. The Gyandoot intranet service provided in Dhar district is an example of such an Interactive service model.

Another important model is the Evolutionary model, which blooms into a complete system through multiple stages of advancement. This Kaizen concept of system mostly starts from an ordinary information dissemination approach and ends up with a fully-blown participative/interactive system. Here participation means involvement of people for issue-based policy-making work. An evolutionary model in this sense is non-static, time dependent and ever growing. This continuously improving flexible and dynamic model redefines its role in a slow but steady fashion starting from broadcasting, moving to transactional, widening from one-way transactional to two-way transactional and so on.

Present State of Governance in India

The Government of India in our country has come out with an integrated plan to employ a system of E-government and E-governance. Initiative has been taken in this direction by the Ministry of Information Technology (MIT). If this initiative takes a full shape, India can become a leading country in joining the global march for E-government and E-governance (see www.mit.gov.in/eg/agenda.htm). It has also invited from each ministry its IT-plan with a vision of arriving at a comprehensive course of action with a planning horizon of five years. The philosophy of planning for MIT is a bottom up philosophy that allows for trickling of concepts upward against the usual planning concept of trickling down. However, for an initial coordination of work MIT has also provided with an overall structure in the form of a common agenda of work. Each department under each ministry has been asked to install its local area network to connect all the officers down up to the level of a section officer and provide them with access to requisite software. It has also stressed upon the urgent need for organizing training programmes to ensure that the net and software facilities can be prolifically used at each nodal desk. The concept of on-line notice board has been mooted so that all interested officers of each department can become aware of the purposes, dates and places of meetings. It has also been proposed that for timeliness and efficiency in the entire office work, surface mail communication system should be supported by e-mail communication system, and if needed be replaced by the latter. MIT is also encouraging mounting of own website by every ministry. Web-enabled grievance handling is on the common agenda to deal with complaints at a faster rate. Further, to bring transparency into the governmental work all the ministries have been asked to make available all the acts, rules, and regulations on both print media and electronic media. To encourage on-line submission of forms or downloading of the same from all places MIT has asked for making the forms available in the website of the respective departments. It has also been persuading different offices to develop internal software to equip their respective office delivery systems.

Positive Outcomes of the Moves Taken so far

In the recent past various initiatives have been taken by different departments to improve the services they provide. They are making use of the state-of-the-art information technology for this purpose. The District Treasury has been computerized in many places leading to overnight simplification of the long procedures prevailing so far. Procedural simplification has removed the delays earlier associated with their services. In many states considerable progress can be noticed in this direction. The home pages of different state governments are available. On-line websites have been mounted to provide up-to-date information, which allows citizens to go for better interaction with the respective governments. For some states, there are websites to educate the citizens on different aspects of governance and meet the queries of the people. Websites of districts are also available to provide district-specific information on subjects like tourism, health and industry. Computerization of various departments like election, treasury, land and land records, land acquisition, motor vehicles, etc. also going on. But these achievements are humble beginning towards administrative reforms. More changes should be taken up with greater zeal. It is expected that in the near future, India's march towards a state of fully developed E-government and E-governance will become a reality and the economic development will reach new height.

REFERENCES

Anandkumar, S.V. and Jeyakumar, S.A. (2002), "E-governance: The Emergence of India Inc.'s New Competitive Tool," Proceedings of the 5th Convention, Strategic Management Forum, pp. S-131-S-136.

Carroll, A.B. (1978), Setting operational goals for corporate social responsibility, *Long Range Planning*, April, pp. 35-38.

David, F.R. (1989), *Strategic Management*, Merril Publishing Company.

Hill, C.W.L. and Jones, G.R. (1992), *Strategic Management Theory*, Houghton Mifflin Company.

Jauch, L.R. and Glueck, W.F. (1980), *Business Policy and Strategic Management*, McGraw-Hill, New York.

Jupp, V. (2001), "The Second Global E-government Study," Accenture Global E-goverment Services.

Person, T. and Tabellini, G. (2000), *Political Economics*, MIT Press, Cambridge.

Roy, D. (2002), "India's Participation in the Global March for E-governance and E-government," *Vidyasagar University Journal of Commerce*, pp. 10-20.

Stiglitz, J. (1998), Development Economics in World Bank, *Frontiers of Economic Development*.

Working Group Report on Convergence and E-governance for the Tenth Five-year Plan, Planning Commission, Government of India.

9

Good Governance and Urbanization for Promotion of Sustainable Urban Development in Bangladesh

MD. SHARIFUL ALAM CHOWDHURY

1. Introduction

Historical background of urbanization

Urbanization is the process of becoming urban. Sustainable urbanization is closely associated with sustainable development of cities and has physical, economic, socio-political and environmental issues involved. Growth of population, human settlements and urbanization are important issues in many countries of the present day world including Bangladesh. Inseparable linkages are observed to exist within these issues. All these three elements are linked together in a dynamic process, which has inherent determinants of cause and effect as well as indicators pointing towards solution to problems arising out of the process. Movement of people in and out of settlements is inevitable due to many reasons. The most important aspect of migration, which has overwhelming implications on socio-economic change, is the migration to urban areas. It is desirable that urbanization is transformed into a positive urbanization process of urban development, which contributes to enhancement of standard of urban life as well as ensures satisfactory contributions to advancement of national economy.

Definition of urbanization

Urbanization is basically a process of migration of people from rural to urban regions, but due to problems of definition of urban areas in different countries and under different conditions, a single comprehensive definition of an urban area is yet to be formulated. For instance, in Bangladesh Population Census Reports, urban areas are defined as settlements with a minimum size of population in a specific area and with certain other conditions, like population density, occupation, extend of the provision and extend of urban services, etc. On the other extreme, in Japan settlements with a population of 50,000 or more are generally counted as an urban area. However, it is important to note that these diversities in size of urban areas and the number of people living there in different densities create complex situation relating to socio-economic needs of the inhabitants especially with respect to provision of shelter, job opportunities, transportation and communication, education and health care, and other urban infrastructure and services which tend to disturb the environmental and ecological balance of the area.

Sustainable urbanization

Sustainable development bears a close relationship with sustainable urbanization. Although in essence, 'sustainable development indicates a process by which present development are met without adversely affecting the ability of the future generations to meet their own needs'. The process includes the strategies of utilization of resources to meet the present needs and conservation for the future. Consequently, the strategy gives a wide ranging of coverage encompassing economic, social, political and environmental aspects of development.

Sustainable urbanization may be looked upon on a different angle of view. The essential pre-requisites for making this policy shift to be effective are political will, honesty, sincerity and patriotism among all parties concerned, starting from the political decision-makers, and administrative set-up down to development project managers, service providing agencies and the common man. It is, therefore appropriate to study the basic characteristics of human settlements, the motivating factors and the proper environment influencing its size, composition and characteristics, migration pattern determining the condition for movement of people towards urban area, rate of urbanization and its effects on urban environment and on functioning of urban areas and then try to find out appropriate strategies for urban development which will ensure sustainable urbanization and desirable social development of the country.

Relationship between sustainable development and sustainable urbanization

It is argued that each of the elements of sustainable development concerns for the present needs and concern for the future generations, has three aspects, i.e. *environmental, social* and *economic*. National economic development, which plays an essential role to positive urbanization, is in itself heavily dependent on progressive urban development. Consequently, regulating the effects of urbanization towards progress and prosperity of towns and cities becomes an arduous task for many of the policy planners, decision makers and urban managers.

On environmental advantage of cities, the following observations were made:

(1) Much lower costs per person or per household for the provision of piper, treated water supplies, sewers and drains, garbage collection, advance telecommunication, and most form of health, education and emergency services.

(2) A greater range of, and possibility for, national redemption, recycling and reuse of and possibility for, the specialist enterprise that ensure this can happen safely.

(3) A much higher population concentration that reduces the demand for land relative to population.

(4) Considerable potential for reducing fossil fuel use in cities where homes and work places used to be heated, through the use of waste process heat from industry or thermal power stations.

(5) A much greater potential for reducing the use of motor vehicles through walking or bicycling or greater use of public transport.

One way of looking at the attraction of cities, influencing the pace of urbanization and the consequent effects on the urban areas, is to assess the advantages and disadvantages, generally produced by functioning of specific cities, with respect to needs and demands of people living and working in the city. The level at which the needs and demands are met satisfactorily relating to employment, housing, infrastructures and services such as education, health, transportation, trade and commerce, law and order, and pollution-free living and working environment, determine the level and standard of life and so the degree of attraction of the city.

Effects of rapid urbanization

As already discussed, urbanization may have predominantly positive or and negative effects. On one hand, migrants provide an important source of labour force required in the industries and other productive institutions. Majority of this labour force may be uneducated and unskilled, but this deficiency can be made up to requirements through suitable training programmes. This way the migrants may be turned into tools of higher production and higher economic output of the city. Thus urbanization may have positive contributions for boosting up economic output and for adding to prosperous national economy as well as further advancement of better urban development standards of living in the city. On the other hand if needs and the demands created by the additional people through urbanization are not provided for, negative effects on urban function may produce worse and an intolerable living and working environment in the city areas characterized by unemployment, lack of adequate shelter giving rise to wide-spread poor housing, squatter settlements, bad sanitation, unhealthy slum areas, resulting in overall environmental degradation, poor industrial production and increasing environmental pollution.

Rapid urbanization may have positive effects, which promote the process of economic, physical and environmental development. For instance, national economic development, upgrade the poverty level and turn the poor into rich in higher proportion. On the other hand, if urbanization is not properly addressed, it can produce serious negative consequences involving unemployment and especially urban poverty and degradation of environment.

2. Good Governance

The concept of "governance" is not new. It is as old as human civilization. Simply put "governance" means: the process of decision-making and the process by which decisions are implemented (or not implemented). Governance can be used in several contexts such as corporate governance, international governance, national governance and local governance.

Since governance is the process of decision-making and the process by which decisions are implemented, an analysis of governance focuses on the formal and informal actors involved in decision-making and implementing the decisions made and the formal and informal structures that have been set in place to arrive at and implement the decisions.

Government is one of the actors in governance. Other actors involved in governance vary depending on the level of government that is under discussion. In rural areas, for example, other actors may include influential landlords, associations of peasant farmers, cooperatives, NGOs, research institutes, religious leaders, finance institutions, political parties, the military, etc. The situation in urban areas is much more complex. Figure 1 provides the interconnections between actors involved in urban governance. At the national level, in addition to the above actors, media, lobbyists, international donors, multi-national corporations, etc. may play a role in decision-making or in influencing the decision-making process.

All actors other than government and the military are grouped together as part of the "civil society". In some countries in addition to the civil society, organized crime syndicates also influence decision-making, particularly in urban areas and at the national level.

Similarly formal government structures are the means by which decisions are arrived at and implemented. At the national level, informal decision-making structures, such as "kitchen cabinets" or informal advisors may exist. In urban areas, organized crime syndicates such as the "land Mafia" may influence decision-making. In some rural areas locally powerful families may make or influence decision-making. Such, informal decision-making is often the result of corrupt practices or leads to corrupt practices.

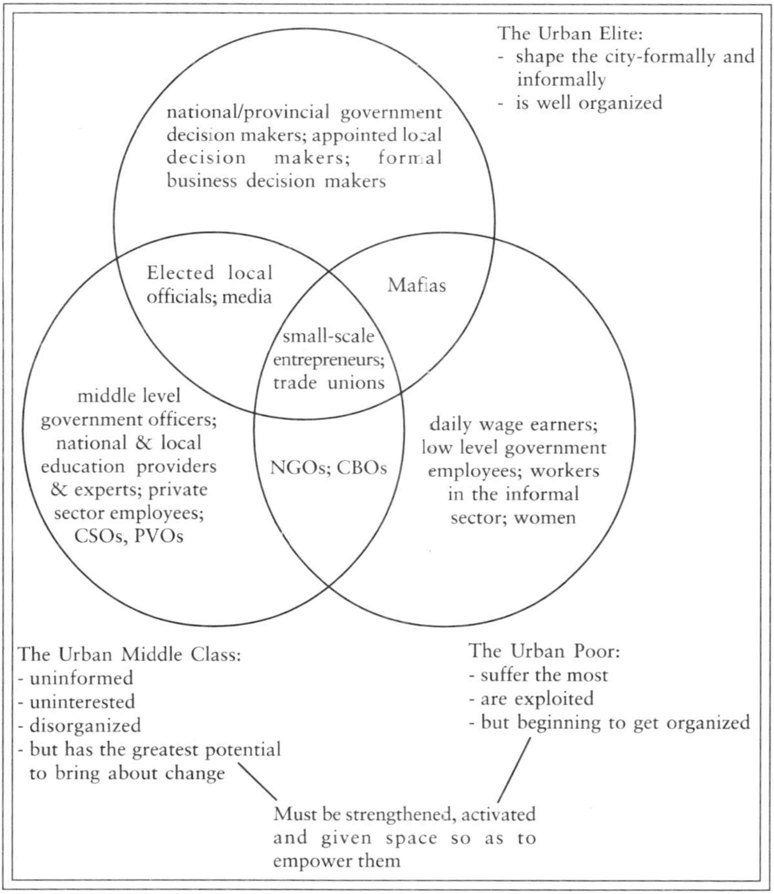

Figure 1: Urban actors, good governance.

Good governance has eight major characteristics as shown in Figure 2. It is participatory, consensus-oriented, accountable, transparent, responsive, effective and efficient, equitable and inclusive and follows the rule of law. It assures that corruption is minimized, the views of minorities are taken into account and that the voices of the most vulnerable in society are heard in decision-making. It is also responsive to the present and future needs of society.

Participation

Participation by both men and women is a key cornerstone of good governance. Participation could be either direct or through legitimate intermediate institutions or representatives. It is important to point out that representative democracy does not necessarily mean that the concerns of the most vulnerable in society would be taken into consideration in decision-making. Participation needs to be informed and organized. This means freedom of association and expression on the one hand and an organized civil society on the other hand.

Rule of law

Good governance requires fair legal frameworks that are enforced impartially. It also requires full protection of human rights, particularly those of minorities. Impartial enforcement of laws requires an independent judiciary and an impartial and incorruptible police force.

Transparency

Transparency means that decisions taken and their enforcement are done in a manner that follows rules and regulations. It also means that information is freely available and directly accessible to those who will be affected by such decisions and their enforcement. It also means that enough information is provided and that it is provided in easily understandable forms and media.

Responsiveness

Good governance requires that institutions and processes try to serve all stakeholders within a reasonable timeframe.

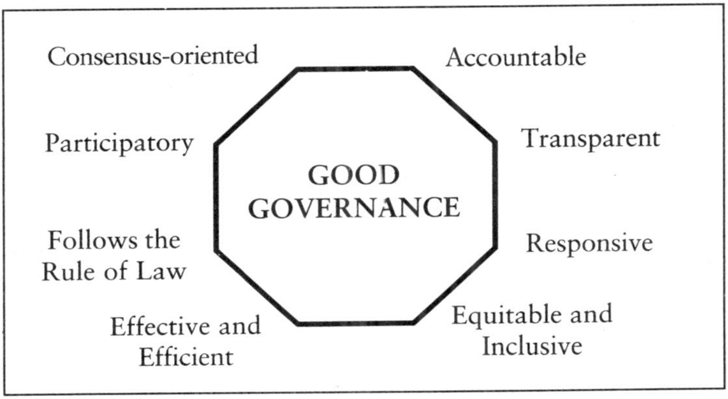

Figure 2: Characteristics of good governance.

Consensus-oriented

There are several factors and as many viewpoints in a given society. Good governance requires mediation of the different interests in society to reach a broad consensus in society on what is in the best interest of the whole community and how this can be achieved. It also requires a broad and long-term perspective on what is needed for sustainable human development and how to achieve the goals of such development. This can only result from an understanding of the historical, cultural and social contexts of a given society or community.

Equity and inclusiveness

A society's well-being depends on ensuring that all its members feel that they have a stake in it and do not feel excluded from the mainstream of society. This requires all groups, but particularly the most vulnerable, have opportunities to improve or maintain their well-being.

Effectiveness and efficiency

Good governance means that processes and institutions produce results that meet the needs of society while making the best use of resources at their disposal. The concept of efficiency in the context of good governance also covers the sustainable use of natural resources and the protection of the environment.

Accountability

Accountability is a key requirement of good governance. Not only governmental institutions but also the private sector and civil society organizations must be accountable to the public and to their institutional stakeholders. Who is accountable to whom varies depending on whether decisions or actions taken are internal or external to an organization or institution. In general an organization or an institution is accountable to those who will be affected by its decisions or actions. Accountability cannot be enforced without transparency and the rule of law.

Urban governance may be defined as a participatory process of management of urban issues and problems for the overall development of urban areas. Broadly speaking urban governance refers to the system of government, concentrating on effective and accountable institutions, democratic principles and electoral process, representative and responsible structure of government, in order to ensure an open and legitimate relationship between the civil society and the state (McCarney, 1995). Governance also defined as "the experience of authority, control, management, power of government" (World Bank, 1992).

3. Urbanization and Urban Governance in Bangladesh

Urbanization in Bangladesh

It is interesting to note that the 'average population of the world's 100 largest cities was over 500 million inhabitants by 1990 compared to 2.1 million in 1950 and less than 2,00,000 in 1980' (*Source*: Islam, 2003). In the area of the subcontinent which is presently under Bangladesh, urban development was very limited during the British colonial period up to 1947. Movements of the population were almost confined to village to village, or one agricultural area to other and even within the village, due to marriage of women or seasonal demand of agricultural labour force. Reasons behind movement of people were also somewhat different during the period of urbanization and migration to urban centers. Joint family system, inheritance, land purchase were the principal factors contributing to land fragmentation as well as land consolidation which operated in a more or less balanced state but gradually with increased population growth.

Transformation of predominantly agricultural economy to industrial economy has been accompanied by high rate of movement of population from the rural areas to urban areas attracted by industrials economy, higher income, urban facilities, which increased the rate of urbanization during the Industrial Revolution of the 18th century through the early part of the 20th century.

One important feature of migration in Bangladesh was due to river erosion, which has been continuing over a long period in the past. At present, it forms an important source of urbanization and immigration to towns and cities of Bangladesh. After Partition of the subcontinent in 1947, development activities in different towns and cities within the area covered by present Bangladesh, continued with accelerated process of urbanization.

Present status of urban governance in Bangladesh

Urban governance is really in bad shape in our country. No city has a vision of its own, almost none of the non-metropolitan cities have any semblance of urban planning or development control, and none have adequate manpower or financial adequacy (CUS: 2001). Almost all cities suffer from terrible environmental problems and economic and social crisis. It is a fact that for metropolitan cities in Bangladesh, there are many challenges and some of these are the problems for development of infrastructure, lack of financial resources, mismatch in policy formulation, lack of transparency, uncoordinated functioning by different agencies and the recurrent national disasters which frequently destroy bridges, roads and tracts. Recently the public authority in metropolitan management is being shared by private organization and CBOs in some parts of Dhaka city due to resource constraints and lack of state driven initiatives in the operation and management issues.

It is noted that decentralization, transparency and people's participation are key to good governance (*The Daily Star*,

June 24, 2001). The ultimate responsibility of urban governance rests with the urban local governments, i.e. the pourashavas and city corporations. The quality of urban governance may be measured on the basis of—decentralization, democratic participation, transparency and accountability, control and leadership, rule of law, equity (economic, gender, etc.), efficiency and productivity, sustainability, networking and information flow, and coordination (CUS: 2001). At present metropolitan governance of Dhaka is composed of three broad types of agencies: national, sectoral and local. Within the sectoral agencies, however, there are some special agencies in Dhaka. Thus, municipalities of agencies exist to guide and control the planning and development of Dhaka and its metropolitan areas. Twenty-two ministries out of a total of 39 (Statistical Pocketbook of Bangladesh, 2000) and 51 agencies are involved in planning, execution and development of metropolitan Dhaka. The sectoral agencies are dominant (66.7%) against the weak position of urban local government (13.7%).

Again in the light of the discussions on principles of urban good governance, attention should be given on a number of specific issues concerning urban areas, i.e. employment and poverty reduction, access to land and shelter, improvement of urban infrastructure, improvement of urban social services, urban transport, planning functions of city authorities, planned physical expansion of cities, land use control, legislation, open space, greeneries and water bodies in urban areas, environmental pollution control, city information center, urban development-related human resource development and planning education; and strengthening urban local authorities.

4. Urban Environment—Living and Working Conditions

In Bangladesh, like many of the developing countries of South-East Asia, tremendous inconsistencies are observed in facing the effects of rapid urbanization by the city management authorities. In most cases, the resources available and the resources needed to meet the needs and demands of the urban population, fall apart with growing deficiency. The followings are the main concerns of the developers, planners and decision makers for sustainable urban area development.

1. **Growth of Population and Employment**
   - (i) *Urbanization and Growth of Population*
     - (a) High rate urbanization added to the existing population put pressure on land, urban infrastructure and services.
     - (b) Unplanned settlements with high density but with an unacceptable level of urban services.
   - (ii) *Inadequate Employment and Income Generation Developments*
     - (a) Unplanned and inadequate employment opportunities.
     - (b) Poor industrial development.
     - (c) Low levels of economic output.
     - (d) Inappropriate growth of trade and commerce.
2. **Provision of Urban Services**
   - (i) *Public Health Provisions*
     - (a) Uncoordinated and inefficient health services.
     - (b) Poor standard of health services.
     - (c) Lack of control of mosquito menace and viral diseases.
   - (ii) *Education Problems*
     - (a) Inadequate education facilities.
     - (b) Poor quality of education.
   - (iii) *Housing Problems*
     - (a) Acute housing shortage.
     - (b) Inconsistencies in provision of housing for different income groups.
     - (c) Squatter settlements.
   - (iv) *Water Supply and Sanitation Problems*
     - (a) Inadequate provision for potable water to residents.
     - (b) Pollution at sources and during distribution of water.

(c) Inadequate sanitation measures resulting in health and environmental problems waste disposal problems.

(v) *Other Services Problems*

(a) Defective electric distribution system.

(b) Frequent load-shedding in power supply.

(c) Inadequate gas and fuel supply.

(d) Telephone communication problem.

(e) Telephone billing problem.

(f) Frequent price hike of essential services.

(vi) *Problems of Leisure and Recreation*

(a) Inadequate facilities for recreation.

(b) Lack of opportunities for leisure and past time.

3. **Provision of Urban Development Infrastructure**

(i) *Transport and Communications Problems*

(a) Unplanned and uncoordinated transportation system resulting in difficulties in mobility of people.

(b) Inefficient transportation and traffic management resulting in intolerable traffic jam and accident risks.

(c) Problems of improper and uncoordinated use of different modes of traffic and transportation.

4. **Land Use and Land Development**

(i) *Land Development*

(a) Sites and services development.

(b) Development and proper use of low lying land.

(c) Development of water bodies.

(d) Land reform and land allocation.

(e) Lack of land use guidelines.

(f) Lack of land use control systems.

(ii) *Land Ownership*

(a) Urban land ownership patterns.

(b) Land values.

(iii) *Tenural Security of the Migrants in Urban Areas*

5. **Policies for Social Development**

(i) *Social Problems*

(a) Social unrest.

(b) Morality of people and national image building.

(c) Religious tolerance.

(d) Political unrest and terrorist activities.

(e) Promotion of national heritage.

(f) Poverty alleviation.

(g) Widespread corruption in national life.

6. **Planning for Sustainable Environment**

(i) *Environmental and Ecological Problems*

(a) Serious environmental degradation.

(b) Disturbances in ecological balance.

(c) Air, water, physical based pollution.

(d) River pollution and its dangerous effects.

(e) Lack of open spaces, parks, playgrounds, lakes, water bodies, low land, river, and shrinkage of the existing ones due to unauthorized occupation and improper use.

7. **Good Urban Governance**

(i) *Urban Management Problems*

(a) Weak institutional framework for good governance.

(b) Lack of honest, sincere and productive manpower.

(c) Lack of skilled and experienced technical manpower.

(d) Lack of adequate research facilities for promotion of development.

(e) Lack of an effective planning process.

(f) Lack of co-ordination among different development agencies.

(ii) *Physical Planning Problems*

(a) Inadequate planning framework.

(b) Uncontrolled development and unauthorized constructions.

(c) Inadequate investment programmers.

(iii) *Problems of Appropriate Political Environment*

(a) Party politics is not favourable to social welfare.

(b) No favourable political environment for institutionalization of democracy in the country.

(c) Lack of proper political commitment to democratic process.

(iv) *Poor Law and Order Situation*

(a) Poor law and order situation resulting in:

(i) murder,

(ii) terrorism,

(iii) theft and dacoits,

(iv) lack of public and personal security,

(v) increasing trend of lawlessness and criminal activities.

8. **Provision for Adequate Resources of Urban Finance**

(i) *Strengthening of Local Government Finance*

(a) Increased power of levying taxes,

(b) Increased central government grants and aid.

(ii) *Power to negotiate Foreign Cooperation*

(a) Find out sources of foreign grants and aid.

(iii) *Increased areas of delegated subjects to local government.*

5. Sustainable Urbanization, Social Development and Governance

Relationship between sustainable urbanization, social development and good governance

The concept of sustainable urbanization is, thus, linked to economic development and is heavily influenced and regulated by social development and political environment. The multi-disciplinary planning process plays an important role in establishing a system of good governance in attaining sustainable urbanization and urban development, because of a complex system involving development where heterogeneous as well as homogeneous elements simultaneously come into play and interact, where coordination is a crucial factor towards achieving the goals of urban development.

Recognized five pillars of a possible poverty reduction strategy are: (i) accelerating economic growth; (ii) promoting education for the poor, particularly primary education and specially for girls; (iii) investing in poor areas to take advantage of strong location effects on poverty reduction; (iv) improved targeting of public expenditures and safety nets to reach the poor better; and (v) forming further partnerships with NGOs to reach the poorest and not-so-poor in ways designed to make a stronger attack on poverty. Discussions with stakeholders, NGOs, the government, poverty researchers, and other donors in Bangladesh arising from this report will help to build support for an action plan and more detailed policy and institutional changes for faster poverty reduction. In line with the capacity-building emphasis of the World Bank's country assistance strategy, these discussions will also help to build consensus on the institutional capacity required to mainstream poverty analysis in policy design and implementation.

On the other hand, the rural urban interaction is manifold. This can be classified as administrative and political, economic, commercial and financial, socio-cultural, educational, information, transformation, services and amenities, etc. What we need in the developing countries is a balanced urban system with a large metropolis at the apex supported by and in turn supporting a large number of small and intermediate towns and cities. Such a system must be organically and generatively linked to the hundreds of thousands of rural settlements both vertically and horizontally. All the coordinated and effective management for the long-term planning will enhance the sustainable growth of cities with the organized social development effort.

In the prevailing socio-economic and political situation in Bangladesh, a new approach to attain effective sustainable development and so sustainable urbanization is necessary because the traditional process of addressing the problems fails to produce satisfactory remedy. In the study of different aspects of sustainable urbanization and social development, decision on the development planning process, consisting of preparation of different types of development plans role of planners, development management and good governance are pertinent subjects, and have been looked into.

Efficient governance by the municipal authorities is not possible without highly efficient and trained manpower. Again it is necessary to evolve an institutional arrangement to undertake planning exercises in each city. The service delivery system of each individual city or town should be planned to embody efficiency, productivity, beauty and environmental sustainability. Efficiency of good governance is related to the functional aspects of cities and to be achieved through physical planning and providing basic urban services with emphasis or equity (Islam: 2001).

Sustainable urbanization includes impact of urbanization on cities, social, physical and environmental favourable to progress and prosperity of the city or adverse effects on the healthy life and efficient functioning of the city. The urban management is primarily the responsibility of and functions better and efficiently under, the local government or municipal authorities. Therefore, degree of attainment of sustainable urbanization and urban development, depends upon the concerted efforts and effective co-operation of local urban government or the municipal corporation, the central government and international agencies.

6. Problems and Constraints of Sustainable Urban Development

Important problem areas and constraints to sustainable urban development

As discussed earlier urbanization have both positive and negative effects on urban development and desirable resizable and sustainable urban functioning. The most sensitive areas of activities, which determine the status of a city whether it is on the path to progress and prosperity or is on a degrading and decaying trend which can be identified as follows:

- Growth of population and employment.
- Provision of urban services.
- Provision of urban development infrastructure.
- Land use and land development.
- Policies for social development.
- Planning for sustainable environment.
- Good urban governance.
- Provision for adequate sources of urban finance.

Case study of Dhaka metropolitan city with respect to urbanization and its consequences

Metropolitan Dhaka has two connotations, first is that of the central city [Dhaka City Corporation or DCC, or Dhaka city as it is popularly known and the other is the Dhaka Statistical Metropolitan Area or DSMA which includes DCC and Keranigonj, Demra, Narayangonj, Dhaka Cantonment, Tongi and adjoining rural areas. The total area covered by DCC is only about 200 square miles. The SMA area is about 550 square miles. The other connotation is that Dhaka Metropolitan Development Plan (1995-2015) prepared in 1995 by RAJUK (Capital Development Authority) contains an area of 590 square miles (1528 square kilometers) DMDP, 1995, Vol. II, p. 1].

It is interesting to study consequences of urbanization in Bangladesh especially in the Metropolitan City of Dhaka. It is important because, it is the capital city of the country and it is being the largest and by far the most significant city which reflects the image of the country in terms of effective achievement of development efforts towards the national goal of enhanced progress and prosperity. A city has distinctive functions. The efficiency in performance of its functions may determine the contribution of the city to national development and economic output.

It is meaningful to study the operational performance in each field of functional elements which regulate the functioning of the Metropolitan city of Dhaka which provides a representative case study and make assessment of performance in different fields of activity which may assist in coming to a conclusion as to the direction to which the development in large cities in Bangladesh is moving.

Metropolitan city of Dhaka and three other Divisional headquarters, namely Chittagong, Khulna and Rajshahi came under tremendous pressure of urbanization and increase in population over the last four decades. In 1986, Dhaka metropolitan city was declared as one of the Mega cities of the world at that time, of 30 cities so designated, in the world. Dhaka was listed Mega city with population over 10 million and position of Dhaka was 30th in the list in order of size of population. At present, Dhaka ranked as 11th Mega city in the world.

The Dhaka Narayangonj-Demra (DND) area is another example of the consequences of failure of pursuing planned and systematic efforts of successfully carrying out sustainable development projects. The failure was due to lack of good urban governance.

Deteriorating conditions and continued pollution of rivers and water bodies and low lands around the city are even worse. Perennial rivers around the city especially the Burhiganga, the Sitalakha, the Balu, Turag, Bangshi, Dhalesware rivers are the nerve centers of the city. These rivers used to provide very good sources of water supply, navigation notably facilitating river transport, open air recreation and most of all, maintaining an ecological balance within the city.

7. Appropriate Strategies and Policy Planning for Sustainable Urbanization in Bangladesh

Promotion of good governance

Productivity of good governance is related to economy of the urban areas while beauty is related to the aesthetic aspects of the city and environmental sustainability is of paramount importance, which can be achieved through realistic planning and governance. The potential benefits of good governance in service delivery system, include the following:

- Creating social awareness.
- Creating synergy to the actions of different stakeholders.
- Empowering the local institutions and organizations initiate actions on their own.
- Helping ensure improved service delivery from the municipality (DCC) and others service providing organizations.
- Helping operate and maintain the systems effectively.
- Increasing ownership and a sense of belongingness of citizens.
- Mobilizing local resources.
- Promoting community involvement in the provision of service delivery.
- Providing option for the citizens to share their views and ventilate their concerns and grievance.
- Reducing the municipals body costs and burden of service delivery.

(SINPA-Bangladesh: 2001)

Integrated planning approach

In order to attain a sustainable urbanization and social development process, an integrated urban planning approach is likely to deliver the goods in the perceptive of socio-economic and political realities of Bangladesh. Large cities, especially the Metropolitan city of Dhaka, are at the center of focus for performing the leading role in planning and development activities in moving towards the goals of sustainable urbanization, social development and sustainable environment.

Expanded role of local government

Expanded role of local government is another important strategy. Although for establishment of a viable and dependable process for sustainable development an integrated effort comprising local, national and international collaboration, is possibly the best approach to follow. The local government especially the municipal corporations have the most important role to play.

Radical reform to pave the way for attraction of industrial investment

Favourable strategies for making adequate provision for development infrastructure and services, land improvement and land availability for development, social development and very importantly proper policy for ensuring sustainable environmental development supported by necessary sources of finance for integrated and coordinated efforts, are needed to be found out.

Ensure public participation in good governance for sustainable development

Community participation in policy planning and development management is another aspect of good governance for sustainable development, which cannot be overemphasized. This can be achieved through appropriate mechanisms for effective urban governance as well as devising pertinent strategies/approaches of participatory urban development programmes and activities.

8. Conclusion

Good governance free from corruption, vested interests and harmful power politics, will ensure social justice, equality, rule of law and establishment of transparency and efficiency in development management. In this regard, urban planning plays an important role in establishing an effective process towards achievement of sustainable urbanization and social development. Therefore, the urban planning institutions should be strengthened. Again, political reforms aimed at introduction of real democratic rule in the country where accepted basic democratic principals will protect and preserve fundamental human rights. In order to achieve desired sustainable urbanization, especially keeping up the present trend of coordinated efforts of the government, the NGOs, and the civil society at large, should be strengthened and further promoted. And all level stakeholders should be involved in planning, designing implementation, maintenance of appropriate projects for sustainable development. And further research, evaluation and monitoring cells should be created in each sector as part of planning process with exclusive responsibilities to carry out a continuous process of evaluation of the performance of what is being done to attain sustainable development, what is the shortfall, if any, and how to regulate the development process on right path, to move faster towards the development goals.

REFERENCES

Bangladesh Bureau of Statistics (2002). "Statistical Pocketbook of Bangladesh 2000," Statistical Division, Ministry of Planning, GoB.

CUS Bulletin (2001). Center for Urban Studies, Number 41, July-December 2002.

DCC (1978). DCC Ordinance 1978, Ministry of LGRD & C, GoB.

Islam, N. & Khan (1997). "Urban Governance in Bangladesh and Pakistan," Center for Urban Studies, Dhaka.

Muhit A. Mohammad (1998). "Dhaka Planning and Development Problems: Department of URP, Bangladesh University of Engineering and Technology, Dhaka, Bangladesh.

Muhit, A.M.A. (2001). "Issues of Good Governance in Bangladesh", Dhaka.

Raman, Golam and Md. Alam, Monirul (2000). "Urban Growth Pattern in Dhaka City and Its Problems of Urban Solid Waste Management" Bangladesh Environment 2000. ed. M. Feroze Ahmed, BUET, Dhaka.

Rahman, Golam and Mallick, Bishawjit (2002). "Promoting Good Governance in Service Delivery System of Dhaka City Corporation" World Habitat Day Souvenir 2002, GoB.

SINPA-Bangladesh (2002). *Facilitating, Local Partner Participatory Initiatives: A Handbook for Urban Platforms*, Potential Press, Dhaka.

The Daily Star, October 18, 2000.

World Bank (1992). "Government and Development."

10

Reducing Barriers to Entrepreneurship as an International Development Strategy: Implementation Challenges and Structural Constraints

PAUL DRAGOS ALIGICA

Summary

The international development community has increasingly shifted attention to a development strategy that implies a major switch of the focus from large businesses to small, from the formal to the informal sector, from big macro and national level policies to micro level targeted interventions, from "great strategies" to local and administrative level approaches meant to improve the environment for entrepreneurs and small businesses. This article discusses the feasibility of such an approach. Using the concrete USAID "Red Tape Analysis" case as a vehicle, the article conjectures that one should not expect "bottom up" policies like the "Red Tape" initiative to deliver as long as they are not part of a larger, structural strategy of reform. The dangers of promoting policies aimed at "removing barriers to entrepreneurship" without understanding the implementation, structural and political economy constraints that affect their chances of success are huge because the disappointing results would lead sooner or later to the rejection of this very promising approach to international development.

Barriers to Entrepreneurship and the International Development Policy Portfolio

The constant effort of the international development community of practitioners and theorists to find a solution to global poverty has gone through many stages or *avataars*: industrialization, indicative planning, foreign aid, investing in technology, fostering education, controlling population growth, making aid loans, or forgiving those loans on condition of reforms (Esterly, 2001; Arndt, 1989). Due to the disappointment with the results, new solutions and approaches have been sought continuously. Recently, the attention has been more and more focused on issues such as liberalizing prices and controls on both domestic markets and international trade; rationalizing tax and tariff structures, including reduction of average rates; liberalizing investment laws and restrictions; and promoting foreign investment and exports (Emery and Spence, 2000). However, there has been a sense that the results have fell short of expectations again. The counter-reaction to that has created a new trend. The new strategies added to the policy portfolio by this new trend imply a major switch of the focus from the formal to the informal sector, from large businesses to small, from big macro and national level policies to micro level targeted interventions, from grand programmes to local and administrative level approaches meant to improve the environment for entrepreneurs and small businesses (Miles, 2004). This trend is not only theoretical or academic but also has gained important institutional sponsors. The new approach has been taken up by major players in international development such as United Nations Development Project (UNDP), World Bank, United States Agency for International Development (USAID) and by many governments involved in either domestic or international development-oriented activities.

The main characteristic of the new strategic vision on development is a focus on the entrepreneurship's environment and the regulatory procedures that small firms and entrepreneurs must follow in establishing and operating their businesses. These procedures (which include registering businesses, administering taxes, obtaining investment approvals, business licenses, intellectual property, sanitary inspections and clearances, construction and building permits, customs clearances, and utility hook-ups) raise production and transaction costs, reduce entrepreneurial initiatives, create barriers to market entry and business expansion and in general weaken enterprise and competitive forces. In short, they are barriers to business. Eliminating them means opening the way to economic growth.

In the emerging literature associated to the new strategic vision, study after study has documented from different angles and in different cases the facts and principles that give the rationale of the approach. For instance, bringing the informal business sector into the legal and the gray economy into the economic mainstream is a principal theme of Hernando de Soto's work. de Soto (2000, 2002), one of the leaders of the new trend, notes that in most developing countries it is costly to function in the formal economy. Formally registered businesses are often overtaxed, registering a business can be a long and expensive process taking months and even years, regulations and government requirements are complex and compliance costs are high. On the other hand, there is a direct relationship between the lack of transparency and over-regulation on the one hand, and corruption, on the other. The opportunities for bribery increase with the complexity of regulations, creating negative spillovers in the entire economy. In a similar vein in his book, *Just Get of the Way: How Government Can Help Business in Poor Countries*, Robert E. Anderson, a former World Bank employee, argues that the macro level and structural policies that foreign experts and development institutions recommend are beyond the capacity of most governments in developing countries to implement. As a result, they more often than not harm the private sector instead of helping it. Fostering a friendly environment for entrepreneurship is the best an international development strategy could do.

Encouraged by the growing interest, the empirical studies trying to explore the issues and to support these views, started to gain in breath and depth. For instance, Morisset and Neso (2003) calculated, based on a fairly solid country database that it can take up to two or three years to establish a new business in many developing countries. Also they found that the associated administrative costs are positively correlated with estimates of the level of corruption, strength of governance, and the degree of protection of the economy. In addition to cross-country quantitative studies, there are other authors dedicated to very specific practical aspects such as transparency and clarity in regulations. For instance, McKinley (1998) argued that fewer requests for clarification reduce administrative costs. Plain language in regulatory practice may be an important factor in improving the environment of entrepreneurship. McKinley reviews examples of 'plain language' approaches and pleads for strategies to reduce error rates, improve compliance, and reduce appeals and challenges, in addition to saving time for understanding regulations.

An additional signal regarding the appeal and the strengths of the new trend is given by the number of international or regional initiatives reflecting or promoting it. A typical example is the FIAS South-Eastern Europe Regional Conference on Self Assessment and Removal of Administrative Barriers to Investment sponsored by the Foreign Investment Advisory Service (FIAS) in Sarajevo in 2003. The event's objective was to overview practices in removing administrative barriers in various Eastern European countries. The discussions were exemplary also because they took place around one of the favourite tools of the new policy 'movement': national surveys of barriers and regulations, in this case the Administrative and Regulatory Costs Surveys undertaken in 2002 in Albania, Bosnia and Herzegovina, Bulgaria, Croatia, Macedonia, Romania and Serbia. On a different continent and in a different geopolitical context, it is worth mentioning that the 'Johannesburg Statement by Co-chairs on Main Building Blocks of Modern Governance and Transparency for Investment' issued at the Organization for Economic Co-operation and Development (OECD), Global Forum on International Investment, November 2003, is emblematic for the promotion efforts. The statement is basically a plea for transparency. Transparency 'encourages domestic and foreign investment in an internationally competitive environment', 'reduces business risks and uncertainties', 'helps combat bribery and corruption' and ultimately 'promotes sustainable investment' (OECD, 2003).

In other words, transparency improves the business environment and that, in the end, leads to an improved performance.

The above-mentioned initiatives are a clear signal that the international organizations have started to incorporate the new approach into their agenda. The World Bank for instance has made important steps forward in building quantitative assessment tools. The Doing Business Database provides 'objective measures of business regulations and their enforcement'. The Doing Business indicators are comparable across 145 economies indicating the regulatory costs of business 'can be used to analyze specific regulations that enhance or constrain investment, productivity and growth' (World Bank, 2004). The Regulatory Reform Programme of the Organization for Economic Co-operation and Development (OECD) is an expression of similar views and concerns and so is From Red Tape to Smart Tape: Administrative Simplification in OECD countries, a publication which 'analyzes proven approaches adopted by governments to reduce and streamline administrative procedures' (OECD, 2003) including reforms such as one-stop shops, time limits for decision-making, regulatory compliance assistance for small- and medium-size companies, and increasing reliance on information technology-based solutions.

Finally, in 2004, UNDP's Commission on the Private Sector and Development, presented their report, "Unleashing Entrepreneurship: Making Business Work for the Poor". The report was described as 'a call to action' to unleash the potential of local small business and the informal, village-based micro-enterprises. The report suggested that 'unleashing local private enterprise, supported by strong, indigenous democratic institutions' is 'a new pillar of development' and called for 'targeted policy reforms and other initiatives' that would spur growth 'in the local businesses that are critical to the eradication of poverty in the developing world' (Martin, 2004). Questions such as how can the potential of the private sector and entrepreneurship be unleashed in developing countries, announce the same shift from a focus on big foreign direct investment to a targeted approach aimed at identifying and addressing the legal, financial and structural obstacles blocking the expansion of the indigenous private sector in developing nations. To sum up, in all cases, both the diagnostic of the problems and the strategies emerging to remedy administrative barriers are relatively unambiguous, and include the use of transparency measures, regulatory reforms, efficiency reforms such as one-stop shops, or technological reorganization or more domain specific responses such as customs reform and trade facilitation.

The Feasibility Problem

One of the most important features of the new trend is the fact that it brings with it a shift of emphasis to the micro level. The small firm or the mere entrepreneurial activity becomes the center of attention. That is in many respects a radical departure from the standard approaches. The question is in what measure is the operationalization of this shift sustainable at the policy implementation stage? Is it possible to create a change in the overall performance of an economy by consistently targeting small economic actors and 'unleashing' their potential? The relevance of this challenge is first practical and only second theoretical.

In order to understand the meaning of the challenge it is necessary to go deeper into the logic and rationale behind the new approach. It is apparent that the roots are in dissatisfaction with the 'great policies', structural change strategies and programmes operating at or through the national and central level. The new approach tries to redefine the terms of the debate. Implicit in it is the suggestion to orient the strategy the other way round: from bottom up instead of from top down. It is assumed that enterprises are able to function and adapt even in an imperfect environment. Yet, degrees of imperfection matter. The idea is to create within the existing structures and institutions as much as possible and whenever feasible, microclimates favourable to small changes affecting positively the performance of small firms and entrepreneurs. It is hoped that once set into motion, these developments will reach a tipping point. Once the tipping point is reached, the critical mass of enterprises and firms will have enough aggregated economic and political power to force a transformation of the entire structure of the system. In other words, if entrepreneurship is a resilient and dynamic phenomenon, even a small improvement in its environment will create cascade effects in terms of performance and social impact. By taking advantage of marginal and niche improvements (such as the reduction of regulatory barriers that block the birth and growth of new initiatives) entrepreneurship will be able at one point to transform the entire system.

There is no doubt that this approach is representing a significant departure from the standard strategic propositions that start with big structural projects and expect a realignment at the micro level to follow suit. But in this case the micro change drives a structural transformation. The question is: Is such an approach feasible? Is it possible to implement a strategy that is in principle based on accepting the institutional and political economy structures more or less as they are and try to concentrate on mere reducing 'the number of days required to register a business', reducing the 'red tape' or increasing 'transparency'? Although theoretically it is possible to build complex adaptive systems models in which a small change at the micro level creates an emergent property structural change, there are many questions regarding the realism and practicability of such principles in international development given the current circumstances.

Precisely because of this potential tension between the theoretical promise and implementation realism, an examination of the empirical evidence from the existing relevant cases is crucial for understanding the promise and the limits of the new approach. Given the fact that it is too early to have a cross-national databases consisting of data tracking the post-implementation phase of the first wave of the new measures, one should settle for the analysis of relevant case studies. The second part of this article will use a case study in order to explore the strengths of the new approach. The analysis will take advantage of the chance of identifying one case that is a perfect example of a project inspired by the new ideas, and will try to identify the most important lessons regarding the tenability of the implementation of the new approach. As a parenthesis it is important to note that the objective of a standard policy evaluation in this respect should not be whether or not the measures discussed at events such as FIAS South-Eastern Europe Regional Conference on Self Assessment and Removal of Administrative Barriers to Investment, managed to reduce the number of days or increase transparency but if (a) the economic growth has improved as a result and (b) if these measures generated structural change. However, the objective of the present investigation is less to assess performance and impact but more to explore the implementation conditions and whether or not a bottom up strategy is tenable as an implementation procedure.

As it has already been mentioned, an outstanding case could help an implementation assessment effort on these lines. USAID run a project that fits well that parameter: In order to identify the relevant barriers in the development of small and medium sized enterprises, USAID launched a multi-country programme on 'red tape' and regulatory procedures that affected the business environment in several developing and transition countries. Following the Red Tape Analysis report, USAID encouraged a series of concrete initiatives to simplify bureaucratic procedures and to clarify the confusing and unpredictable regulatory and legal environment in some of the countries analyzed. The important thing is that those concrete initiatives were based precisely on the notion that the approach should fit the existing political and institutional structures and make the best out of them, trying to get as much change in the direction of improvement as allowed by them.

Out of the countries where policy initiatives were advances, Romania is a special case. The implementation of the Red Tape project was run by the IRIS Center from Maryland University at College Park. The IRIS and USAID experts knew from the beginning that they were engaged in a test aimed at determining the extent to which improvements could be made within the existing general political-institutional setting. The entire approach was designed carefully and most of the specific interventions were aimed in such a way as to depend as little as possible from the central level decision-making structures. Thus, it is appropriate to conclude that the Romania initiative was a very good experiment and exploring and assessing it offers a very telling insight into the workings of the new approach.

With this end in view, an assessment research design based on content analysis, interviews and field work was planned for 2003 and implemented starting that summer until the beginning of 2004. The analysis reflected in this article is elaborating the ideas of the assessment report and thus is based on systematic field work in Romania following in a very concrete way the trail of the Romania Red Tape Initiative. However, in considering those conclusions one should not forget the exploratory nature of the entire effort and the intrinsic generalization limits of such analyses.

The Romanian 'Red Tape' Analysis Case

USAID objectives regarding the private sector were defined within the parameters of the new approach and were meant to improve the business environment for small and medium-sized enterprises. The goal was to streamline the legal and administrative processes required for a Romanian enterprise to register and operate. In order to identify the relevant barriers in the development of SMEs. In 2001 USAID through IRIS Center drafted a report on Red Tape and regulatory procedures that affected Romania's business environment. This report contained information and an analysis of the regulatory framework, as well as economic data generated by interviewing 200 small and medium sized enterprises throughout Romania. The report presented the barriers that a company was faced with in the field of registration, licensing and approvals, fiscal obligations, utilities, land ownership, construction and various regulatory and legislative obligations.

The Red Tape Analysis ideas were influential in the creation of a Government of Romania Action Plan for improving the business environment, which was approved by Government Decision 1189 on August 23, 2001 and amended via Government Decision 209 on February 28, 2002. Also, most deregulation recommendations within the Red Tape Analysis were incorporated into a new NATO accession action plan coordinated with NATO and the Ministry of Foreign Affairs. But more important than that, USAID was not satisfied with only having the ideas of the Red Tape report captured in official documents. Instead, it developed a series of initiatives aimed at simplifying bureaucratic procedures and at clarifying the confusing and unpredictable regulatory environment. Out of them, three deserve a special attention because of their objectives and levels of operation and implementation.

Local Approvals—Five Step Programme

Eighty cities in Romania were called to participate and ultimately 29 of these cities were invited to take part in a six-month programme. The project was designed as a private and public sector partnership in order to reduce the time and effort necessary to obtain approvals and other related site development authorizations to operate and register an SME. This was to be accomplished through both the elimination of some approvals, reduction of the paperwork involved in processing and fostering mechanisms for increased communication and transparency between officials and SMEs. Five steps were defined. Each step corresponds to a particular barrier identified within the initial 'Red Tape Survey': (1) Eliminate the operating authorization issued by city halls in order to reduce the redundant approvals that a business needs to obtain. (2) Reduce time in local approvals process in contract processing for Local Community Sewer Authority, Local Water Management Authority, Local Supplier of Thermo Energy and Local Garbage Removal, by allowing for Health, Environment and Fire Brigade approvals and authorizations to be applied simultaneously. (3) Increase transparency in local approval processes by conducting public hearings/debates on business environment decisions issued locally, by establishing an office within city halls as points to register complaints against both the government and individual businesses. (4) Reduce time in building construction permit process—by using the concept of a 'one stop shop' facility. (5) Enable simultaneous issuing of the fiscal code and registration certificate.

Transparency

The initiative to increase transparency was aimed at developing administrative procedure codes that create transparency in the public decision-making process. A transparency code includes stipulations such as prior notice of upcoming decisions and pending regulations, as well as mechanisms for meaningful private participation in the decision-making process. The transparency project worked with local communities and was adopted in Giurgiu, Sibiu and Timisoara. The transparency codes adopted in these cities were superseded by the National Transparency Law (Law no. 52) passed by the Parliament of Romania on July 21, 2003. The national law did not modify the use of transparency at the local level. Rather, it is aimed at ensuring the continuity of transparency across localities.

Payroll Reporting and Inspections Regime

Although it was not a local level approach, the 'Payroll Reporting' initiative is noteworthy for two reasons. First because the solutions suggested did not require legislative changes and second because they operated through a systematic stakeholders' mobilization. Payroll Reporting identified that the Romanian payroll reporting and inspections regime was subject to excessive red tape and administrative duplication, a time-consuming and costly burden for SMEs. This finding was corroborated with a subsequent report drafted by World Bank—FIAS (Foreign Investment Advisory Service), which identified labour reporting as a barrier to investment in Romania. The project aimed to improve the efficiency and to reduce corruption in payroll reporting and inspections by promoting a set of principles such as: centralization of payroll reporting and consolidated declaration forms, reduction in payroll reporting frequency and/or computerization of reporting, simplification of the payroll reporting procedures for SMEs and improvements in targeting of inspections. In order to reduce the red tape in this area without going through thorough legislative amendments it was recommended that the monthly declarations be converted into a unique declaration that would be filed with the Pension

Houses, inter-institutional communication of the information needed by the other involved state institutions, replacing the six payment orders to the State Treasury with a special payment order in which the payments would be in separate accounts, and the State Treasury oversee the payments in the separate accounts arranged by the business. The project was implemented in coordination with representatives of the Ministry of Labour, the Ministry for SMEs and all the relevant social fund agencies, the World Bank, European Union, USAID, US Embassy, business environment representatives (National Council of SMEs and other representative SME associations, including regional organizations).

These three policy projects offer a very good illustration of how an entrepreneurial environment policy agenda looks like. As regarding their relevance, it should be noted again that the USAID-IRIS experts were aware that they were engaged in a test aimed at determining the extent to which improvements could be made within the existing general political-institutional setting. One can distinguish between the local level—a case when the implementation and decision-making process falls under the responsibility of the local public administration, the territorial representative offices of various governmental institutions, the civil society and the business environment (e.g. 'Local Approvals') and the central level—the case of policies with focus at the national level, the Government, the Parliament, national agencies, etc. They were aware how difficult and time consuming and inconsequential was to go through the central level, governmental and legislative processes. Therefore they decided to try a new, targeted approach. Thus, it is appropriate to conclude that the Romanian Red Tape initiative was not only a good illustration of the entrepreneurship centered agenda but also a very interesting social sciences quasi-experiment.

Lessons from the Romanian 'Red Tape' Case: Implementation and Structural Challenges

Examining the substance and implementation process of each of these programmes was thus more than a mere assessment follow up study but felt like a contribution to a policy science.

The USAID-IRIS programmes and the analyses they were based on, took as a starting point the investors and the sequence of events related to the bureaucratic process associated with their activities. Their modus operandi was to identify problems or clusters of problems and then to address them with specific initiatives. A large number of problems were thus identified and a large number of ideas emerged as potential solutions to those problems. When evaluated in the light of initial expectations one may consider that many of these solutions were not very successful, however, if expectations are gauged by the success of other, similar projects, there were a number of accomplishments that must be acknowledged.

One of the most important things revealed by the implementation analyses was that the routes, conditions and factors affecting the implementation process and its success were crucial and deserved special attention. Irrespective of how analytically correct the identification of a specific barrier to economic activity is, the success of any solution intended to overcome that barrier will be determined to an overwhelming extent by the existence of a series of policy hurdles. Thus, as a result of an overview of the way the IRIS-USAID policy programmes were implemented, the issue of factors, conditions and barriers to policy initiatives emerged as critical. The set of programmes growing out of 'Red Tape' survey was an extremely important social experiment pushing to the limelight the important issue of the factors that determine the fate of such micro and local level policies aimed at eliminating barriers to investment, and entrepreneurship.

In this context the follow up study identified two related but different outstanding categories of determinants: (a) the political economy and the interpersonal networks factors that influenced the success of the implementation of the reform policies of the type analyzed and (b) the importance of the distinction between different decision arenas/institutional levels, i.e. the distinction between the level at which the targeted problem is located and the level at which the solution addressing it is implemented. The two determinants were closely intertwined, but for analytical reasons they should be approached as separated.

The implementation of the IRIS-USAID policies intended to improve the legislative and regulatory frameworks for business shows that on the one hand, those dimensions of the strategies relying on both local and national action were more successful than those who relied directly and exclusively on action at the national/center level. On the other hand, the post-implementation analysis concluded that in the case of the local approaches the magnitude of change induced was limited. At best one hoped that local institutions could optimise within the existing institutional framework. They were able to change things, but as expected, only within existing limits and in the end that proved not to be enough. The existing institutions and regulatory parameters determine the degree of change and most of these parameters and institutions were set in various degrees by the 'center' and not at the local level. In order for a reform to be effective and efficient, it takes more than local initiatives to optimise within the existing conditions. A local policy often means elimination of redundancies, increased efficiency in the application of a law, and so on, which requires structural modifications, hence a central policy, i.e. a policy aimed at affecting higher institutional levels or decision arenas. An economic policy implementation strategy must consider the political economy and institutional circumstances of each level and the interplay between them before starting an initiative.

Because the Red Tape initiative could be seen as a test aimed at determining the extent to which improvements could be made within the existing general political-institutional setting it is appropriate to conclude that it was a very good experiment in terms of exploring the capacity of various institutional and policy levels involved. The results reveal the fact that it is important to identify the level to be addressed for a specific policy and that opens up the possibility to explore the issue of calibrating and coordinating policy reforms at different levels. Corruption could be used as a very interesting example of inter levels linkages. There are two different types of corruption: first, there is the inherent corruption, which can be treated as a local social behavior. Second, there is the high level corruption, which supposes developed connections involving both vertical and horizontal social networks. The vertical chain of such a business is anchored in all levels and structures. In one of the cases studied, the mayor was obliged to resign because of political pressure from the county level structures of the governing party, after he opposed a group involved in stealing wood, that included local officials and local police officers, connected at the county and from there at the national level. In such circumstances it is difficult to think of 'local' solutions when one knows that anything done locally could be undone by the 'center'. Another interesting example illustrates the inter-level linkages between the business financing, licensing and permits systems. All the rural entrepreneurs interviewed financed their businesses from their own resources or by borrowing from friends. The low occurrence of loan financing of rural entrepreneurship is due to the fact that both bank loans and EU funds can be obtained only at the county level or at best, from neighboring towns. The level of information regarding the financing opportunities and the transparency of the process was very low, while the collateral and formalities required in other towns make these opportunities very costly. Local solutions could not address those problems without dealing with higher institutional and policy levels.

The analysis of the 'Red Tape' initiatives also revealed the importance of the policy initiation and lobbying capacity of the implementer for overcoming the status quo lobby and implementing the policy. The importance of the business community and the civil society involvement in the successful reform activity throughout the three years (2000-2003) of the 'Red Tape' programme is worth noting. The lesson is that for a policy to be implemented it is important to have the active support either of a political party or of the civil society and/or the professional associations that could overcome the lobby of the bureaucratic and economic interests that promote the status quo.

This set of insights opens a broader perspective on the initiatives aimed at identifying and removing barriers to economic activity. The way the policy process, inspired by an expert assessment is structured by political parties, local communities and interest groups, and the way they use the institutional or administrative levelers they have to block or further a policy change initiative is crucial for the success of the policy. Reducing the barriers and reducing 'the number of days needed to register a business' is more complicated than one may think. In order to be successful, an intervention at one level may require an intervention and a mobilization of forces at another level. There are networks or interest that cut across levels and tie them together.

The significance of the political economy processes surrounding initiatives aimed at removing barriers to economic activity is in this respect one of the key lessons emerging out of the 'Red Tape' exercise. The implementation phase matters and the definition of problems and their solutions might have been different if from the very beginning the 'implementation processes' is considered explicitly and systematically at the beginning of the initiative. A formal agreement of support from the government or party in power is insufficient: interest groups, coalitions and institutions matter. There are barriers to 'reducing barriers'. If they are not taken into account from the very beginning, they could derail the entire process.

In summary: (1) In terms of strategy and conceptualization the approach developed by USAID-IRIS was efficient in identifying the barriers to investment. The approach identified correctly a set of problems and their solutions, from a specific conceptual perspective: that static compliance costs of regulations imposed on start up processes are a critical barrier to entrepreneurship in Romania. (2) The success of the implementation of the solution was more local and fragmentary and indirect than expected but was reasonable if compared with analogous programmes. (3) The local-central dynamics revealed by the experience draws attention to the important notion of institutional levels or decision arenas and the linkages between them. (4) The limits of the approach were not determined primarily by the conceptualization or methodology but by the inherent barriers to policy initiatives. The issue of 'barriers' to policies aimed at removing 'barriers to entrepreneurship' emerges as critical. Those barriers could be identified as political economy related. The actors needed to endogenise the policies identified by outside agencies or experts in order to overcome the interest groups and institutional inertia supporting the status quo. These barriers were very strong in the Romanian case and they necessitated special attention. One could imagine many strategies to remove them. But irrespective of strategy, a focal point vital in designing them is the notion of 'policy ownership in the policy process'. That points to the very important notion of 'policy ownership', the voluntary and credible commitment of responsibility for a programme of policies.

Lessons from the Romanian 'Red Tape' Case: Policy Ownership

The study of the Red Tape Romania initiative leads to the identification at a deeper and less visible level of a general dysfunction in the economic policy-making and implementation process in Romania. That dysfunction affected the Red Tape implementation but was not limited to it. Any economic policy, irrespective of its analytical quality and its justification would be mired and blocked by the maze of interests and institutional inertia that characterise this process. As long as the policy process is not tightened up and well structured in terms of political support, any initiative, no matter how analytically and pragmatically grounded, will likely be dissipated, eroded and emasculated in the implementation phase. The question is at what level policy ownership should be mobilised. Local level is important indeed but due to existence of powerful interlinkages, the central level is in the end, decisive. The rest of the articles will focus on this issue as a vehicle for illustrating the depth and complexity of the problems involved in the new approach to development (and for that matter in any development policy initiative).

The International Monetary Fund (IMF) defines policy ownership as 'a willing assumption of responsibility for an agreed programme of policies, by officials in a borrowing country who have the responsibility to formulate and carry out those policies, based on an understanding that the programme is achievable and is in the country's own interest' (IMF, 2001). This concept is important because policy-providing outsiders and transitioning governments frequently have different perspectives or agenda regarding the substance and timing of reform (Boughton and Mourmouras, 2002). The conditionality of much foreign assistance requires that dissenting leaders nominally agree to changes envisaged by the aid-providing outsider in order to receive loans. But nominal agreement for the sake of obtaining funds does not mean genuine involvement and support of policies advised by the international development community. Without solid commitment to reforms proffered by organizations like USAID, national leaders are unlikely to undertake desired policy changes but incompletely or superficially.

In the specific case of Romania it was interesting to see in the context of the Red Tape Analysis in what measure policy ownership (or the lack of) may represent indeed a problem for the international development initiatives. The analysis documented the declarations of formal support given by the Romanian Government in many instances to the USAID-IRIS agents. Indeed the Government was declaratively supportive but it was difficult to document genuine involvement and ownership into the entire process. However, the crux of this investigation is given by the answers to a questionnaire regarding the economic policy process by top Romanian economic policy decision makers that were involved at one point or another in the economic reform process at the top tier. Were investigated: ex-ministers of finance, ex-ministers of privatization, two ex-prime ministers, ex-ministers of reform, secretaries of state, chairs of the parliamentary economic commission and several top academics that played key advisory roles. The objective was to explore the political economy of economic policy-making and to reconstruct this process using the inside perspective offered by the relevant players through an application that offers a glimpse on the way the economic policy-making is perceived by the very people that are involved in it. The responses of thirty-eight top economic decision makers to a 33 questions survey (the rate of response was 80 questionnaires/ 38 responses) and ten in-depth interviews offered a solid generalization basis.

Both the results of the interviews and the results of the survey were in line with the initial assessment of the dysfunctional state of the economic policy decision-making process but goes even beyond that. The economic policy process is perceived as incoherent by the very actors that implemented it. The political parties (theoretically the main vehicles for the definition and implementation of policies) were considered fairly ineffective, and the interest groups and bureaucratic and administrative inertia reigned supreme. There was no clear institutionalized process for articulating policies or for supporting economic policy initiatives. As a result, when policies are defined and supported by foreign development agencies, policy ownership and responsibility are weak and diffused. This was amplified in the 1996-2000 period by the existence of a coalition government and after 2000 by the lack of a strong opposition party. A brief overview of some of the responses given by the top decision makers is very illustrative and offers a clear image from another angle of the situation the IRIS-USAID effort has encountered in the field while working with Romanian counterparts to implement its initiatives.

Almost 75 per cent of the top decision makers consider the process of implementing economic policy measures more efficient if it takes place through informal channels compared to only 25 per cent who consider the process of economic policy implementation more efficient if it takes place through the normal, formal channels. About 70 per cent of the top decision makers responded that the parties' economic policy programmes did not take into consideration the interests of large social groups and classes, and on the contrary, that they were driven by group and party interests. Over 90 per cent think the economic policies implemented by the parties reflect the general interests and preferences only in a limited measure. Over 80 per cent of the respondents consider the economic programmes proposed by parties incoherent, namely that they were a contradictory mixture of liberalism, socialism, social democracy, and so on. It is worth noting that 85 per cent of the decision makers surveyed felt that the economic policy of their party was not reflected in the economic policy of the coalitions (governments) from the previous years. From this we conclude an almost total lack of responsibility of ownership for the policies.

Moreover 85 per cent of those surveyed think that the extent that political parties managed to create appropriate organizational structures aimed to formulate the economic policies is 'more likely small' and 'small'. In a similar way 75 per cent of those surveyed consider that the extent that political parties managed to create appropriate organizational structures, in order to support their economic policies in the Parliament and Government is 'more likely small' and 'small'. Over 70 per cent of respondents consider that the political parties did not function as efficient mechanisms for selecting the experts and decision-making persons in economic policies. 70 per cent of the top decision makers characterise the performance of the parliamentary economic commissions as 'more likely inefficient' or downright 'inefficient'. Over 80 per cent consider the concept of 'lack of political will' relevant as a diagnosis of the situation of the economic policies in Romania during the previous 10 years and 90 per cent of the respondents consider that in the stage of discussing and negotiating economic policies the communication process between the participants was 'more likely unsatisfactory' and 'unsatisfactory'. Almost 90 per cent think that politicization of the ministries is a real phenomenon and that it is a major impediment to the economic policy-making and implementation process. According to them the assignment of the public officers on strictly political criteria, the too frequent change and the subsequent incompetence of the public officers and the frequent change in organizational structure of ministries are the top forms this phenomenon takes. Finally, it is interesting to note that almost one-third of the respondents consider that Western economic institutions and political decision makers act relatively coherently against the

Romanian economic interests. That says a lot about the mindset through which initiatives like the 'Red Tape' are perceived.

In these circumstances it is not surprising that even a formal agreement between an external economic aid institution and the government in power and the publicly declared support of the government could not secure a sound foundation for the implementation of a package of economic policies (even one local and limited as the one emerging out of the Red Tape Analysis). As long as the policy process is not functional, the responsibility and the effort for such initiatives will be generated more often by accident than by institutional design. These conclusions are even stronger given that the very people in charge of the process confirm them. The image that emerges substantiates the notion that the implementation phase of economic policy is riddled with barriers and challenges that are far stronger and more complex than expected.

As a general conclusion one could conjecture that Red Tape-like initiatives, couldn't be as successful as expected in countries like Romania due to the dysfunctional economic policy process that generates weak support and weak 'policy ownership' among potential reformers. Under these conditions, regardless of international development community's ability to promote entrepreneurship-related initiatives or economic reforms, it is the institutional and policy system of the country in case the one that creates the conditions for a successful implementation. Since it is ultimately public officials who implement or fail to implement reforms, it is important to ensure that the economic policy process is defined by an institutional structure that is functional and that has the incentives that encourage policy ownership by these public officials. In other words, absent a strong economic policy institutional mechanism and a strong policy ownership element built into the policy-making process, removing barriers to entrepreneurship efforts like those discussed, are unlikely to achieve optimal results despite having correctly identified necessary policy changes. However, building economic policy institutional mechanisms is not a task that could be accomplished at (or only at) the local level. This vital precondition of removing the barriers to entrepreneurship should be addressed through the standard top-down approach.

Conclusions

The study of the barriers to entrepreneurship policy implementation points to the fact that factors pertaining primarily to the center (national level) institutions and political processes are crucial for the elimination of those barriers. Eliminating barriers to entrepreneurship by focusing on the local level requires bold policy initiatives at the center. Although local level efforts aimed at improving the bureaucratic and administrative process might be successful, they have clear limits and it seems that the accumulation of such small-scale successes can rarely lead to a tipping point.

To create the policy process needed to generate policy ownership is a huge task. Policy ownership is important but it is a result of structural features of the institutional and political system. One is forced again to look at the central level and at structural interventions and initiatives. The interlinking between levels, the networks of political economy interests that unite social actors require that type of effort. In other words, one could conjecture that one should not expect initiatives like the Red Tape initiative to deliver as long as they are not part of a larger, structural strategy of reform. A strategy of reform and development thus seems to depend in the end, in a decisive way on the central level initiatives and the policies targeting them. The success may look more like the result of the convergence and wise sequencing of the bottom up and top down approaches. If one is seriously considering that fact, the chances of making the regulatory and transparency initiative designed on the bottom up model successful, increases. If not, we should be aware that the dangers of promoting policies aimed at 'removing barriers to entrepreneurship' without understanding the implementation and structural constraints that affect the chances of success are huge. One may expect that very soon, the disappointing results would lead to the rejection of this very promising approach to international development. That would be indeed a disastrous result because removing barriers to entrepreneurship is and should be a fundamental component of any sensible economic development policy portfolio.

REFERENCES

Anderson, R., 2004, *Just Get Out of the Way: How Government Can Help Business in Poor Countries*. Washington DC, Cato Institute.

Arndt, H.W., 1989, *Economic Development: The History of an Idea*. Chicago: University of Chicago Press.

de Soto, H., 2000, *The Mystery of Capital: Why Capitalism Triumphs in the West and Fails Everywhere Else*. (New York: Basic Books).

de Soto, H., 2004, *The Other Path*. (New York: Basic Books).

Easterly, W., 2001, *The Elusive Quest for Growth: Economists' Adventures and Misadventures in the Tropics*. Cambridge, Mass: MIT Press.

Emery, J. Spence, M.T., Wells, L.T. and Beurhrer, T.S., 2000, "Reducing Red Tape Analysis: Administrative Barriers to Investment" (FIAS Occasional Paper 14).

Emery, J., M.T. Spence, 2000, "Administrative Barriers to Investment in Africa." FIAS Occasional Paper 14b.

FIAS South Eastern Europe Regional Conference on Self Assessment and Removal of Administrative Barriers to Investment, 2003, http://www.fias.net/Conferences/SEEurope%20(Feb.%202003).htm.

International Monetary Fund , 2001, Strengthening Country Ownership of Fund-Supported Programmes, http://www.imf.org/external/np/pdr/cond/2001/eng/strength/120501.htm.

Martin, P., 2004, "The business of helping others: Global poverty won't end until entrepreneurs are allowed to thrive." Ottawa Citizen Special.

McKinley, V., 1998, "Keeping It Simple: Making Regulators Write in Plain Language." Regulation 21(4): The Cato Institute, Washington, D.C.

Morisset, J. and Neso O., 2002. "Administrative Barriers to Foreign Investment in Developing Countries," World Bank The Policy Research Working Paper Series: Working Paper 2848, Foreign Investment Advisory Service (FIAS), Washington, D.C.

Organization for Economic Co-operation and Development (OECD), 2003, *From Red Tape to Smart Tape: Administrative Simplification in OECD Countries* (OECD Publication Services, Paris).

Organization for Economic Co-operation and Development, (OECD), 2003, *Johannesburg Statement by Co-chairs on 'Main Building Blocks of Modern Governance and Transparency for Investment'*. Global Forum on International Investment, Johannesburg.

Tomlinson, B., 2001, *Unleashing Entrepreneurship: Making Business Work for the Poor,* The UNDP Commission on the Private Sector and Development, A CCIC Commentary

World Bank, 2004, *Doing Business Database*, http://rru.worldbank.org/DoingBusiness/

11

Relational Strategy of Institutional Reforms and Urban Governance: An Assessment for Dhaka, Bangladesh

MD. SHARIFUL ALAM CHOWDHURY & MD. AHSANUL KABIR

State of the Problems

The municipal governments throughout the country are the main agents of urban governance and it is a challenge for them to build an efficient, transparent, accountable and people-oriented development institution. How these objectives can be achieved were discussed throughout this paper. However, it remains necessary to strengthen the capacity of municipal governments. To this end, an efficient and trained work force at the municipal level is to be created. Preference should be given to quality rather than the quantity. Frequent elections may help to develop a democratic process at the local level which may make the elected representatives more people-oriented. In all City Corporations, including Dhaka, such reforms and restructuring would be necessary. To initiate such reforms, the legal framework and ordinances may need to be changed. Similarly, other autonomous bodies such as Rajdhani Unnayan Kartripakkhya (RAJUK), DESA, WASA, should also undertake reform measures to bring about qualitative change in their operations. Recently, Dhaka WASA has reformed its structure of governance, but this is still not sufficient. The proposed Commission on Urbanization may identify an agenda for reforms on governance of the urban sector. Careful attention needs to be given to ensure representation for the common people in each of the local government authorities, while reform activities are undertaken. Strong private sector involvement is needed to promote urban development. The private sector is therefore to be given preference, wherever appropriate. Development partnerships between the public and private sector may help to promote rapid development of the urban sector. Adequate institutional arrangement and reform may be necessary to facilitate such a partnership.

Institutions like the Parliament and the traditional 'watchdogs' bodies are often designated as the essential pillars of the governance structure. The effective functioning of these institutions could be instrumental in curbing corruption and ensuring good governance in a young democracy like Bangladesh. These institutions, along with a vigilant and organized civil society, could enforce transparency and accountability of the political leaders and government officials, who are entrusted with the maintenance and improvement of governance standards. This underlying premise explains why often fundamental and radical reform measures are advocated for these institutions in order to make them more autonomous, functional and efficient.

The institutions in Bangladesh work under various constraints. The 'watchdogs' like the Public Accounts Committee of Parliament, the Office of Comptroller and Auditor General and the Bureau of Anti-Corruption lack structural strength, autonomy and authority to enforce their decisions. The Police are often subjected to unfair political influence. The civil society has remained disunited and succumbs to pressure from political quarters. Consequently, widespread corruption and non-accountability have degraded the state of governance and has brought about immense sufferings to the general public.

Political Party Reform

Most of the essential aspects of political reforms have already been addressed in the Fair Election Component of this report. The reasons for recapitulating those measures is to underscore the fundamental necessity of democratizing political parties in order to enhance their capabilities to ensure democracy in, and accountability of, the governance system. The present state of politics has led to an erosion of commitment of the political leaders to bring about the needed changes such as administrative reform, strengthening of 'watchdog' agencies and strengthening of institutional checks and balances to curb corruption. Furthermore, the present system of politics encourages corrupt practices. Politics need to be disciplined to allow infusion of committed people. It can be brought about in the following ways:

- **Political Party Registration:** Political parties should be registered and recognized as formal institutions. Criteria for registration and continuance (or cancellation) of registration should be clearly laid down with necessary safeguards to avoid misuse of registration/de-registration. Such criteria may include financial regulations and accountability, regular meetings at designated tiers of leadership, exercise of internal party democracy by way of, for example, the election of party leaders.
- **Regulation of Finance:** The sources of political funding are stated to take the form of private donation from various vested interest groups including the bank loan defaulters and protectors of organized criminal groups.
- **Budget Allocation for Political Parties:** A certain portion of the budget should be allocated for the financing of the political parties. In turn, the political parties will have to submit an audited account to the C&AG or PAC. To ensure healthy democratic practice it is advocated that a certain portion of the national budget should be allocated for the nurturing of political parties and institutions.

Administrative Reform

A separate task force is covering administrative reform. Therefore, this paper does not focus on the administrative reform, except certain areas of administration that directly lead to corrupt practices. These areas are government procurement, tendering process and collection of income tax. Free flow of information is one of the most important prerequisites for introducing transparency and accountability in administration. The civil servants by and large value secrecy and are absolutely unwilling to share information with citizens about the decision-making process. A number of actions have been recommended to ensure transparency and, thereby, considerably empower citizens and contain corruption.

- The proposed Right to Information legislation should be framed immediately. This could enforce transparency in the decision-making and execution process and considerably prevent corrupt practices.
- Civil servants, long accustomed to transact public business under a veil of secrecy, should be appropriately trained to bring about necessary changes in their attitudes and work habits.
- International standard for tendering process should be strictly followed. In particular, measures must be taken to curb irregularities and use of muscle power in bid submission.

Independence of the Judiciary

The rule of law is not being enforced by the judicial system impartially and promptly. The integrity of judiciary, particularly the lower strata, is being questioned.

The reasons for the above situations are many. These include lack of independence of the judiciary from the executive branch, inadequate training of lawyers, poor standard of legal education and lack of supervision and monitoring of the functions of the lower courts.

Possible remedy to improve the judicial system:

- Separation of the lower judiciary from the executive
- Repeal (simplification and modernization) of existing statutes and greater public scrutiny prior to new enactments.
- Better pay structure for the judiciary as a whole.
- Quick recognition of good service, particularly from the lower judiciary.

The Judicial Administrative Training Institute (JATI) should be strengthened to become a premier institution for training District Court judges, lawyers and support staffs as well as a support and resource facility for training Supreme Court judges. The judiciary should be given control over JATI through a governing body reconstituted to consist of a majority of judges from all levels of the judiciary. A modern curriculum for JATI should be developed. Full-time instructors should be created within JATI. Reform of the judicial system will create an enabling environment for the civil society to make more effective use of public interest litigation.

Bureau of Anti-Corruption

Corruption has been identified as such an obstacle to economic development, and the impact of this greatly outweighs other factors such as political instability, lack of infrastructure, regulatory uncertainty and inflation. The argument is that if a state can reduce corruption by strengthening institutions and ensuring their accountability, the economy, after a time lag, will record higher levels of growth.

In order to curb corruption it is important to have an independent and efficient anti-corruption agency. Unfortunately, the agenda of the Bureau of Anti-Corruption in Bangladesh is seriously compromised by a number of factors, including institutional weakness, irregularities and absence of political will.

- An autonomous standing committee should be formed with judges, senior public officials and leading citizens to oversee the activities of the BAC as well as authorize investigations into ministries, corporations and other agencies by a statutorily appointed and protected public prosecutor.
- Recruitment standard for BAC should be made higher. Higher-ranking officers should be recruited. Currently, inspectors, who generally rise from the ranks, sometimes even from that of constable are the investigation officers of BAC. They are unskilled. This leads to a system of working that is not satisfactory.

- A mechanism should be put in place to enable BAC to make use of the power it has through Acts, rules and regulations, which are quite adequate for BAC to discharge its functions.

Comptroller and Auditor General

The Office of Comptroller and Auditor General in Bangladesh is constitutionally entrusted with the examination of financial transaction and compliance with rules and regulations. This institution is over-burdened and it lacks efficiency. It does not have the capacity to determine the priority areas of audit and often corrective actions aren't taken on its findings.

- Audit activities must be separated from accounts.
- The office of the Comptroller and Auditor General should be allowed to function independently. It should not remain dependent on Ministry of Finance, especially in matters of budgetary sanctions and manpower. The Rules of Business of the Government need to be reviewed as the present ones have considerably curtailed the authority and autonomy of the C&AG guaranteed by the Constitution.
- Provisions for higher education and training should be made for auditors. Inadequately qualified and poorly trained personnel, who cannot perform quality audits, man the C&AG's office. The accounting system has changed and the auditors need to be more familiar with the new systems of accounting.
- The C&AG should be given full independence for reconstituting its organizational and manpower structure in accordance with its present requirements.
- Global comparison in the field of auditing should be carried out. Its cost-effectiveness should be evaluated through comparisons with other countries.

Ombudsman

The Constitution of the Republic of Bangladesh has provided for the office of the Ombudsman under Article 77 with power to investigate any action taken by a Ministry, a public officer or a statutory public authority. The office of the Ombudsman has not yet been created nor has any Ombudsman been appointed. It is strongly felt that an efficient, independent and objective network of Ombudsman office could contribute immensely to prevent and control corruption, irregularities and malpractices in almost every sphere of governance.

- A network of Ombudsman should be set up immediately with responsibilities for all departments of the government.
- Ombudsman should look into the all areas of unnecessary harassment including irregularities in issuing passports, registration of lands, official permission for construction of different structures, and different kinds of licenses and permits.

Parliament

An effective parliament is a body of elected people that acts as a bridge between the wider society and the state. Within that scheme of things parliament should serve as an institution to safeguard public accountability and maintain the highest of standards.

Parliament has a particular role to play in raising issues and putting them on the national agenda. In order for its recommendations to be effective, the operation of other supporting institutions like the market place, the civil society, others, are vital. But the primary task lies in strengthening the parliament itself.

- Mechanism should be put in place to ensure regular meetings of the parliamentary committees. Accountability of the government cannot be ensured if the meetings of the parliamentary standing committees are not held regularly
- Provision for the ministers to face a no-confidence motion should be put in place.
- A mechanism should be put in place to seek public opinion in case of bills where public interest is involved.

- The question and answer session should be made effective by scheduling specific days of the week for the purpose and ensuring the participation of the ruling party and the opposition.
- Mechanism should be put in place to ensure neutrality of the Speaker.

Responsibilities and Failures

Originally the Dhaka Municipality was created under the District Municipal Improvement Act of 1864. The city administration became a Corporation in 1978. In 1982 the adjoining municipalities—Mirpur and Gulshan were absorbed in Dhaka Municipal Corporation increasing its area to 360 square kilometers. The Dhaka Municipal Ordinance 1983 provided the legal framework for the Corporation. In 1990, it was renamed the Dhaka City Corporation. Since 1990, amendments have been made in the ordinance mainly to democratize the governance of DCC. Some of these amendments have enabled the direct election of the mayor and 90 ward commissioners, one from each of the 90 wards, and indirect election of 18 women commissioners by the other members in 1994 for a five-year term.

For batter governance has been floated the idea of ward level neighborhood committees to provide opportunities to residents to residents to assemble on a regular basis among themselves and also with their commissioners. But due some particle problem the idea fizzled out. In the process, an opportunity was lost to enhance popular participation and empower people. The authority further approached the Ministry of Local Government, Rural Development and Cooperatives (LGRD & C), to which the city corporation belongs, with the idea of a "metropolitan government" which would allow the Mayor to have increased power, including police power, to deal with the pressing problems of city, particularly terrorism and violence. It was hoped that under such a system it may be facing the problems of lack of coordination amongst the various service agencies; due to some shortcoming this idea could not be implement. In the changed political scenario, the relationship between the city government and the central government would improve. Meanwhile during the heavy monsoon, problems of water logging and traffic jams in the city escalated. The authority approached the central government for implementation of his proposal which required that the government cede its authority, and hand over control of many of its service-delivery organization like the Dhaka water and Sewerage Authority (DWASA), Dhaka Electricity Supply Authority (DESA), Bangladesh Telephone and Telegraph Board (BT & TB), Dhaka Metropolitan Police (DMP) and the capital Development and Planning Authority or the Rajdhani Unnyan Kartripakkha (RAJUK) to the city government. Again central government was found to be reluctant and came up with an alternative proposal for better inter-agency coordination and cooperatives (LGRD & C) as the convener and the Mayor of Dhaka as co-convener.

The members of the committee included heads of all basic service providing organizations terms of reference of the committee state that: (i) the committee would ensure the overall management of Dhaka City Corporation and the efficient running of services; (ii) decisions of the committee would be considered decisions of concerned governmental departments, agencies and semi-government organizations, subject to legal conformity and budgetary allocation; and (iii) the committee would sit at least once a month and if necessary, the convener or co-convener can call meetings at short notice. This is an anachronistic arrangement for a number of reasons. There has not been any shift of power in favour of DCC. The status of the Mayor as 'city-father' qualified to look after the city of his own, appears to have been undermined by making him second in command after the LGRD & C Minister. Apart from this image problem, it will be an extremely useful experience to examine the workings of the Coordination Committee and to see whether it is a viable mechanism to run the city more efficiently.

Institutional Arrangements

Governance in Dhaka is shard by a number of agencies and department which can be categorized under public sector, the elected local government, the private sector of the both formal and informal NGOs and other civil society groups. In this section of the paper, the structures of the various actors and their respective roles in the governance for the city, is perceived by the citizens as the principal agency for the management of the city.

Public Sector Management

The governance system of Dhaka within the jurisdiction of DCC includes components of both national as well as municipal governance, the private sector and the NGOs. Dhaka, being the capital city, accommodates key office of three organs of the state, i.e. the legislature, the executive and the judiciary. Also Dhaka is the headquarter of secondary and tertiary levels of civil administration, the Division and the District as well. Public sector institutions actively involved in the development of Dhaka can be broadly categorized into three types, i.e. national sector, special and local. Some 19 ministries and 40 national governments organizations are involved in the planning and development of urban affairs on Dhaka. Of them 15 ministries are directly responsible for urban administration and development in the city. These are: Local Government Division of the Ministry of Local Government, Rural Development and Cooperatives, Ministry of Planning, Ministry of Home Affairs, Ministry of Environment and Forest, Ministry of Communication, Ministry of Irrigation, Water Development and Flood Control, Ministry of Land, Ministry of Heath, Ministry of Post and Telecommunication, Ministry of Energy and Mineral Resources, Ministry of Social Services and Women's Affairs, Ministry of Education, Ministry of Youth and Sports and finally the Ministry of Defence with exclusive territorial jurisdiction. The other national level organizations are the National Economic Council, and the Board of Investment which play important roles in development, policy planning and management of Dhaka.

A number of sectoral agencies under various ministries provide extension services. For example, Public Works Department (PWD) is responsible for constructing government offices and other public buildings; Housing & Settlement Directorate (DSD) now National Housing Authority in the development and distribution of serviced plots and construction of medium-sized and multi-storied flats; Local Government Engineering Department (LGED) with DCC for low-cost sanitation, infrastructure and improving physical environment in slum areas; Department of Environment (DOE) for combating air and water pollution; and the Department of Social Welfare (DSW) in organizing and providing community services and fostering community-based organizations.

The special development authority is the Rajdhani Unnayaan Kartripakkha (RAJUK) which is responsible for urban planning, land development and building, and controls throughout the Dhaka Mega city region, which is several times larger than DCC area. On the other land DWASA is responsible for building and maintaining water supply and sewerage in Dhaka and DESA is entrusted with the responsibility of distributing electricity to inhabitants of Dhaka. BT & TB is providing telecommunication and satellite network to the city-dwellers. Titas gas transmission and Distribution company (Titas) supplies gas to the citizens for domestic and commercial/industrial use. Bangladesh Road Transport Authority (BRTA) runs the public transport system. DMP is a special purpose law-enforcement organization for maintaining law and order of the city. The Cantonment Board (CB) is responsible for planning, maintenance and development of areas within the cantonment. Physically the cantonments exist as enclaves within the DCC area.

Although a number of public sector agencies are responsible for providing service to the citizens, the quality of such services is far from satisfactory. The only agency whose services are regarded reasonably good by the citizens is the Titas Gas Transmission and Distribution Company and citizens' perception of DCC services is also poor.

Private Sector Management

The economy of Dhaka is overwhelmingly dominated by the private sector, both formal and informal. The formal private sector includes economic activities such as construction, manufacturing that is garments, textile, leather, plastic, printing, chemical and pharmaceutical are the major ones, besides commerce and services.

In the manufacturing sector, garment industries have profound contribution to the urban and the national economy. Such industries are extremely labour-oriented, currently employing nearly a million people in Dhaka, most of whom are poor women. While the national policy was to encourage such industries in Dhaka city, at least at the initial stage, no comprehensive strategy was adopted for employee's housing, leading to a further increase in the number of already proliferated slums and squatter settlements. A large number of industrial units operate as informal sector enterprises and do so normally outside controls often causing environmental problems.

At Prissy in the housing sector, a number of private real estate groups are involved in developing land and housing commercially. The capital city started as site and service facility, the industry has moved gradually to completed flats in multi-storied apartment buildings for the rich and upper middle class people. Most of these buildings are located in the high-density central city, putting pressure on the inadequate infrastructures, resulting in drainage and sewerage problems, shortage of water and electricity, and traffic congestion, etc. This is tolerated only because of the alliance between private development regulations. The private household for the middle class and the lower middle class which together constitute nearly 40 per cent of the city's population. The private informal sector's involvement is visible in developing hundreds of slums and squatter settlements in and around the city. The private sector has long been involve in the transport service. The manual transports like cycle rickshaws are all operated within the informal sector. Intra-city buses run under a formal private sector system although services are poor. Recently the sector has also ventured into luxury intra-city bus transport and now metered taxis are introduced.

Provision of utility services like electricity, water, sewerage, sanitation, garbage disposal and management gas for domestic fuel and industrial use, and telecommunications are largely managed by public sector agencies. The formal private sector has only recently become involved in telecommunication services. The informal private sector serves the urban poor communities with drinking water. There is also some community initiatives in solid waste disposal and in other important areas of urban social services as health, education and recreation the role of the formal private sector is increasingly becoming important, especially for the middle and upper income groups. While the government policy is favourable, the response of the private sector is also encouraging, and is already quite robust. This is evident even in the provision of university education, specialized hospitals and technical institutions in the private sector, i.e. it plays a very significant role is providing various services to the citizens and In the process the private sector also causes many problems in urban development and governance.

Non-Government Organizations

Non-government Organizations (NGOs) are contributing significantly to socio-economic and political changes aimed at furthering development agenda for the poor in Bangladesh. NGOs have certain characteristic advantages such as rapid response, flexibility in financial and operational matters and a generally closer relationship with the people.

In urban areas, NGOs involvement has increased significantly in the last few years and has brought about noticeable significantly improvements in the living conditions in many of the poor by providing credit, skill training, and building awareness. The NGOs are initiating dialogue between the key political decision-makers and the poor. Some Government-NGO collaboration is beginning to take shape in the urban sector, such as in a proposed major project squatter resettlement.

Donors

International donors also play significant role in the governance process in Bangladesh both nationally and locally and in urban governance influenced in decisions as well. Some urban programmers are designed by external agencies and are merely implemented by the city authority and these programmers are ideal for the city governance system today. Among the more influential donors are the World Bank, the Asian Development Bank, UNICEF and UNDP. The Asian Development Bank is currently assisting Dhaka City Corporation in an effort to improve the management system of the Corporation while the World Bank supports a major project on the transportation system of the city.

The Role of Civil Society

An active civil society can bring about the needed political commitment to initiate necessary actions towards curbing corruption. It is common knowledge that political scenario of Bangladesh is generally dominated by the private gains of the politicians. This has been possible due to lack of transparency in the conduct of the affairs of the political leaders and bureaucrats. The present scenario is unlikely to change unless an active civil society stands up to the unethical practices of a minority few. The needed measures such as political party reform, administrative reform, a neutral judiciary, effective police and strong 'watchdog' agencies will not materialize into reality unless an active civil society demands such changes.

- Strengthen and broaden the education system to contribute to increased citizen involvement, emphasizing both rights and obligations of citizens.
- Make arrangement for involvement of civil society organizations in the work of parliamentary committees, in the work of parliaments generally and in election monitoring activities.
- Empower local and private organizations like union parishads, consumer organizations, citizens groups/ associations.

More than one civil society network may be established in order to exchange opinion and information. Such networks may be city-specific or extend across many towns and cities. In some cases networks may be international or regional. The civil society should observe whether the authorities are meeting out the conditions (or indicators) of good urban governance. Civil society may place continuous pressure on the authorities by legal and other means. Only a well-educated and motivated group of individuals could reach out to the general public and encourage them to believe in the principles of democracy. The general public should be informed of their rights. Only then can they be mobilized to create pressure on the government to bring about the necessary changes that would improve the quality of life of the citizens of Bangladesh.

Urban Slum Improvement Project in Dhaka Metropolitan City—Bangladesh

Dhaka is one of the fastest growing Megacities in the world. Slums pose one of the biggest problems of the city. Around 12 per cent of the total population of the Dhaka city live in slum areas, which are very densely populated with a population density of 750 people per hectare. These areas have few or no basic utility services, including portable water, sanitation, drainage, etc. Slum Improvement Project (SIP) under the Local Government Engineering Department (LGED) was established in 1985 in five municipalities to address the social and environmental problems affecting slum dwellers.

Through the Slum Improvement Project (SIP) participatory approach, the Local Authority in partnership with urban communities, public and private institutions has made a breakthrough in providing an integrated package of basic physical, social and economic infrastructure services to the urban poor. Of all SIP components, the micro-credit programme has been found to be particularly successful and most attractive. Many poor households have increased their income using this facility. The SIP has significantly raised levels of awareness particularly in health and sanitation among slum dwellers, resulting in significant reductions in the incidence of numerous diseases. The SIP has empowered poor women through community involvement, particularly through the savings and credit program, thereby realising the overall status of women in families and communities.

Urban Governance in Environment and Public Health: Surat's Experience, India

Prior to May 1995, the city of Surat was not only faced with financial, administrative, socio-political and legal problems but was also one of the filthiest cities in India. In September of 1994, the city was traumatised by a plague outbreak. This outbreak coupled with poor working conditions and non-attendance to grievances further demoralised the staff of the Surat Municipal Corporation. Basic municipal services such as street cleaning, collection of solid waste, water supply and sewerage services, drains, street lights, parks and gardens, roads and schools were only covered by about 45% of the city residents. Morbidity rate due to water-borne and water-related public health diseases was high. To make matters worse, both the elected representatives (councilors) and the media had no interest in the SMC's functioning. Capital expenditure on long-term assets stood at Rs. 300 million with expenditure on salaries and allowances accounting for about 47% per Revenue Budget.

In May 1995, a new Mayor was posted to the city as the CEO. He undertook a one-week extensive tour of the city and held consultative meetings with all levels of municipal employees. He decentralised all his administrative and financial powers to ten commissioners (six zonal chiefs together with four functional heads of water supply, sewerage, town planning and finance divisions). A consultative decision-making process among all the eleven commissioners was introduced. The resulting decentralisation and empowerment of work units broke the departmental barriers and lifted the morale of the staff. A micro-planning exercise based on extensive field input was carried out to lay down equitable norms for effective and efficient provision of services to the citizens with best use of the available resources.

The council entered into partnerships with the private sector, who provided street litterbins in exchange of advertising rights. Instant penalties on littering were also introduced and this increased the amount of revenue collected. CBOs, mainly women groups in the slum areas, were used to raise awareness on the need to widen the roads so as to make provision of other services easier. The media realised the positive role it played in spreading public awareness and has taken up the role of social auditing of SMC's operation.

The citizens were involved in the decision-making process through a grievance redressal system and feedback mechanism. A sense of citizenship and pride was developed, as the citizens were aware of their civil rights to quality services. Inculcating public awareness and civic participation among the citizens brought about transparency among council officers and workers. Also, a transparent system for routine works such as maintenance was worked out for contractors. During the whole process, the media was used to highlight the situation and to create public awareness. Morale of the staff at the lower echelons is being sustained by an innovative system of public rewards. Within a period of 18 months Surat had turned from the filthiest city to the second cleanest city of India. The internal revenue collection increased due to efficient tax recovery, transparency in tax assessments and plugging of loopholes in tax administration. A sense of pride among the sanitation workers was restored, through provision of proper equipment and their grievances taken into consideration. Provision of basic services increased to over 95% of the residents, while capital expenditure also increased by about 450%.

Conclusion

This policy briefly represents a doable agenda for the establishment of good governance in Bangladesh. Even though it may not be an exhaustive list for any incoming government it could, nevertheless, be a starting point for reform in many of sectors discussed. Certainly most of the issues raised in this policy brief merit immediate consideration by the political parties. In view of the rising expectation of the citizens at large it is imperative that some of these measures are translated into policies for immediate implementation. Complacency would give rise to greater frustration, which needs to be avoided at all costs.

REFERENCES

Ahmed, F. (2000). "Poverty Incidence in Bangladesh '99: Regional and National Estimates," Regional Seminar on Poverty Monitoring Survey, '99. BBS-CIRDAP: Dhaka.

BBS, (2000). *Statistical Pocket Book of Bangladesh, 2000,* Bangladesh Bureau of Statistics, Government of Bangladesh, Dhaka.

CUS Bulletin (2001). "Center for Urban Studies," Number 41, July-December 2002.

DCC (1978). DCC Ordinance 1978, Ministry of LGRD&C, GoB.

Islam, N & Khan (1997). "Urban Governance in Bangladesh and Pakistan," Center for Urban Studies, Dhaka.

Islam, N. (2001). "Urbanization in Bangladesh and Future Strategy," in N. Islam (ed.).

Muhit, A. Mohammad (1998). "Dhaka Planning and Development Problems: Department of URP, Bangladesh University of Engineering and Technology, Dhaka, Bangladesh.

Muhit, A.M. A (2001). "Issued of Good Governance in Bangladesh," Dhaka.

Rahman, Golam and Mallick, Bishawjit (2002). "Promoting Good Governance in Service Delivery System of Dhaka City Corporation" World Habitat Day Souvenir 2002, GOB.

Raman, Golam and Alam, Md. Monirul (2000). "Urban Growth Pattern in Dhaka City and Its Problems of Urban Solid Waste Management," Bangladesh Environment 2000, ed. M. Feroze Ahmed, BUET, Dhaka.

SINPA Bangladesh (2002). "Facilitating, Local Partner Participatory Initiatives: A Handbook for Urban Platforms," Potential Press, Dhaka.

Task Force on Urban Governance, (2001). CPD—Centre for Policy Dialogue, Dhaka.

Task Force on Urbanization (1991). "Report on the Task Force on Social Implications of Urbanization," Task Force on Bangladesh Development Strategies for the 1990s, The Planning Commission, GOB Dhaka.

The Daily Star, October 18, 2000.

Urbanization, Urban Planning and Development and Urban Governance" Centre for Urban Studies (CUS), Dhaka.

World Bank (1992). "Government and Development."

Contributors

Dhammika Herath. <herath@padrigu.gu.se> Ph.D. Student, Gothenburg University, Department of Peace and Development Research, Sweden.

Tapomoy Deb. <tdeb1969@rediffmail.com> M.Phil. (Management), MBA (HRM), MSW (PM&IR), PGDHRD, DLL and B.Sc. (Hons.) Physics, is a rank holder throughout his academic life. He is a practicing HR Manager with wide corporate experience in Human Resource Management.

Gina Buijs. <gbuijs@pan.uzulu.ac.za> Gina Buijs is Professor of Anthropology and Development Studies and Assistant Vice-Rector Academic at the University of Zululand, KwaZulu-Natal, South Africa.

James Petras. <jpetras@binghamaton.edu> Dr. Petras is Professor Emeritus at Binghamton University. He has taught at 14 universities in China, Latin America, Canada and Europe. He is the author, co-author, and editor of 61 books translated in 27 languages. He has published 624 professional articles and book chapters.

Sadik Hasan. <sadik_hasan@yahoo.com> is an Assistant Professor of Public Administration at the University of Chittagong, Bangladesh. He received Master of Social Science (MSS) degree in Public Administration from the University of Dhaka, Bangladesh with honors. He also received the Master of Public Administration (MPA) degree from the University of Baltimore, Maryland, USA in 2000.

Bertil Egerö. <bertil.egero@sou.lu.se > Department of Sociology, Lund University, Sweden.

Rana P.B. Singh (b. 1950), <ranapbsingh@dataone.in> Professor of Cultural Geography at Banaras Hindu University, Varanasi, UP, India. He is the *Founding President* of the Society of Pilgrimage Studies, and of the Society of Heritage Planning & Environmental Health. He is executive member (South Asia) of the IGU Initiative 'Culture and Civilisations for Human Development', CCHD (Rome), and also International Research Forum, IRF, on SAARC (Tokyo).

Dilip Roy. <diliproy@vsnl.com> Professor Dilip Roy has an excellent academic record. He secured the first class first position in both B.Sc. (with honours in Statistics) and M.Sc. (Statistics) and each time he was awarded with gold medal by the University of Calcutta. He did his doctoral work in Management from the Indian Institute of Management, Calcutta. He also did Ph.D. in Statistics from the University of Calcutta. He carried out post-doctoral work in Dalhousie University of Halifax, Canada.

Paul Dragos Aligica <paligica@yahoo.com> is a political economist. Currently he is Senior Fellow at the Mercatus Center at George Mason University, Faculty Fellow at the James Buchanan Center for Political Economy, and Associate Professor at the National School of Political Science and Public Administration in Bucharest. In addition to his academic work, he has served as an expert to large international consulting firms and as an advisor or project partner to institutions such as the United Nations Development Programme, the World Bank, European Union Organizations, NATO and the United States Agency for International Development.

Md. Shariful Alam Chowdhury. <payelbuet@yahoo.com> is basically a Town Planner. He received his Bachelors Degree in Urban and Rural Planning (URP) from Khulna University, Bangladesh. He is presently in Chittagong Development Authority (CDA), CDA Building, Court Road, Chittagong; under the Ministry of Housing and Public Works; Government of the Peoples Republic of Bangladesh.

Md. Ahsanul Kabir. <makabir@bttb.net.bd> is Associate Professor, Urban and Rural Planning, School of Science, Engineering and Technology, University of Khulna, Bangladesh. He received his Masters Degree in Spatial Planning and Geographic Information System (GIS) from Asian Institute of Technology (AIT), Thailand and Durham University, United Kingdom.